Doubt

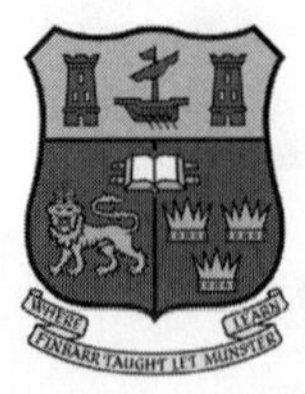

University College Cork
Coláiste na hOllscoile Corcaigh

Theories of Modernism and Postmodernism in the Visual Arts

A BOOK SERIES FROM ROUTLEDGE AND
UNIVERSITY COLLEGE CORK

James Elkins
General Editor

VOLUME 1
Master Narratives and Their Discontents
James Elkins

VOLUME 2
Ways around Modernism
Stephen Bann

Doubt

Richard Shiff

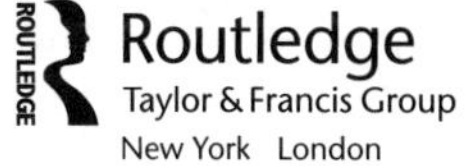

Routledge
Taylor & Francis Group
New York   London

Routledge
Taylor & Francis Group
270 Madison Avenue
New York, NY 10016

Routledge
Taylor & Francis Group
2 Park Square
Milton Park, Abingdon
Oxon OX14 4RN

Printed in the United States of America on acid-free paper
10 9 8 7 6 5 4 3 2 1

International Standard Book Number-13: 978-0-415-97309-0 (Softcover) 978-0-415-97308-3 (Hardcover)

Library of Congress Cataloging-in-Publication Data

Shiff, Richard.
   Doubt / Richard Shiff ; with an introduction by Rosie Bennett.
      p. cm. -- (Theories of modernism and postmodernism in the visual arts ; 3)
   Includes bibliographical references and index.
   ISBN 978-0-415-97308-3 (hardback) -- ISBN 978-0-415-97309-0 (pbk.) 1. Modernism (Art)--United States. 2. Art, American--20th century. 3. Art criticism. 4. Greenberg, Clement, 1909-1994. I. Title.

N6512.5.M63S54 2008
709'.04--dc22   2007017640

Visit the Taylor & Francis Web site at
http://www.taylorandfrancis.com

and the Routledge Web site at
http://www.routledge.com

CONTENTS

There is a gap in accounts of modern art. Some of the best historical work has been done by scholars who have not wanted to contribute to the large-scale questions of what modernism might be or how nineteenth-century art might fit in the lineages that led to postmodernism. That is one side of the gap. On the other is a common pedagogic literature intended to introduce modernism to beginning students; it is generally not written by the scholars whose work is central to the developing discipline, and it is not often cited. Between these two extremes there should be a kind of writing that is at once attentive to the grain of history and responsive to the different and often contentious accounts of modernism as a whole. Such writing is rare for a variety of reasons—some of which are embedded in the ways modernism itself has been understood. So far, there have been only a few exceptions, notably T. J. Clark's *Farewell to an Idea* and the multiply authored *Art since 1900*. Aside from those two enormous, contentious, and problematic texts, there is almost nothing between the sides.

In this series major scholars in the field consider the shape of the twentieth century: its essential and marginal moments, its optimal narratives, the strengths and weaknesses of its self-descriptions. I hope that the series as a whole will be helpful for those who find, as I do, that it can be revealing to put a little pressure on the assumptions that are made in recent scholarship regarding what is or is not crucial to an understanding of twentieth-century art. There is a growing literature, for example, on surrealism and its afterlife. In what ways does that scholarship imply that a version of surrealism is central to a description of some contemporary art? Or to take another example, How does cubism sit with accounts that rely on modernism's political aspirations? Where is Clement Greenberg, his ghosts or avatars, in current historiography?

Large questions like these are the subject of this series. If we do not try to assemble the best theories, to winnow the worst, and to prepare a clear collation, then what does it mean to continue to write about art in an age of increasing pluralism? I hope it means more than playing in an era that is happily "after the history of art," in Arthur Danto's phrase.

I have mixed hopes for this series. On the one hand, I doubt the ideas these authors set out will comprise a consensus, or even a satisfactory, survey. On the other hand, I believe that there is not an indefinitely large number of cogent, informed, and committed versions of how the century went: On the contrary, I think only a handful of separate and simultaneous conversations sustain our sense of what modernism was, or is, and it is possible to gather and compare them.

A parallel might be made to physics here: Physics turns on what are called grand unified theories (GUTs) and theories of everything (TOEs), in the sense that physicists work with those possibilities always in mind so that the smallest theoretical demonstration or technical innovation gains significance by its potential connection to the literally larger questions. In the event, many things may happen before the small-scale result can ever effect its ideal theoretical impetus, but that does not vitiate the fact that in physics it is absolutely crucial that large-scale theories exist to drive local inquiries. Art history is different in many ways, not least in that art historians need not think of large-scale problems at all. Yet in art history reticence regarding larger problems is sometimes taken as a virtue, and that, I think, is questionable. It is as if the most prominent physicists—the Steven Weinbergs or the Stephen Hawkings—were silent about the basic laws of physics, or as if the most active and creative physicists were committed to looking only at specialized phenomena, leaving the form of the physical world, and the direction of physics, to others as a matter of speculation. What I mean to suggest is that there is a point beyond which attention to the fine structure of historical events is no longer the necessary virtue of good historical work but rather becomes a strategy of avoidance that can threaten the coherence of the enterprise as a whole. In that sense, larger questions are not unhelpfully large or irrelevantly large, as they tend to be taken to be, but are crucially large.

The risks of avoiding going on the record about larger questions of twentieth-century art are nicely illustrated by a recent exchange involving English critic Julian Bell, American art historian Michael Fried, and nineteenth-century German realist painter Adolf Menzel. In the London *Times Literary Supplement,* Bell reviewed Fried's book on Menzel, praising Fried's readings of individual works and his rigor but remarking that it is unfortunate Fried chose not to connect this book, his first on a German artist, with his decades of work on the French tradition. How is Menzel linked, Bell wondered, to the sequences of French painters that Fried had studied in the past? How is modernism affected, if at all, by this alternate genealogy? They are good questions, hastily posed but essentially accurate. Menzel is not—cannot be—an isolated figure somehow beyond the streams of modernism, if only because the critical terms Fried brought to bear on modernism figure throughout his book on Menzel, driving Fried's inquiries and informing his judgments. It is the aim of this series to provide a space where challenges like Bell's can be taken seriously without becoming either ephemeral polemics or floating generalizations of the sort most useful to first-year students.

The books in this series were originally lectures, each given on two successive evenings at the University College Cork, Ireland, over a period of three years from 2004 to 2006. Each pair of lectures was followed by a seminar discussion, part of which is included in each book. The authors were encouraged to respond to previous efforts: The notion was that the series might grow to resemble a protracted exchange in which each person has months or years to consider how to respond to what has been said. That speed seems entirely appropriate to a subject as intricate, and as prone to overly quick assertions, as this.

I wrote the first book to provide a preliminary survey of the field, although I avoided describing the work of the authors in the series. That absence should not be taken as a lack of interest (the opposite is true): it is meant to provide a fruitful starting place for meditations I hope will follow. Readers may begin the series with any book, but taken as a whole, and read in sequence, the series is intended as perhaps the world's slowest, and I hope best-pondered, conversation on modernism.

—J. E.

INTRODUCTION

TO FIX ART HISTORY IN MEMORY

Rosie Bennett

The title of this book deserves some explanation.[1] In an age where art history is "an ever more academicized critical discourse where questions are now expected to receive answers," Richard Shiff (b.1943) presents a challenging alternative.[2] By embracing doubt as an epistemological tool, he poses the question of how specific histories of art come to be constructed. His intellectual scepticism and his insistence on the value of doubt do not result in some half-baked relativism. Instead, his rigorous writing (in the taut house-style of analytical art history) insists on clear thinking about art that compels conviction. In particular, his writing takes issue with a style of self-referential art writing seemingly "licensed" by Roland Barthes, whom he nevertheless admires.[3]

In a 1995 interview, Shiff identified himself as a self-critical art historian whose work remains concerned with art historiography; he concluded this interview by asserting that Modernist art is not dead.[4] Shiff is a graduate of Yale (PhD 1973), who holds the Effie Marie Cain Regents Chair in Art at the University of Texas at Austin, where he directs the Center for the Study of Modernism. His scholarly interests span the field of modern art from early nineteenth century French painting to post-war American art. Although he is probably best known for his book *Cézanne and the End of Impressionism* (1984), his research has always addressed critical and methodological issues in the history of art.[5] As well as contributing to academic books and journals, he has written many catalogue essays for major museum retrospectives on the work of Donald Judd, Bridget Riley, Barnett Newman, Robert Mangold and Chuck Close, to name just a few recent examples.[6] Shiff's art criticism is, I think, somewhat enigmatic, in part because it appears both in traditional art history journals such as *The Burlington Magazine* and *The Art Bulletin* as well as in more experimental journals such as *Artforum* and *Parkett*. Shiff is both an amateur painter and the proud custodian of a number of Willem de Kooning customized-paintbrushes.[7] He appears equally at home in an artist's studio, as he is in painstakingly cross-referencing Walter Benjamin's footnotes at the Bibliothèque Nationale in Paris.[8] As the history of interpretation is one of his ongoing areas of concern, Shiff prefers to translate directly from source languages (principally, French and German) while working through the effects that mistranslations have had on scholarship. One of the appealing things about his writing is his willingness to return to his own work (to a familiar lineup of artists, artworks and ideas); alternatively, one can see this as a willingness to allow past work to return to him, as though he were renewing a conversation.

The subtitle of his book *Cézanne and the End of Impressionism* (1984) identified his areas of concern as *A Study of the Theory, Technique and Critical Evaluation of Modern Art*. A close reading of this book, together with his co-edited book *Critical Terms for Art History* (1996), paints a portrait of this art historian as a stickler for the historicity of practice, the epistemology of art history, the etymology of words, and the genealogy of concepts.[9] As a product of its time and as a contribution to the "politics of representation" debates in the 1980s, *Cézanne and the End of Impressionism* is concerned with the cultural construction of concepts like "individuality" and "originality," rather than with forwarding mythologies about Cézanne — the man, his "genius," his "symbolism," his "originality," and so forth.[10] Shiff noted that Cézanne's critics (in the late nineteenth century) had imposed the dominant but now clichéd set of modernist values that continued to prime art historical accounts. For Shiff, it is not possible to return to some pre-Symbolic moment of historical innocence when facing an artwork, because the work's rhetoric affects how we see: it is critical discourse that establishes an artist's cultural meaning.[11] To this end, he notes that critical accounts are rhetorical, feeding "more on one another than on any extended engagement with the painter or his works."[12] Even in the Cézanne book, the double focus that characterizes Shiff's later scholarship is evident: notably, he explores the key concepts of the book not just by relating them to the surrounding critical literature, but also by situating them in relation to Cézanne's experiments with techniques of painting. Because contemporary interpretations of a given artwork remain part of its ongoing history, Shiff's writing identifies the artwork, its criticism, and its interpretation as inter-related material practices, even as it investigates them.[13]

In writing the introduction to *Twelve Views of Manet's Bar* (1996), Shiff observed that the twelve essays differed not in relation to factual data but as to how "the nature of the artistic and historical discourses should be construed."[14] Previously, scholars had "acted as if a comprehensive knowledge of the vicissitudes of visual motifs within the history of culture (a kind of panoramic vision of Western art) would yield a fundamental understanding, independent of the politics of the moment."[15] However, a problem arose when "what was said about Manet's combination of intellectual and emotional liberation would be said also of Jackson Pollock seventy years later."[16]

Shiff characterized the critical currency in operation in the mid-1990s as "the play of dematerialised cultural signs."[17] He observed that the deployment of French theory by "critical" art historians tended to dematerialise physical objects and social relations, treating them primarily as linguistic constructs. However, he noted that academic discourse tended to attribute linguistic signs with a materiality that rendered them too opaque to facilitate communication.[18] Although Shiff is happy to name Cézanne's early critics (Emile Bernard, Maurice Denis, and Joachim Gasquet) as Catholic-revivalist, chauvinist, and royalist respectively, he is notably more reticent to name his contemporary targets in art history and criticism.[19] Nevertheless, his book reviews have taken issue not only with "the social history of art" (T.J. Clark's *Painter of Modern Life*), but also with "formalism" (Michael Fried's *Manet's Sources*) and the "new art history" (or "visual theories") associated with the MIT journal *October* (Yve-Alain Bois's *Painting as Model*).[20] Comparing these critical reviews with Shiff's more positive book reviews betrays his allegiance to experiential scholarship (notably in the work of David Sylvester, Fred Orton and Leo Steinberg, for example).[21]

Shiff's own writings are rhetorical, well-crafted inquiries into the very act of writing art history and into the various writerly poses and intellectual fashions that converge on visual artworks. To this end, he has identified three discourses that converge on visual art: that of the artist, that of the critic, and that of the historian. He characterises art as a mode of belief, criticism as a mode of doubt, and history as dispassionate judgement.[22] If Benjamin's cultural criticism could be crudely (and incorrectly) characterised as a "one-way street," Shiff sees historical judgement as two-way traffic: For him, the relation to history is a reciprocal one: a concern not just with how we judge history, but also with how history judges us.[23]

With this idea of historical judgement in mind, he began his essay "Flexible Time" (1994) with a pointed question: "As subjects who write, how do we characterize art history in a self-consciously post-modern era, as we privilege differentiation and multiplicity?"[24] Such a question may stop readers in their tracks: it makes us conscious not only of what we choose to read and write but also of the way in which we do so. Ever mindful of academic fashions that fail to take a longer historical overview of the terms of their debates, Shiff cuts through heavy theorizing in order to understand the ideological ends of certain theoretical debates.[25] While theory has become the means through which orthodoxies and received ideas are challenged, he argues that we must not treat theory as an ahistorical matrix: theory too has its history; the rise and fall of academic fashions. For him, art and art history are engendered through the theory and practice of previous schools of thought and through the complex social, cultural, political and technological relations operative in a given society at a given time. Given that self-definition, we might reasonably ask two interrelated questions: What, for him, is art history? And how might an art historian responsibly write a history of art?

Following Shiff's tendency to let sources speak for themselves, he claims that history is "a construction, a figuration, perhaps just as fictive as the most fantastic paintings and sculptures."[26] Consequently, he advises readers to "consider history [as] a collecting and organizing of data with the details… understood as having been figured through desires, languages of representations, and social ideologies."[27] If history is a construction, then knowledge cannot pretend to be objective. For Shiff, any attempt to represent a historical project as unified and universal is to trade in illusions of continuity that would "render 'history' and the social relations it represented as unchangeable."[28] His writing takes issue both with the false neutrality of inherited art history (à la John Rewald) and with the contemporary penchant for "oppositional posturing."[29] For Shiff, the art historian is as immersed in history as is the art object under consideration; the way in which professional art historians respond to art works reveals their own cultural and social formation.[30] He claims that in order "to give the history we write 'reality'… we must figure this history so that it becomes productive."[31] Shiff's own work demonstrates a remarkable sensitivity to the problems of objectivity in art history. He notes that "it is difficult both to operate as an interpreter of history, committed to multiplicity, and to recognize at the same time the potential for positivistic (ideological) totalization *in one's own method*. The times, however, call for this uncanny ability."[32]

When asked by *Artforum* in 1995 to discuss an artwork that had special significance for him, Shiff chose Jasper Johns's *Alley Oop* (1958) because it made him "feel close to the hand of the artist."[33] For Shiff, *Alley Oop* "stimulates the viewer's hand into reflex action, making the viewer feel as though they might paint *Alley Oop* themselves."[34] The work also facilitated what he called the "passional freedom… to observe freely… letting [the viewer's] centred esthetic sense respond to the given patterns."[35] These curious statements, culled from a mid-career piece of writing, are symptomatic of Shiff's working method. His is a method that is not limited to situating art in an historiographic frame, but one that also commits the art historian to a materialist approach to the art object itself, to the making of the art object, and to how the art object figures through art writing. He looks closely at both the artworks and at the writing that purports to look at them: equal attention is paid to the rhetoric of the writings on art and the rhetoric of the object that the writing inevitably transforms into history. For Shiff, historiography is not an adjunct (some sort of value-added) that supplements the discipline; rather, historiography constitutes art history. Shiff's bodily response to *Alley Oop* betrays a tradesman's knowledge of the application and history of the artist's technique: he brings the same detailed attitude to the craft of art history, observing that "the maker (of history) handles history critically, with care. He makes it and remakes it and makes things with it, as if it were a tool in the hand."[36]

In a 1997 review of David Sylvester's experiential art criticism, Shiff observed that Sylvester's work needed to be read closely, so that his subtle moves would not be "mistaken for a lesser talent."[37] The same can be said of Shiff, whose methodology somewhat defies simple categorization. While his materialist take on *Alley Oop* fits uneasily with standard socio-historical accounts of art, it is nonetheless a rebuff to the voguish postmodernism that currently dominates the discipline. This is not to say that Shiff's writing attempts to recapture some modernist fantasy of a metaphysical or transcendental aesthetics. On the contrary, when he deploys the various dominant methodologies that now constitute the discipline (as a historian who is actively interested in art historiography must inevitably do), it is to historicize their relevance to the artwork under consideration.

While Shiff recognises that historical objectivity is now an obsolete cultural construct, he also says it is "an idea that remains known to us."[38] For him, an art historian's judgments are based not on fashionable gleanings but on sifting through the history of interpretations. Consequently art history cannot but have an aura of objectivity about it.[39] Benjamin's materialist criticism, he says, simultaneously produced an aura while handling the "shocks" of modernity. By contrast, he laments that much contemporary art criticism seems exclusively concerned with its own aura.[40] Art criticism has lapsed into poetic writing that exists for the sake of writing alone. Shiff's concern is always with forwarding some understanding of scholarship rather than "recognizing, manipulating, and appropriating potentially meaningful discursive convergences."[41]

Shiff, of course, acknowledges that to act as an art historian is no easy task because the art historian's view is likely, as he says, to be "contaminated by either art or criticism."[42] Nevertheless, he insists we should strive to be more objective. For Shiff, art history is "criticism" (a mode of doubt) when it "becomes cognizant of its own subjectivity and politics, of the fact that it advocates something," and art history is "art" (a mode of belief) "whenever its commentary… becomes itself a figured representation."[43] Hence art history is an inter-textual, linguistic construct. It is both an account written in a literary manner (a narrative account) and the "reality" (the events /the historical facts) that the account describes.[44] History is "the "reality" that the account describes" because history is obliged to assume a conventional form if it is to be received as history.

Shiff's 1995 essay "Critical Reflections" is a complex and polemical piece of writing. In this essay (interestingly published in a journal of art criticism), he distinguished the work of art historians from that of art critics; he identified himself as an art historian, while at the same time acknowledging his debt to the cultural critic, Walter Benjamin. In "Critical Reflections," Shiff also claimed that art historians build up their knowledge gradually, over time and through the arbitrary accumulation of information; this might explain why he repeatedly returns to the same familiar lineup of artists and ideas in his own writing. What he takes from Benjamin's criticism is the critic's tacit ability to "handle" the shocks of modernity:Shiff is interested in the way Benjamin's odd juxtapositions reproduce in his readers an experience of shock.[45] The value Shiff finds in Benjamin's "analogous technique" is its ability to act on its "readers *in lieu of explaining.*"[46] Shiff puts Benjamin's technique to work in his "Critical Reflections" essay to demonstrate the arbitrary nature of historical awareness built up over time and through the availability of texts: the three texts that Shiff "activates through contiguity" (Octave Mirbeau's 1892 essay "To be a Painter", Clement Greenberg's 1946 review of an exhibition of Henri Rousseau, and a 1962 *Art in America* commentary on art and industry) are all concerned with the relation of art to industrialisation. In juxtaposing these three texts rather than repeating a clichéd narrative, Shiff's essay "acts on its readers in lieu of explaining."[47] In this respect, his own juxtapositions seek to return to visibility the shock effect that these three texts once had the capacity to produce.

While Shiff notes that "handling shocks" may be an "unseemly gesture for refined academics," it nonetheless remains a gesture he subscribes to; otherwise, his writing approaches that of the critic in lacking "physical agency or impact."[48] However, he notes that the historian's critical distance comes at a cost. In historicizing Benjamin's writings as a product of their time (even though they also speak to us of our time) we tend to "canonize and auraticize" them, losing the "shock" value (the materialist value) of Benjamin's work.[49] Because Shiff is concerned with the reciprocity of historical judgement rather than just with the auratic quality of Benjamin's criticism, he tasks art history with the job of putting Benjamin's "analogous technique" to work. By subjectively grating together discontinuous events and texts, we encounter our own consciousness of history and find any illusions of historical continuity shattered: "Until the present moment of juxtaposition, the past event remains incomplete, its implications unrealized: the present gives to the past a form it otherwise lacks. Yet the present needs a fragment of the past to provide its own direction."[50] Consequently, Shiff describes his own method of handling history as follows: "I'm drawn to the chance illuminations that arbitrary sequences of documents provide. I take the judgemental statements of others and arrange them in a form appropriate to me. In the process, various cultural expressions seem to combine into plausible argument. I sometimes call this 'analogy,' because it involves a set of discrete elements, distilled from an array of 'facts,' creating resemblances that in turn imply sequences, evolutions, oppositions, and reactions."[51] What emerges, then, from the diversity of Shiff's writing is his acute awareness of embodied subjectivity, situated knowledges and the phenomenological intersubjectivity of the interpretative act. Shiff is not one to shy away from saying "I." What this vocalisation of the first person singular does is both entrench the discipline more firmly in its historical moment and accept responsibility for what is said.

The rigorous materialism and self-reflection that Shiff brings to historiography and to the writer's role in the production of art history is reflected in his analogous concern with art as a material practice and the artist as a maker of art objects. This is evidenced by his detailed interest in the material processes by which art is produced. When he intervenes into the field of art criticism, this emphasis is particularly stark, as he constantly reminds critics not to lose sight of the art objects that they purport to represent. His reviews of Howard Hodgkin's and Lucien Freud's American retrospectives, for example, attest to his frustration with the fashion of subordinating art-objects to theory. In relation to the critical reception of Lucien Freud's work, Shiff accuses Linda Nochlin and Donald Kuspit of "biting at sexualized bait."[52] While Shiff considers that Freud's unvarnished canvasses invite close material inspection of how paint goes on canvass, Nochlin and Kuspit can't see Freud's paint because they are primed towards the "genital fixation" that characterises our culture.[53] In his review of the Hodgkin retrospective, Shiff makes a point of ignoring the artist altogether, preferring instead to put "his questions to [twenty years worth of] paintings."[54] For Shiff, Hodgkin's paintings must stand independently of their maker and of the emotive blurbs that are customarily attached to his work. Shiff quite literally sidesteps the usual interpretations of Hodgkin's work which tend to interpret his "brilliantly colored bars, arcs, waves, and dots" as though they were "renderings of people, situations, scenes or events," and thus representative of Hodgkin's "effort to convey a state of emotion."[55] Ever the historian, even when he writes art criticism, Shiff puts the self-confessed ahistorical Hodgkin within art history's remit: Shiff expresses annoyance with his suggestive titles because they evoke "bad criticism by those who would otherwise do better."[56] For Shiff, it is precisely because Hodgkin's "titles have the effect of setting up a game" that it is "good reason not to play this game"; not to cede critical territory.[57] In light of such "games," Shiff's claim that he felt as though he might paint Johns's *Alley Oop* himself is not to be read as hubris: rather for Shiff seeing and making, and writing about that seeing and making are equally stressed and materially linked practices: all take time; all are built up over time; all attest to physicality and process.

Throughout his work, Shiff makes a point of letting his readers know that the art object comes first, and if it doesn't do so, then it should. In his discussion of John Rewald's carefully mapped chronologies, Shiff notes that whenever questions arose, Rewald tended to privilege documents over his own experience of an artwork.[58] By contrast, while Shiff acknowledges his debt to Rewald's painstaking collection of data on Impressionism (he calls him the dean of Impressionism) Shiff's own writing emphasises the importance of the phenomenological encounter with the artwork or art-historical text. Flicking through the forty-seven black and white images in *Cézanne and the End of Impressionism*, one cannot avoid the sense that Shiff's bodily engagement with artworks has become more central to his approach to art since that book. It may be that, as the scope of his writing has developed, he has done what many other art historians have neglected to do: he has taken the time to look. This is particularly significant at a time when a material understanding of technique seems to be increasingly absent from the art-historical register. Shiff's writing takes account of the materiality of artistic processes; of the fact that artists do not merely address social or generational concerns, but also convert surfaces into pictures.

While acknowledging that we live in a fast-image culture, Shiff is uneasy with some of postmodernism's implications not just for art history, but also for art. For example, he compares the high critical exposure given to artists such as Sherrie Levine to the relative neglect of artists such as Vija Celmins and Chuck Close.[59] Shiff attributes this to the fact that the work of Celmins and Close operates more on the level of materiality and physicality (which have hitherto been concerns outside the scope of theory). By contrast, Levine's work, which so-readily leant itself to exploring the postmodernist mortgage on the concept of originality, has been theorised as if it only operated on the level of sign and image.[60] Working against the grain of contemporary discourse, Shiff finds the work of Close and Celmins compelling because it is work that repays close looking. In Shiff's writing, compelling art takes time: compelling art has its own temporality, absorbs its viewer, arrests attention and grabs hold of the field of vision, as *Alley Oop* did for Shiff.[61]

In his article "Realism of Low Resolution" (1996), Shiff sidesteps the usual "Realism" debates that dominate the social history of art, because the realism that interests him is the realism of material specificity, specifically the materiality of translating one medium into another medium.[62] An image of low resolution is one in which the technique makes itself unavoidably present by disrupting the possibility of a transparent view of the image depicted. Though he does not refer to Benjamin in this particular text, thinking the art-making process in terms of translation is analogous to Benjamin's theorization of "The Task of the Translator" (1928): for Benjamin, translation resists imitating the original; instead, it reveals what in the original remains incomplete and in motion.[63] For Shiff, all artwork is a translation because "artists are acutely aware of phenomenological distinctions between seeing and making."[64] In this article, Shiff explores how Chuck Close uses grids to transfer his Polaroid photos into highly layered and well-worked paintings that can take the artist up to a year to complete. Shiff is not at all concerned with whether Close captures anything of the photographic realism of the polaroid in his paintings. Instead, he is interested in the way viewers relate to the work. As he said of Close's work, in quite a different context, "in a face as Close reveals it, everything is featured: the appearance, the mark, the work and an entire set of cultural values."[65]

From what has already been said of *Alley Oop*, readers cannot but note that Shiff (like his heroes Walter Benjamin, Clement Greenberg, Leo Steinberg, and Donald Judd) is always the archetypal spectator. He characterises viewers either as active (as he himself has learnt to become) or lazy. He advocates that the value of looking at work by artists like Close, Celmins, and Georges Seurat, is not to be found in moving away from the canvas so that distance might assist in making the artist's touch cohere into realistic (ocular) images. Rather it is the opposite — it is in getting up close and personal with the work. For Shiff, "touch" remains important, as it is situated between objective fact and the spectator's subjective response: the artist is also a spectator of his/her own work. He describes the spectator's act of visually tracing the artist's translation of one medium into another as an act of mimicry that reveals the materiality and physicality of the artwork's production and the artist's reciprocal encounter with the world.

What emerges from Shiff's writing is a concern that the *appliqué* of interpretation has replaced an understanding of the *appliqué* of paint. This potentially reduces the materiality of artworks to the immateriality of anamorphic images that are viewed from the wrong viewpoint.[66] He seems weary of the wholesale application of academic trends because the easy deployment of conceptual metaphors and categories of appraisal, threaten to reduce artworks to little more than illustration. Instead, he contextualises overarching postmodernism and "politically committed" social histories of art, refusing to simply apply them or to take them at face value. This is especially evident in his appreciation of Levine's work. Contrary to established perceptions of her as an artist who appropriates iconic images, Shiff examines Levine's work in terms of how she makes. The Levine that figures in his account is (to borrow a phrase from Freud) a character "wrecked by [her own] success."[67] In the 1980's, her work was reduced to a critique of the inherited signs of romantic notions of originality. Levine happily embraced this fashionable reading at the time, only to find herself somewhat precluded from trying to claim the originality of her own work later in her career. Shiff's demand that an artist's work cannot be seen outside of its critical interpretation, and his insistence that critical interpretation also has a history that needs to be addressed, remain the most enduring elements of his methodology.

What Shiff's response to *Alley Oop* suggests is that his phenomenological approach to his own subjectivity (his physical mimicry of how Johns put paint on canvass) is a self-conscious attempt to move beyond the established, as well as the "new" epistemological paradigms that are operative within art history. From our perspective, to look back to the moment of Shiff's formation and entry into the discipline as a Cézanne scholar (under Rewald's deanship) is to perceive that art-history's firmly buttressed disciplinary foundations have now subsided under a field of force: Where once the discipline had privileged a transcendent disembodied subject and universal objective truth claims, Shiff has introduced the importance of an embodied looking that does not lose sight of historical context. He describes his time-consuming, highly interested, close observation of Johns' *Alley Oop* as the "touchstone for my thinking about physicality and process" — though his writing is never just concerned with the physicality and process of the artist.[68] His work, I think, never loses its focus on the ways in which artists (such as the ill-fated Levine) "struggle to regain [their] culture's lost indexicality in a world formed by… excessive iconicity." At the same time, he remains equally committed to addressing how art historians engage art objects through their literature.[69]

Doubt

I. Pragmatic Doubt

We cannot begin with complete doubt. We must begin with all the prejudices which we actually have ... Let us not pretend to doubt in philosophy what we do not doubt in our hearts.

—Charles Sanders Peirce, 1868[1]

Charles Sanders Peirce was an artist-philosopher. A doubter, he was also a believer. He trusted the analytical procedures he devised and his skill at deploying them. Even more, he trusted his intuition, a skill at guessing, whether evaluating an incomplete set of data or judging the significance of the slightest sensory discrimination. To guess and then commit to the hypothesis was for Peirce as basic to human patterns of reasoning as more formal, seemingly more conclusive, methods of proof. At times, proof would come to pass as mere feeling, "a single feeling of greater intensity ... belonging to the act of thinking the hypothetic conclusion ... Hypothesis produces the *sensuous* element of thought."[2]

However much Peirce believed in his ability to prove or, if need be, to guess, he reserved a degree of doubt for his conclusions. Doubt is not distrust. He knew that his judgments, whether rational or emotional, could be no more than relatively reliable—no more certain than the degree of certainty that he, in his fallibility, could achieve. A degree of certainty is the reciprocal of a degree of doubt: "I used for myself to collect my ideas under the designation *fallibilism*; and indeed the first step toward *finding out* is to acknowledge [that] you do not satisfactorily know already." What remains obscure in the physical sciences as well as in the abstract disciplines of mathematics and logic seems minor by comparison with the darkness that descends on speculative work in the human sciences: "In those sciences of measurement [such as geology or meteorology] which are the least subject to error ... no man of self-respect ever now states his result, without affixing to it its *probable error*; and if this practice is not followed in other sciences it is because in those the probable errors are too vast to be estimated." Having made his statement without identifying those "other sciences"—was he thinking of economics? psychology?—Peirce confided wryly that he was "a man of whom critics have never found anything good to say."[3]

By "critics" Peirce meant his academic peers: those of comparable authority who differed in being less willing to assign the doubt factor and to admit that it bore on their professional judgment. Peirce was an academic whistle-blower. He could have referred to professional critics of every type. Although their work is by nature speculative, critical thinkers often claim for it an authority beyond the arbitrary and fallible, believing that—or perhaps merely acting as if—they were able to distinguish the determinate from the indeterminate, the certain from the uncertain. We value critics for the reliability of their judgment in fitting an object or situation to an appropriate category, announcing its proper identity. Challenging the categories themselves is far less common than arguing over their fit or inventing additional ones to contain an experiential overflow. There are nevertheless times to doubt what the categories and the procedures designed to serve them indicate we should believe, and there are times to believe—to trust to intuition and feeling—what the same patterns of rationality may indicate we should doubt. To believe and to doubt with neither more nor less than a beneficial quotient of self-doubt becomes a useful psychological skill, an intuitive self-discipline.

Effects become causes; it happens

In 1965, the American pavilion at the São Paulo Bienal featured the work of senior artist Barnett Newman. Six younger painters and sculptors accompanied him, among them Robert Irwin. When *Artforum* published a preview of the group enterprise, only Irwin's page appeared without illustration. He explained the situation as if to say that any object of his creation was ... what it was:

> I am concerned with *specifics* and reject the generalities of photographs. Every element in painting has had both an identity and a physical existence – identity has always lent itself to being transferred in both photographic and literary terms. The physical existence *never* has.[4]

Identity "always" lends itself to transference; the physical existence "never" does. Rhetorically, Irwin allows no exception, no doubt. His statement of faith amounts to a general definition, even a theory. Yet he constituted this generalized identity for the sake of specificity—the definition of a class by the name of *physical existence*, a class that whenever invoked would have but one member: *This* object happens to have *this* physical existence. A person senses its specific quality, this appearance. It comes to pass—no explanation, no theory needed. Such a class is either a very weak category or no category at all. Categories are classes preestablished by an order of identities. The reproductive practice of photography is such an order, Irwin argued, "a whole system of logic which allows [only] certain kinds of information to come in ... and our essential state of consciousness is formed by that logic. ... And what we're saying about photographs is absolutely true for words."[5] In his understanding, the representational orders of photography and language accommodate the data of new experience by determining meaningful qualities in advance, including like with like by whatever means of resemblance and excluding whatever remains.[6]

Irwin set representational "duality" against the type of art he sought, experiential classes of one member. Duality as he conceived it had little to do with ambivalence or doubt. It was instead a matter of reference—a relation between two entities that would channel the experience of both into the form established through their relation. "Duality *in art*," he claimed, "is a language of romantic sentimentality using the art forms to recall past experiences and feeling … Duality works as a language of expediency with the ability to facilitate mass communication and education … Its accuracy is limited to the concept of ideas as absolutes." An identity that can be photographed or illustrated is an expedient, communicative duality, explaining one thing in terms of another, ultimately working toward an encompassing concept (like modernism and other art-historical categories). Identity, in this sense, is inherently self-differing; it signifies one thing but also some other thing, and then still another. Yet, because an identity offers ready answers to all questions about itself and its class, it coalesces into a teaching, a common doxa. It develops an order ever less open to adjustment. Any material object, but especially an Irwinian object of art, has the potential to resist the importation of identity and so resist doxa and ideology as well. Irwin argued furthermore that people themselves form a resistant barrier: "The duality's truth is very questionable when confronted by the *constant state of change* (and therefore lack of absolutes)—the inconsistencies, irrationalities and emotions of the human equation."[7] Judgments of identity—dualistic sameness and difference—fail to respond to the changing human spectrum of doubt and belief.

By opposing the human experience of physical existence to the abstract dualities of identity, Irwin implied that every identity becomes a commodious category with which any number of disparate events, phenomena, and bits of data have the potential to be associated. The interpretive, representational linkages would appear to enrich the cultural significance of an object, duality after duality; yet, from another perspective, they reduce and impoverish the object. Whereas things that exist are singular, each identity becomes multiple, acquiring ever more members of its class, sacrificing the unlike for the like. Statements of identity are subject to perpetual transfer in spatial relay and temporal delay, with identity itself functioning like a proper noun or even a pronoun. (A personal identity, a person's name, however unique, fits innumerable configurations of personality and emotion.) As a linguistic place-filler—a concept, not a physical condition—identity becomes ever more self-differing. With one statement of identity leading to another, each is equivalent in some emerging sense, yet also a variant that requires as its glossing validation the next in a temporal sequence or enumerative series.

We have become so familiar with modernist—yes, modernist—notions of self-difference that some critics—Rosalind Krauss is a case in point—regard self-differing as if it were an absolute, a *condition* (the term to which Krauss often resorts).[8] Self-differing appears as a condition of all human experience, if only because experience is necessarily temporalized: It moves. Experience changes, so the self differs from itself (as Irwin suggested). Yet notions of self-differing feed on a corresponding desire, also modernist, for selfless immediacy. As much as the latter, the former is our nineteenth-, twentieth-, and twenty-first century doxa—the not-so-hidden flip side of Romanticism, notably explored in the writings of Paul de Man.[9] Krauss insists that "the [immediate] subject can never become identical with himself," that is, with the temporalized self. She opposes the experience of the temporalized self to a phantasmatic "all-at-onceness [that] suspends the temporal dimension."[10] But neither version of the self, immediate or temporalized, can be regarded as absolute if both are to be addressed as "conditions." Conditions of what? There is nothing conditional about self-difference if it is a defining quality—nothing that you can feel: A fish, whose condition is to exist in water, would not feel wet.[11] If the self always self-differs (never integrates), then self-difference becomes its identity, not its differential condition, and to differentiate the immediate from the temporalized as viable descriptions of conscious experience becomes pointless. All is belief; nothing is left to doubt: no self-difference within this critical consciousness who writes of self-difference.

In general—though generalization rubs this argument the wrong way—a differential or "critical" term loses its efficacy when regarded as an absolute that "always" applies, that is, when we designate it as the correct term under all conditions, rather than as the more beneficial term under specified conditions. With absolute identity, ideological assertion substitutes for critical analysis and hypothesis. Difference is as ideological a notion as sameness. Krauss has used the art of Marcel Broodthaers to develop the thematic of temporalized self-differing. To the same purpose, another critic might have chosen the photography of Bernd and Hilla Becher, the self-portraiture of Andy Warhol, the Woman series of Willem de Kooning, or even the landscapes of Paul Cézanne, as well as any number of other examples of work from the nineteenth and twentieth centuries that, by the nature of its process, format, or installation, induces a viewer to become conscious of orders of difference and temporalized plays of memory. A viewer today, perhaps primed with or conditioned by this orientation, is likely to ignore specifics to focus on generalities that integrate each perceptual unit of information and establish links between them. Self-difference is itself identifiable as a thematic shared by modernist and postmodernist art; in this respect, there is hardly a difference (more on this to follow). Were we to seek all indicators of self-difference throughout the art production of the modern centuries, we would severely reduce the differential, and therefore critical, potential of the phenomenon. So perhaps critics should let the various manifestations of self-difference lie—except in cases where it seems most pointed, there on the surface, begging to be noticed for what it is (as in Broodthaers, but also the Bechers, but also Warhol, but also de Kooning, but also Cézanne ...).

By identifying a work, a supplemental photographic illustration or verbal description would reestablish or merely affirm the very ordinary split in experience that artists of Irwin's generation were combating. They sought to mark out a physical realm of experience that would resist mundane self-differing: the gap we perceive between reason and emotion, mind and body, identity-by-name and identity-by-feeling. Illustration and description become codified, semiotic memories of this experience, distinct from "physical existence" (as Irwin referred to it). Memory is a form of identity-by-name. In memory, we reason out the circumstances of life by exemplification, taking an instance or a fragment as tantamount to the totality of a situation, so that manageable generality effaces unwieldy specificity. Imagine that, because of amnesia, you have no sense of identity and would not know how to recognize your own established character. You would no longer be in a position to evaluate any particular act you performed by knowing your own category, by having the capacity to declare, "How like me to do that," or "I wouldn't have done something like that." Instead, you would be reduced to relying on how it felt to do what you did, how the act happened to happen in its "physical existence," as if no memory at all were involved. Every judgment would be specific to the singular, undifferentiated constellation of qualities at hand—a challenging and discomforting prospect.

A photographic illustration or verbal description is less of a fact, more of a theory; like a memory, it "abstracts from experience" in order to relate to an existing system of representation.[12] Irwin and a number of his contemporaries were striving for an absolute of physical presence with the potential to occupy all channels of human attention at once, rendering memory and representational associations nugatory; in colloquial terms, his work would call for the response, "You'll have to see for yourself; description would be useless." Whether or not an artist succeeds in reaching such a physical and perceptual absolute—theory says no, this is impossible—what mattered to Irwin and others was their faith in the value of the attempt. The cultural significance of their art would be found in the nature of their activity and in the viewer's experience of the result, rather than in the interpreted reference of the work as a sign. The physical existence, the material condition that an artist produces, has its "effect," its sensory appearance. A viewer infers a motivational cause from this effect, a correspondence between the perceived form and a plausible reason for an artist's having configured it. A form that seems to have little potential as a sign can, of course, be perceived as intended to have little meaning. Such a dynamic of cause and effect is a hypothetical guess open to doubt.

A statement from Peirce is relevant: "Belief and doubt may be conceived to be distinguished only in degree."[13] If belief and doubt belong to the same experiential category, then a doubt is a weak belief; we feel doubt when belief is weak. Reciprocally—but oddly—a belief is a strong doubt: When the doubted fact gains degrees of acknowledgment, it becomes a belief. The saying, "He protests too much," which turns a negative into a positive, alludes to a similar situation. The potential for confusion here is not due to paradox but results from our having two identifying terms for a single continuum of feeling—a common situation, a variant of mundane self-differing.[14] When we concentrate on the extremes of the binary opposition, we fail to see that the middle is also an extreme—the extreme of the two other extremes, both their limit and the *terrain vague* where they meet as one, so that the one becomes the other.[15] You can be as certain (an extreme of conviction) of a doubt as you are of a belief: "Doubt and belief are two states of mind which feel different, so that we can distinguish them by immediate sensation."[16] Believing in your doubt, you can act on it, use it as a corrective. Reciprocally again, doubt may result from acting on a belief. The psychological complexity of doubt and belief entails that sensations of *coolness* and *warmth* (to choose one binary example) constitute only a crude analogy: two identifying terms that overlap on a single continuum of corporeal and emotional temperature. On another continuum, *sadness* and *happiness* form a closer analogy to doubt and belief but still a relatively crude one.

Working through the same postwar historical context that affected Irwin and many other artists, the polymath Michael Polanyi, in 1958, assumed a philosophically aligned, but different perspective from Peirce: "Doubts, which we now sustain as reasonable on the grounds of our own scientific world view, have … only our beliefs in this view to warrant them."[17] The warrant may come from our investigative method, which generates the doubt—not as a sign of failure necessarily, but as an indication of the fact that, although observation may have no limits in terms of what a person (*some* person) is sensitive enough to feel, our method sets a theoretical limit to what level of observation we collectively deem sufficiently reliable. The question remains, To what degree are we—each one of us, singly or together—willing to trust and act on feeling, especially when no theory supports it?

There was nothing absolute or "pure" about the notion of a felt physical presence that Irwin and other late twentieth-century artists entertained. Their experience of physicality occurred on a continuum affected by conditions of awareness, attentiveness, likelihood of perceptible resemblance, and other contingencies. Physicality came in degrees, like belief, doubt, and analogous psychic and sensory states. We might regard all such states as emotional, to avoid differentiating between psychic (mental, intellectual) and somatic (physical, corporeal) feelings as if they derived from distinct sources. We feel our emotional state in both our thinking and our bodily sensation. Emotion is a cause (a motivating force) as well as an effect (our being moved or having been moved). Peirce's philosophical confrere William James warned against drawing a distinction where none was justified: "The stream of thinking … is only a careless name for what, when scrutinized, reveals itself to consist chiefly of the stream of my breathing. ... Breath [is] the essence out of which philosophers have constructed the entity known to them as consciousness."[18] *Stream*, connoting fluidity and continuity, is an appropriate metaphor when applied to emotional states, at once psychic and somatic, which resist being fixed by identity. The question, What (How) do you feel *now?*, requires a bit of fabrication, because answering it converts the feeling into a memory, if it has not already passed—come to pass—of its own accord. Perhaps thinking is an emotional abstraction or condensation of what the body already has sensed, though sensation may be an emotional abstraction of what the mind already has thought.

Differential writing

Few today would dispute the belief that a writer writes history from his or her own perspective, according to his or her interests, values, and even emotions, whoever this writer may be, and whether or not the writer acts apart from ideological constructs that may be unknown—present yet outside the scope of attention. To assert that as we construct the history of the past we reflect who we are creates no scandal. Nor is there much controversy over the claim that every history, no matter how credentialed its author, must be subjective. Most academic writers nevertheless remain averse to suggestions of subjective arbitrariness, even when they shift from writing an art history of events and causes to practicing art criticism. They are loath to acknowledge that being subjective entails being arbitrary in one's judgments. They argue among themselves as if only one position had a right to prevail, as if one subjectivity deserved to dominate. Perhaps this is merely to assume the pose or posture of critical argument—the identity or category into which participants in academic debate believe they must fall. They have an emotional need to differ and to identify themselves with the authorship of their argument, which amounts to self-differing (stepping outside your own position, speaking from it as if it were objective and apodictic). Exaggerated difference solidifies an identity limited to those who, at any given moment, hold one position out of many, presumably the proper one.

To the extent that academics fail to recognize how much alike they are, they volunteer for self-difference without always admitting self-doubt. Each stresses the degree to which his or her beliefs form a distinctive pattern, neglecting to acknowledge its closeness to the pattern of cultural contemporaries with whom each nominally differs (difference by self-identification only). In recent years, we academics—I would be hypocritical not to include myself—have favored at least two means of personal absolution from the rampant subjectivity we treat as if it were our individual discovery. One technique is to present history as a narrative account, writing it from an overtly personalized perspective about which the writer can claim objectivity (or subjective transparency), because each of us recognizes his or her individual desires, whether by longing or through their satisfaction. As Peirce reasoned, we know the difference—the self-difference—between the I as a structural position and this I who is oneself, the most natural holder of the rank of grammatical subject: "I know that *I* (not merely *the* I) exist." We observe the will—not the motivation—of other subject-positions; but it is this I, who is oneself, who experiences intention and desire.[19] Yet, seated in the I, desire does not necessarily belong to anyone in particular: It may circulate; it may be social; it may be borrowed from the expression of others, like a figure of speech.[20] Theory tells us that the I is either a preexisting literary figure or a product of ideology. To your experience, to my experience, it will not feel so. An unscientific guess: When young children refer to themselves by their proper names and resist use of the pronoun *I*, we attribute their language to their incomplete intellectual development; but perhaps this is also evidence of an instinct for self-preservation in the form of self-sameness—a linguistic intuition against the self-differing grain of language, soon suppressed by a culture of socialization and typing.

By appropriating a first-person, narrative voice, a writer sidelines theoretical qualms over the inherently collective nature of subject positions. Such a writer asserts the personal self's centered authority. A first-person narrative—the use of a strong I, so to speak—establishes a self-revealing document, a sense of specificity and physical existence, an I-saw-this. Here, as in several other instances (see the previous section), my example comes from Krauss. My two predecessors in this series, James Elkins and Stephen Bann, have invoked her work as representative of criticism from a postmodernist position. In their different ways, Elkins and Bann undermine the strict division that such a category promotes. They emphasize the need to track through the earlier years of modernism, seeking the parallel emergence of postmodernist values. At the very least, this type of investigation counterbalances the tendency of critics of contemporary art to regard those notions that they turn to last—in this case, the postmodernist syndrome—as if these must be last in a chronological sequence of historical events. Far be it from a critic to recognize a cultural phenomenon belatedly. Nevertheless, the more attention critics bring to a particular cultural practice in the present, the more likely they are to perceive the same practice in the past. Such a critical program of inverted discovery is Benjaminian, or, in Bann's sense, Nietzschean.[21] I have joined in this program, too.[22] Attributing a branch of the enterprise to Krauss's later work, Elkins eliminates a one-dimensional chronology by alluding to "postmodernism as a form of resistance that takes place within modernism."[23] If this is so (it is my conclusion as well), then postmodernism would be better named *metamodernism* to capture the irony of its stance of resistance and doubt toward modernist mythologies—not after the fact, not belatedly, but in their making. On his part, Bann stresses the tradition of interest in curiosities (redundantly: an interest in objects of interest) as opposed to aesthetically purposeful objects of design. Bann's involvement with curiosities—from the early modern *Wunderkammer* to the decontextualized surrealist object to the postmodernist installation—follows from his view that "the preconditions of Postmodernism cannot be understood without reference to the preconditions of Modernism."[24] I concur.

Setting a tone of physical presence (I-saw-this) in a publication of 1999, Krauss inaugurated an account of Jackson Pollock with a cinematic voice-over, establishing the immediacy of her contact with the artist's widow. Perhaps not so immediate, because it is a memory, therefore an established class of identity, presumably filtered by the writer's sense of purpose: "I remember the expression on Lee Krasner's face that afternoon in her apartment."[25] The reliability quotient of a remembered glance at a passing appearance must vary; Krauss has stated in its favor that such an account "gain[s] a certain power as witness."[26] We might read her assertion as ironic—or not—since the power would be (merely?) rhetorical. If regarded as an empirical judgment, the witnessing of a look becomes a case of strong belief derived from a slight sensory discrimination. Peirce: "We gather what is passing in one another's minds in large measure from sensations so faint that we are not fairly aware of having them, and can give no account of how we reach our conclusions."[27] De Man: "From the moment the narrator appears in the guise of a witness and recounts the events as a faithful imitation, it takes another witness to vouchsafe for the reliability of the first and we are caught at once in an infinite regress."[28] Something is amiss in referring to empiricism as a pretense to objectivity, as Krauss often does.[29] Empiricists are radically subjective, trusting their personal sense data as opposed to detached, rational analysis; *subjective* and *objective* are fluid descriptors indeed. Krauss's empirical observation of Krasner's look would amount to a judgment founded in prejudice. Peirce again: "We must begin with all the prejudices which we actually have."[30] Enlisting this memory impression as a synecdoche for the tone of dismay in her account, Krauss reported Krasner's objection to thematized, extra-artistic interpretations of Pollock—his art as psychologically driven, or as spiritual and even religious.

Krasner complained of those who gave an identity to Pollock's art, as if they were displacing its presence, its physical existence, fitting their descriptions to speculations on its motivation.

Nothing compels a reader to doubt Krauss's narrative, which bears all the conventional marks of authority: the first-hand witnessing, the primary source, the emotional candidness of the conversational exchange. But for these very reasons, why would the narrative require the rhetorical embellishment of a cinematic voice-over? Why the initial hypersubjective observation ("I remember ...")? Of course, this is a familiar literary trope, a stylistic effect, and could be ascribed to a writer's professional concern to animate the text. But enlivening entails consequences. Roland Barthes once warned of the seductiveness of this manner of glossing a look: "Sometimes, however, the text produces (invents) an entirely new signified which is retroactively projected into the image, so much so as to appear denoted there."[31] Krasner's look was itself being thematized—by metonymic association, not analysis. Krauss's account of the look (of scorn?) set her scornful narrative in motion, as she began to tell a story of Pollock's reception cast with heroes and villains.

A second technique, ubiquitous, sets the subjectivity of today's writer on a plane different from that of all past writers, treating their subjectivity as a fixed, objective fact, sufficiently detemporalized so as to hold still in its ideological frame. Define the frame, and you contain and master the subject. Often now we use the histories we inherit from previous scholarship as a guide to writing a new history of the past, because a summation of the common points of the existing histories—according to our current prejudice—exposes to critical readers the values and ideological inclinations of those past writers and the social systems in which they participated. Our presumed awareness of their ideological limitations (their frame) relieves anxiety over our own. With the professed aim of using an archive of individuals to gain insight into a past era, we effectively reason the other way round, from general to particular, beginning with the inherited summation: from an established knowledge of the shared beliefs of the era under scrutiny to the (unconscious) motivation of each of its individual agents. I am tempted to call this method the *metacritical fallacy*, the assumption that we see the blind spots of others. To the contrary, we see only those we do not share, most likely a mere fraction, especially when the object of our study resembles us because of elements of a common culture. The situation forces us to concentrate on spots not shared—that is, on difference—the islands of overarticulated cultural signs, rather than the undifferentiated sea of our physical, phenomenological existence.

The more we write, the more we indulge in personal absolution, differentiating our enlightened position from benighted arbitrariness and ungrounded judgment. If I have the impression that my mentality differs from that of the majority of my contemporaries (always a risky assumption), it may be that I have a relatively high tolerance for chance as the bearer of meaning and readily admit to arbitrariness. The question I raise is this: Why do our current practices of critical absolution assume their present forms? We have a decided habit of accepting a secure link between individual artists and the prevailing ideological structures of their time. Such a link is a highly idealized notion that amounts to a vast, reductive generalization; it "abstracts from experience." We interpret the actions of individuals as members of identity groups, as if shared identity entailed shared motivation. Long ago, romantic artists and critics—especially at the naturalist end of the romantic spectrum—privileged concepts of individual experience, originality, and genius to escape this generalization, this typing by class and lineage. They sought relief from an unhappy mix of regulation and anarchy that Franz Kafka would later inscribe in a single sentence: "The Law is whatever the nobles do."[32] For *nobles*, read *the authorities, the dominant class, the man*, or whatever your self-image requires. "We"—that is, professional critics, academics, writers of a class privileged to write—no longer accept central aspects of the romantic strategy of resistance to imposed social order. We have become wary of the logic of concepts of originality and genius. Yet we remain faithful to the testimony of individual experience. Consider again the nonironic use of narrative subjectivity in recent art-historical writing—I am ambivalent about this. Or, take the example of Irwin and his involvement with utterly specific physical existence—I usually feel comfortable with this, resigned to the fact that analytically questioning certain feelings, rationally doubting their reality or significance, may never yield intellectual, not to mention emotional, profit.

It seems that the historiographical method of reading ideology and identity politics into past history works less objectionably for studies focused on the nineteenth century and still earlier periods. The same method becomes problematic when we deal with the more recent past and with people whose lives overlapped with our own, people we may have known and conversed with as individuals, those who in some respect shared our world, even if only by being the contemporaries of others we know or once knew, such as our parents and grandparents.[33] (Elkins and Bann, as scholars whose investigations extend back before modernism, recognize the extent of this problematic difference to a greater degree than is typical of scholars who deal exclusively with issues of the past hundred years or so). The closer the human object of study, the less self-certain we are in reducing individuals to sets of generalized ideological values, although it can be done.

It has been done, and continues to be done, perhaps all too often—often enough, at any rate, to seem as natural as an academic cliché. It comes as no surprise to read that people lack knowledge of "the underlying economic and social causes of their own disorder and moral insecurity": This is Meyer Schapiro's statement of the common position, published in *Marxist Quarterly* in 1937.[34] He was referring to the plight of artists removed from him by only a generation or two. No need to commit to Marxist thought to take such an analytically objective view of the felt subjectivity of others. To resist conclusions of this sort requires an acceptance of doubt and a certain Peircean self-discipline.[35] Compare this similar statement, from an exhibition catalogue essay written forty years later by William Rubin, consistent with a critical lineage that included Schapiro: "Few if any artists are entirely conscious of their enterprise, and therefore of the manner in which the changing directions in their art may transcend the frames of reference imposed by their moment in time."[36] "Few if any": Rubin hedged, leaving the possibility that certain exceptional artists do become aware of the exigencies of "their moment in time." But who would be in a position to identify and verify such demands with authority? Is it the critic, and for that matter, only a critic who lives a different moment? Regardless of the degree of immediate awareness, Rubin argues, artists are most unlikely to recognize the larger implications of their aesthetic stance. They are not prophets.

In fact, this interpretive trope of the unconscious artist has long been used by socially-oriented critics to rescue from moral irresponsibility art that they considered beneficial to society. Artists, Théophile Thoré wrote in 1845, may well engage in "an unreflective process, [and are] not obligated to be cognizant of its rationale."[37] Artists escape self-representation and self-differing; they dodge the pitfall of identity. If they do not consciously join a political team, the critic assigns them to one. In this way, they assume a moral position in the world of their contemporaries, but without suffering the emotional etiolation and other detriments that would come with greater social self-consciousness. (Nietzsche: "Each of us will always succeed in becoming [self-]conscious only of what is not individual but 'average.' ... Whatever becomes conscious ... involves a great and thorough corruption, falsification, reduction to superficialities, and generalization.")[38]

Whether the issues are socio-economic (Thoré and Schapiro) or matters of aesthetic evolution (Rubin), the possibility that artists might lack conscious knowledge of both the causes and the implications of their achievements ought to be obvious.

Why single out artists? Is it reasonable to expect any person to be *entirely* conscious of anything, especially *underlying* causes? Emotional wildness is a fact of life that reason does not control—or so we feel. Underlying causes can hardly be apparent: They underlie. And underneath them, there ought to be still more disruptive causes. Beneath the "economic and social causes" are the psychoanalytic ones. And beneath the psychoanalytic causes are more economic and social ones. If reality is a configuration of effects to be sensed and known, we would expect the causes of specific effects to be located either in the past or hidden within the present; otherwise, the causes would be indistinguishable from their effects (in the same place, at the same time). We claim to reveal underlying causes by imaginative, speculative insight, that is, by critical acumen. Connecting present to past and here to there, the interpreter assumes a position of omniscience unavailable to an artist or, for that matter, any mortal. (It does not empower you to be reminded of the things of which you will never be conscious, by someone who claims to know them already. Omniscience is not infectious.)

More to the point, the interpretation explains the interpreter, not the artist, not the object of interpretation. Interpretations reflect interpreters' interests and are emotionally expressive. My theory, whether social or psychoanalytic, explains me, not you. So the critics are the ones who need to be "entirely conscious of their enterprise"—aware of both its results and its causes. This self-consciousness would provide them with self-knowledge. Self-revelation can be shifted from a writer's conceit to an observer-interpreter's method. But perhaps this would come to—would happen to be—no more than a dubious, pretentious exercise.

An incomplete understanding, a state of doubt, is troubling. To be discomforted in this way can be intellectually stimulating; but, emotionally, we usually prefer the satisfaction of convincing ourselves that we know full well what we observe and do. Security lies in believing that we act with a conscious, rational purpose, or, at the least, are able to articulate a meaningful purpose immediately after the fact. If someone lacks consciousness of the nature of his or her actions, it is the other person. I am often reminded of a backhanded question from Wittgenstein: "Imagine that someone unconscious (anesthetized, perhaps) were to say 'I am conscious'—should we respond 'He ought to know'?"[39] With our comforting habits of consciousness in place, we describe the looks of others as if we had immediately perceived the underlying motivation for these superficial appearances. Effects ought to have causes; and, by metonymic sleight-of-hand, enumerative description slides into analytical explanation. Effects *become* causes. If I observe that a certain visual composition has both a range of warm and cool colors and is balanced—and, especially, if I present these two facts of observation in this order—my description is likely to be read teleologically as an argument from the range of color (as a productive device or cause) to the state of balance (as its intended result or effect). My descriptive representation will have been motivated in someone else's reading, whether this was my intention, my realization, or not. Motivation is an irresistible intellectual attraction, an attractive nuisance. The effect, the material condition that a work of art presents, brings with it the "effect"—that is, the appearance—of its own pictorial cause. The result of this cause-effect logic is what a critic tends to observe and describe. Any acceptable manner of describing a set of effects will imply the nature of their causation. Recall Polanyi's point that a belief in scientific method "warrants" a certain level of doubt in response to investigative conclusions, no matter how they may be reached. Artists who do not interpret themselves, who neither identify the sources of their project in a personal, historical past nor announce the future of their accomplishment—those who appear less than "entirely conscious of their enterprise"—risk relegating their intentions to an unconscious that someone else will define, whether by critical science or critical guesswork. To the artists, it will hardly matter. Of what they are unconscious they will experience no doubt.

Feeling thoughts

> When it comes to art, watch out for thinking.
>
> —Clement Greenberg, 1983[40]

> It's evident that what is to be known can't even be described. ... We sit and look out and see ... and know, but cannot analyze doing it.
>
> —Donald Judd, 1990[41]

As a student during the 1960s, I developed an interest in all aspects of art, not only the physical, feeling side of art making, but also the reasoning side: philosophical aesthetics, artists' statements, and interpretive critical writing, especially when it inclined toward theory. I enjoyed the feel of handling materials. I also liked the feel of theorizing. So I was pleased to discover that a challenging, academic kind of art criticism existed, to counterbalance its journalistic manifestations. I doubt that I realized then the significance of what Elkins now notes—that daily newspapers and commercially-oriented art magazines, along with the occasional "pronouncements of [conservative] politicians," contain the bulk of the ethical arguments over art. Such sources associate the value of art with its capacity to induce a "fully immersive experience," a consequence (so the most conventional argument goes) of an artist's skillful application of illusion. The beneficial social effect—which may simply be benign or even anodyne, as opposed to actively beneficial, more diversion than illumination—is, in Elkins's slightly ironic words, that we "forget ourselves for a while." What causes this type of self-forgetfulness? It can be a range of illusionistic practices from "commercial portraiture" to "digital video games."[42] Art that induces acute sensory awareness and intensified feeling does not simultaneously activate remembrance or reflection on the self. As Peirce wrote, "The element of feeling is so prominent in sensations, that we do not observe that something like Will enters into them ... strong, clear, and voluntary consciousness ... a consciousness of duality or dual consciousness. Feeling is simple consciousness, the consciousness that can be contained within an instant of time[;] it has no parts and no unity."[43]

As I was first learning about art, I was annoyed by the newspapers, popular magazines, and television programs that, without any embarrassment or self-questioning, broadcast philistine complaints about a general loss of skill among modern artists—the kinds of skill leading into expected forms of "immersive experience." Familiarity with studio work allowed me to see that such complaints were poorly informed, based on reductive, hierarchical definitions of skill that favored deliberative planning over open experimentation, technical resolution over imaginative conception, delineation over coloration, and—certainly, stridently—illustrative representation over most forms of "abstraction," from expressionistic figuration to nonobjective construction. Bann recalls how irritated he was to observe much the same syndrome in a professional theorist of great accomplishment, for E. H. Gombrich had presented "the whole production of the twentieth century to date under the heading of 'Experimental Art.'"[44] I detected analogous prejudice in the majority of my university professors in art history. They were at ease in explaining excellence in linear drawing, but most of them rarely referred to color, whether in terms of harmony or dissonance; and many bristled at twentieth-century art as if it were giving their profession a bad name. They found it too abstract in form and too theoretical in concept to coordinate with the rhythms of aesthetically cultivated souls.

The social-history orientation that took hold during the 1970s and 1980s constituted a compromise. In lieu of an analysis of pictorial structure and style, it instituted a broad iconographical investigation that extended beyond traditional symbolism and allegory to the identification of specific sites, events, and conditions to which an image might have alluded. The social history of art turned from philosophical aesthetics to more concrete matters of cultural politics and gender; and it accommodated products of popular culture as objects worthy of the historian's attention (a class of objects overlapping with, but different from, Bann's curiosities). With social history, art history became at once more socially responsible and more fun, if only because less rarefied—talk of images of prostitution being more familiar and engaging than talk of picture planes (formalism) and linguistic shifters (structuralism). Social history held more popular appeal in having a moral message and provoking a common interest in other people's mores and anxieties. In Elkins's words, "most of social art history takes place in a turbid middle ground where particularly academic if not conservative choices of artworks mingle with liberal politics."[45] If the conservatives had long before appropriated the dominant ethical arguments for art, the liberals countered by appropriating its social analysis. They also attempted to repossess for their own purposes some of the more conservative representational images, which offered rich opportunities for social interpretation. I have the unscientific impression that within the American culture wars, this trade-off—the liberals' social-political analysis for the conservatives' ethical-aesthetical analysis (both of them negative in tone)—seems to have brought political advantage to the conservatives. The majority of Americans remain more sympathetic to art criticism that combats aesthetic evil (what the popular press judges fraudulent) than to art criticism that exposes evidence of social malaise (the "unconscious" ends of what intellectuals judge to be dangerous ideology and corrupt cultural practice).

* * *

During the 1960s, I occasionally encountered the term *postmodernist* as a bit of jargon not yet in general usage. It had little political valence. What the attentive audience for art now recognizes as the trappings of postmodernist practice would have been known by other names—or by no name at all, just the specifics of observation. Along with Elkins and Bann, I wonder why a theoretical or stylistic syndrome acquires its name precisely when it does—not later, not earlier—although it can happen by chance without much logic to the recoverable chain of events. A separate question is whether the consequences of such naming and identification augment the culture, deplete it, or merely distract its intellectuals from other matters.

Elements of parodic postmodernist practice existed in an artist such as de Kooning without need of a name. Like Newman and many other late modernists, he objected to naming and categorization.[46] He also hesitated to let his works go, changing rather than finishing them, as if fearing that they would become separated from the flow of his studio practice and the ordinary rhythms of life that motivated it. De Kooning's work was a Jamesian "stream" of breathing, feeling, and thinking ("For Bill, painting was like exercising his humanity, like breathing").[47] By frequent use of transfer (imprinting a wet painting onto a second surface), de Kooning kept what was effectively a daily journal of his encounters with imagery. This allowed him to borrow freely from his past work to make something new, and he used imagery from other artists just as liberally. He was an appropriator who claimed no original vision of the world, a position he would have found arrogant, not for philosophical or even cultural reasons, I suspect, but because of temperamental factors fostered by his personal history—like Peirce, he was a lifelong debunker. De Kooning also mixed the imagery of high and low forms of art, leaving the logic of his choices ambiguous and unresolved. During the late 1960s and early 1970s, he made drawings around the theme of the Crucifixion (Figure 1). Most of these images are clearly

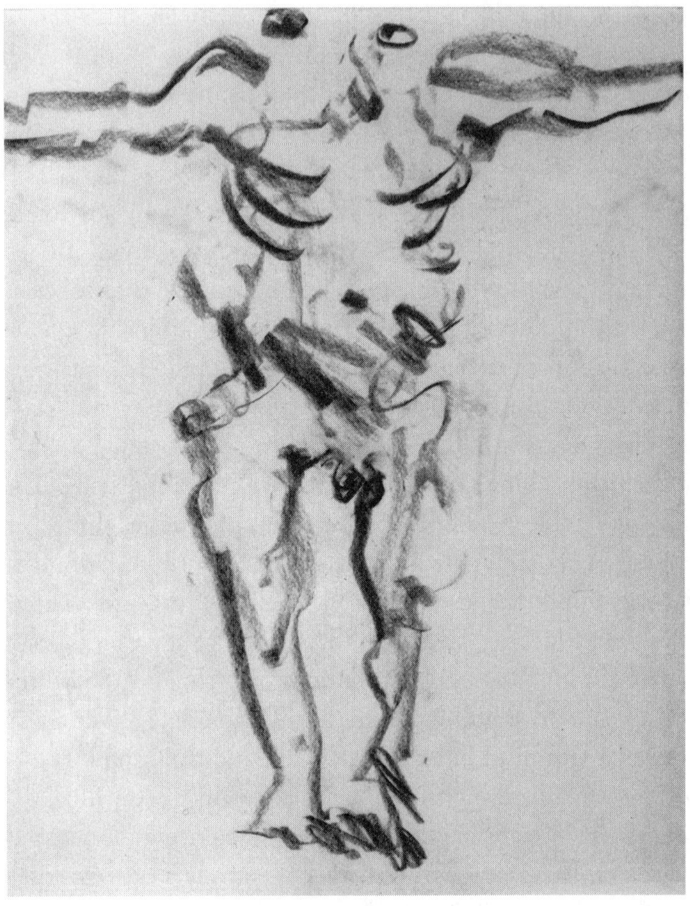

Figure 1   Willem de Kooning, (no title), c.1966. Charcoal on paper, 10 x 8 in., private collection. © 2007 The Willem de Kooning Foundation / Artists Rights Society (ARS), New York.

representational, even though de Kooning produced a significant percentage of them by drawing with his eyes closed.[48] Yet some are so abstract that a viewer unfamiliar with the artist might not discern the representational theme (Figure 2). In any given case, it becomes difficult to determine whether de Kooning's Crucifixion figure derives from the work of a museum master (viewed directly

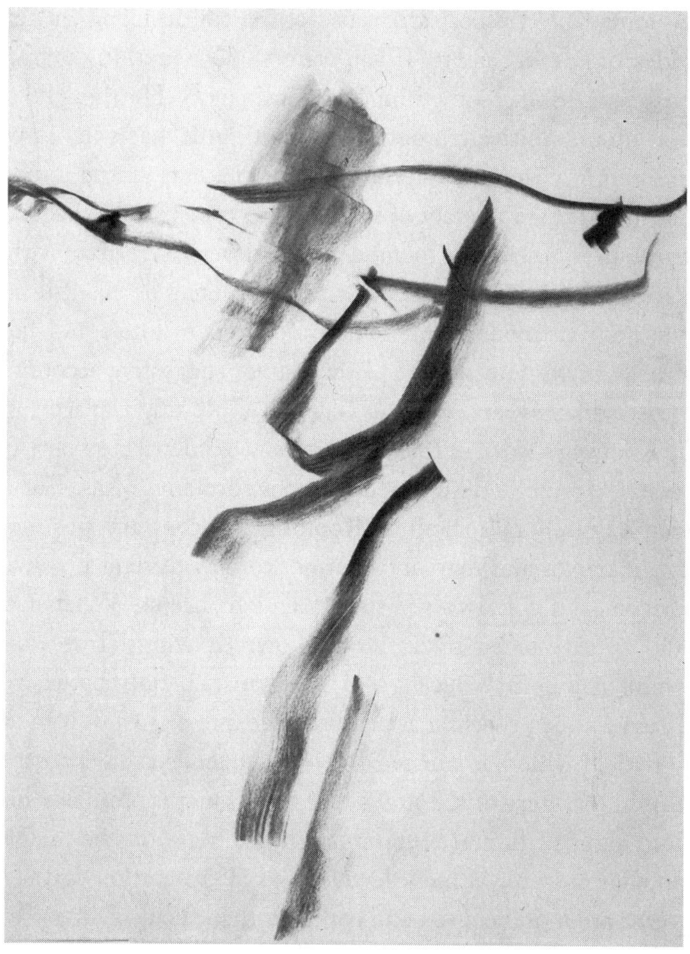

Figure 2   Willem de Kooning, Untitled, c.1970-75. Charcoal on paper, 23 13/16 x 17 7/8 in., The Willem de Kooning Foundation. © 2007 The Willem de Kooning Foundation / Artists Rights Society (ARS), New York.

or seen reproduced in a book) or from the mass-produced, kitsch images found in the homes of Long Island neighbors.

Today academics might say that de Kooning was a rhizomatic figure, creating his imagery on a Deleuzean plateau, that he was someone for whom the suggestion of possibilities would be more meaningful than the authoritative delimiting of a form.[49] He undermined hierarchies, any sense of logical development, and the idea of advancement: "If you want to do something extraordinary ... try doing something very ordinary."[50] He thought the notion of a definitively progressive avant-garde was silly, as was avant-guardism applied to politics. He represents a type of postmodernism before the fact of its name—a type that Elkins associates with a resistance to modernism developing from within canonical practice: "Postmodernism works like a dormant illness in the body of modernism: When modernism falters and fails, postmodernism flourishes."[51] Given Bann's suggestive account of the postmodernist art object as "curiosity," we might place some of de Kooning's work in this category, since it departs so far from normative aesthetic design and assumes so many forms. But art academics rarely talk about de Kooning as a contrary, postmodernist character and may not even notice how deviant his imagery becomes, if not always in form then in concept—What status should we give to his tracings of his own drawings? Instead, de Kooning has been typecast as a modernist, if only because he had already been typecast as an abstract expressionist. Given this designation, which he resisted, critics have tended to see abstraction in his imagery of the 1970s where they might profitably have noticed signs of figural representation and plays on the imagery of popular culture. Whichever way the interpretation drifts, its concerns are more focused and confined than those of an artist at work "breathing."

Categorizations of de Kooning bifurcate: His art is as plausibly a set of abstractions as it is a set of representational images; his technique may seem systematic, or it may seem no more than intuitive guesswork. Critics sometimes explain an artist's practice by identifying its "internal logic," the logic of the artist's self-motivation (Do "external" logics exist as well?).[52] This is an act of interpretative description, likely to be more of a reflection of the interpreter's emotional needs than of the artist's, and an arbitrary choice in relation to the aesthetic practice in question. With the exception of instances of unusually "immersive experience," artists do not determine the mentality of their critics. A confluence of the two emotional forces occurs by chance, hardly affected by the conceptual abstractions of an ideological framework. A person's ideological beliefs may, however, interfere with perceiving chance as chance. Ideology can disguise chance as an "underlying cause" or an "internal logic." Still, temperament remains in play within the ideological frame. My temperamental tendency to acknowledge chance and the doubt it raises makes me wary of imputing the rule of a logic to the practices of another. Given this dynamic, I begin to doubt whether either of the two conceptual abstractions I have just invoked—ideology or temperament—has an independent, absolute reality. The one keeps calling forth the other as a kind of check or antidote.

* * *

In 1948, Clement Greenberg gave significant critical support to de Kooning, admiring him as a painter of abstractions. But in 1955—and, it seems, earlier—he registered his disappointment at the artist's reversion to representational figure painting: "I happen to find de Kooning's *Women* pictures [of the early 1950s] inferior by and large to his previous work."[53] The situation was of course more complicated than a division of abstraction and representation, with the one appealing to the elitist art critic and the other appeasing the journalists and populists, for the public was more directly offended by de Kooning's new pictures on the theme of Woman than by his "abstract," less obviously representational images. The offense registered consciously because representation was something the public believed it understood, as opposed to abstraction, to which it may have objected in principle but could hardly critique in detail. De Kooning's failings as a representational painter could be specified (see Part II).

A bit later, in 1958, Greenberg reintroduced Newman to public attention. He was a more radically abstract artist than de Kooning had ever been at his most abstract. For a number of years during the mid 1950s, Newman was nearly invisible as an exhibiting painter. How now to categorize, how to identify him? "The truth of art lies for him, as for any genuinely ambitious artist, somewhat beyond what he *knows* he can do."[54] Here the italics are Greenberg's, but his precise phrasing may have been inspired by Newman's talk of himself, the artist's self-assessment. If art is always beyond what one knows, then a painter, however adept, would need to reach beyond his or her conscious pictorial skills, both manual and conceptual. The "beyond" in this instance is neither absolute nor unlimited. Nor is the state of abstraction that it implies "pure," as Greenberg indicated that same year: "The arts are to achieve concreteness, 'purity,' by dealing solely with their respective selves—that is, by becoming 'abstract' or nonfigurative. Of course, 'purity' is an unattainable ideal. … But this does not diminish the crucial importance of 'purity' or concrete 'abstractness' as an orientation and aim."[55] As Greenberg imagined this *approach* to the "unattainable ideal" of purity—to a materiality absolutely concrete, an absolute specificity—he came close to proposing an "internal logic," a method of making the approach. Yet he remained the empiricist observer, describing the course of events of the recent past rather than predicting the near future.[56] His statements of advocacy concerned behavior and attitude rather than a prescription for specific results:

> We have had enough of the wild artist. … We stand in need of a much greater infusion of consciousness than heretofore in what we call the creative. We need men of the world not too much amazed by experience, not too much at loss in the face of current events, not at all overpowered by their own feelings.[57]

This is Greenberg in 1947, in a context to which I return, different from the situation of 1958. Possibly, however, Newman in 1958

Figure 3   Barnett Newman, *Uriel*, 1955. Oil on canvas, 96 x 216 in., The Barnett Newman Foundation, New York. Photograph by Bruce White. © 2007 Barnett Newman Foundation / Artists Rights Society (ARS), New York.

satisfied what remained of Greenberg's quasi-Apollonian desires of 1947:

> Apollonian art in which passion does not fill in the gaps left by the faulty or omitted application of theory but takes off from where the most advanced theory stops, and in which an intense detachment informs all. Only such an art, resting on rationality but without permitting itself to be rationalized, can adequately answer contemporary life.[58]

Theory predicts and prescribes what an artist can do, both before and after the fact; practice shows an artist what he or she is doing during the fact, the event. For Newman to operate "beyond what he *knows* he can do" would amount to his feeling his way through his own thinking, "tak[ing] off from where the most advanced theory stops." In 1965, when asked about *Uriel* (Figure 3)—a large, horizontal painting of a decade earlier, in which an expanse of pale greenish-blue covers about three quarters of the width—Newman explained that he had "wanted to see how far [he] could stretch [the color] before it broke."[59] His action had no internal logic to guide it and no purity of a formal kind, solely purity of heart and emotion.

The purity of which Greenberg spoke was not to be believed as a fact. It was instead a creative fiction to be believed in a different sense, its actual existence strongly doubted: "We should remember that no attempt at a 'pure' work of art has ever succeeded in being more than an approximation."[60] An artist or critic could nevertheless trust in the social benefits of this fiction. At a relatively early stage (1947), Greenberg applied the notion of purity to Pollock as it might have been applied to Newman—as sensory immediacy and material concreteness. Pollock was hardly an Apollonian figure yet someone a critic could invest with his belief: "Pollock's art ... dwells entirely in the lonely jungle of immediate sensations, impulses and notions, therefore is positive, concrete."[61] Purity in the form of concreteness allowed mid twentieth-century American artists to meet the standards of their society halfway, communicating with and therefore affecting that society. Greenbergian purity—that is, its approximation—would result when an artist strove to respect the core conditions of his or her particular medium, the nature of its physical existence (invoking Irwin's understanding once again). There was cause to take this technical approach to art. It corresponded to the "general direction [in] thought ... toward a stricter conception of the positive [and to] our increasing faith in and taste for the immediate, the concrete, the irreducible." An avant-garde art that approached pure, concrete abstraction also approached the sensibility of a bourgeois, conformist American public, ill-disposed to such an abstract, concrete art except for the crucial fact of its positivist immediacy, its materialism. Within its historical and social context, abstract art was as appropriate to the emotional needs of its public as an art of "hypostatizing reason" had been to a different public before the advent of the positivist, industrial era. And before the celebration of reason, an art of "revealed religion" had served the needs of a still earlier era.[62] Like a Marxist, Greenberg took a long historical overview, thinking about underlying causes. Like Marx's older contemporary Auguste Comte, he arrived at a canonical historical sequence, Western culture in a nutshell. First, religion or spirit; next, philosophy or intellect; finally, science or sense: revelation—rationality—positivism. Just as religion had ruled over one historical period and reason had guided the next, so raw, concrete sensation and its empiricism were directing life in Greenberg's own time. His analysis differed from a more doctrinaire Marxist or deterministic account by attributing an acute critical consciousness to artists, at least some of them. Aware of the materialism of their culture and its drawbacks, they were fighting fire with fire: Newman with his expansive, "stretched" color; de Kooning with his hyperactive line, even if compromised by representation; Irwin with his effects of light, specific to the moment (this last, not Greenberg's choice). The more aggressive among the modern artists were challenging the public directly: So you think you want physical existence; well, here's the real stuff; deal with it.

Where was the purity and concreteness, however imperfect? What kind of positive, immediate sensation or knowledge would lie "beyond" what an artist or any other person "knows"? Given the various arguments intellectuals made from within the modernist context, two answers come to mind, although these are not precisely Greenberg's responses. The first possibility is a body of skills and capacities called *tacit knowledge*: a person possesses tacit knowledge yet is unable to articulate or explain it, as if it were never fully conscious in an intellectual way, although perhaps conscious in a physical, somatic way. This is Polanyi's notion, from his book *Personal Knowledge*.[63] We might argue that de Kooning had tacit knowledge in abundance; it enabled him to make Crucifixion drawings with his eyes closed. Animal life, including humans, thrive on tacit knowledge. We all have it, though some of us appear to have more. Such knowledge is like a feeling rather than a thought. Artists who work within a particular medium or a set of related mediums tend to be strong in tacit knowledge because they learn so much through hands-on experience. Their habits and skills acquire a tacit component.

In 1958, Greenberg addressed Newman's art and Polanyi published *Personal Knowledge*. As chance has it, during this same year sociologist C. Wright Mills, Schapiro's colleague at Columbia University, identified the enemy of the hands-on as the "cultural apparatus ... standing between men and events." Culture acted as a filter or governor on experience, shaping its dualities, enforcing protocols for communicating images and ideas. A certain limitation and reduction resulted: "Communications not only limit experience; often they expropriate the chances to have experience that can rightly be called 'our own.'" According to Mills, the "cultural apparatus" consisted of "all those organizations and milieux in which artistic, intellectual and scientific work goes on ... [as well as] the means by which such work is made available to small circles, wider publics, and to great masses."[64] A culture of institutions, protocols, and representations performed in a way analogous to Irwin's photographic illustrations: "a language of expediency ... [of] mass communication."[65] At about the same time, Schapiro made some analogous observations: "The theory and practice of communication today help to build up and to characterize a world of social relationships which is impersonal, calculated and controlled in its elements, aiming always at efficiency." Modern abstract art countered this control with what Schapiro called a "high degree of non-communication." Differing from efficient communication, "painting and sculpture ... induce an attitude of communion and contemplation. They offer to many an equivalent of what is regarded as part of religious life: a sincere and humble submission to a spiritual object" (not far from Elkins's account of the philistine's "fully immersive experience" but lacking its component of representational realism, that is, illusion).[66] This intersubjective, communal aspect of art may have accorded with Newman's views, but not with Greenberg's.[67] If Schapiro regarded the abstractionist's stress on "the mark, the stroke, the brush, the drip, the quality of the substance of the paint itself" as "signs of the artist's active presence," Greenberg viewed these same features as aspects of *material* presence—the physical existence or external quality of sensation that would concern Irwin and many of his contemporaries, members of the generation to follow.[68] He failed to see how either religion or quasi-religious values (a nonspecific spirituality) could remedy excesses of positivism.[69] The art that impressed him was more of a stimulus to sensory distraction than to spiritual communion. Directed at a materialist culture, the proper antidote was homeopathic, not allopathic.

* * *

You cannot prove a negative, they say. Nothing indicates that there might not be a logic or rationality to tacit knowledge, but we defeat the notion by regarding it as logical. If there were a significant difference between voiced and unvoiced knowledge, what would it be? Perhaps we acquire the logic of the distinctly tacit realm by means that are other than logical. This speculation, reasonable enough, leads to the second kind of knowledge that lies beyond knowing: We call it intuitive, a result of nonlogical thinking. Intuition, however, may be nothing other than an advanced application of logical reason. With intuition, logic is too subtle or too complex, and its result comes too quickly for it to feel like deduction, as opposed to a hunch or guess. Recall Peirce's statement: "Hypothesis [guessing] produces the *sensuous* element of thought."[70] I wonder whether what we call genius, insight, and intuition, is for the very quick thinker the same process that other people grasp only as slowly pondered reasoning. Logical thinking may be nothing more than a skill, but when skill operates at an extraordinarily high level, it begins to feel like tacit knowledge. There can be a difference, presumably, between how the mind is working and how one feels that the mind is working. I say that I have a hunch, when "in fact" I am reasoning by deduction—but doing it very quickly. This may explain why we doubt our intuition less than reason tells us we ought to doubt it. Slow reasoning expresses distrust of fast intuiting.

Given this consideration, critical evaluation becomes ever more arbitrary. A few years ago, I centered an essay on a remark by Donald Judd, who, recommended by Newman, had exhibited along with Irwin at the 1965 São Paulo Bienal. Judd was not only one of the most inventive of late twentieth-century artists, but he was also an accomplished art writer, especially clever with words. He was adept at wryly explaining his own creativity, as in the statement of 1983 that particularly interested me. Without quite using the term *intuition*, he said this about its play:

> I've always considered the distinction between thought and feeling as, at the least, exaggerated. ... Emotion or feeling is simply a quick summation of experience, some of which is thought, necessarily quick so that we can act quickly. ... Otherwise we could never get from A to Z, barely to C, since B would have to be always rechecked. It's a short life and a little speed is necessary.[71]

Judd was describing what might be called *fast thinking*—intuition. Another term would be *guessing*. Whether we call it unusually fast logical thinking or hypothetical guesswork, this process has a specific feel to it. People know when they experience their own fast thinking because they have the feeling of a kind of enthusiasm or inspiration. Here, intuition does double duty: We sense what it is that we need to know, while simultaneously we know that we are sensing, as opposed to reasoning. We think so fast that we cannot reconstruct the logic of our conclusion, and we have the feeling that we are doing just that—we are intuiting and are aware of it.[72] We are also conscious that we do not know with certainty what we know; this is the factor of doubt. Intuition entails doubt as much as belief. At such moments, we cannot represent ourselves, give ourselves the identity of a logical position. We cannot explain why we have come to think as we do; this amounts to a factor of belief, for we know that we do think a certain way. Intuitions inspire faith in those who have them, but do not allow the one who intuits to demonstrate the truth of the insight to others. The solution is to dispense with proving the truth.

"It's a short life and a little speed is necessary," Judd would say. In another context, but in the same year, 1983, he wrote, "It's not possible to prove a proposition about the world [that is, to generalize about material specifics]. One can only assert, point and list characteristics."[73] Judd's statement implies that there are always more characteristics to be identified. To place the object under a verbal category and then define the category is to terminate the process of discovery. Normative schematics and metaphorical descriptions together constitute the fantasy world of the general and conceptual. They can only lead away from the sensory world of the specific and the real.

The historical and critical evaluation of works of art has extraordinary arbitrariness and chance built into it. It follows an unpredictable sequence of identifications and associations, which open a work to the whim of every subsequent interpreter and the application of every conceivable meaning. But to say this is circular. For *arbitrary* means dependent on judgment, as opposed to a more secure kind of causation. Any judgment is arbitrary, guaranteed only by the authority arbitrarily invested in the judge. Judges are arbiters. One way to write history, including art history, and even art criticism, is to take note of how artists make choices, how they choose to move one way when they could just as easily have moved another way. Judge the artist as the judge. My own knowledge of events comes to me in an arbitrary manner since my work is dependent on the availability of archives and the proximity of other forms of documentation (a spatial factor) as well as the limited time available for writing (a corresponding temporal factor). Under these normal conditions of research, whatever information arrives, perhaps because of a fortunate conjunction of space and time, assumes disproportionate significance unless I arbitrarily choose to resist the order of chance occurrence. Why resist? No compelling reason. "It's a short life and a little speed is necessary."

As I was preparing the lectures from which this essay is derived, the chance occurrence of a book sale put a text from Heidegger in my hands, which led me to read a particular passage in Leibniz, because Heidegger had referred to it; and reading Leibniz caused me to consider that complexity is (according to Leibniz, at least) the enemy of intuition.[74] Would I have intuited this—this fact beyond knowing? I do not know. Leibniz claimed that we have intuitive knowledge of primary sensations and relations, but not of more complicated, multifaceted situations. All this—from Heidegger back to Leibniz and forward again to other discussions of intuition—seems to have provoked in me the arbitrary intuition (the hypothesis) that Judd's achievement could be described this way: He developed the capacity to maximize complexity within a fabricated object that retains a quality of perceptual wholeness. Judd was intuiting a genre of aesthetically complex but unitary forms that would not be reducible to a hierarchical order of less complex relationships.

If fast thinking is a way of processing a great amount of conceptual and sensory data with the efficiency of a single deduction, then Judd designed his constructions to provide the intuitive feel of material complexity that remains simple and whole. He either had a talent for, or acquired the skill of, visual fast thinking. This leads to the conclusion that minimalist art like Judd's is not so minimal, even though minimalist art by someone else may be. Here the task of critical evaluation is complicated by the existing categories: A viewer is likely to miss whatever features of an object fail to suit the connotations of a category arbitrarily selected as appropriate to the object. The combinations of interior and exterior spaces in Judd's wall and floor boxes are remarkably complex, especially given the stated display height for these structures, one that encourages viewers of average size to peer into and around them. One of Judd's insights was that a box-like structure, if projected abruptly from the wall, at right angles to it, would create a genre of object and a corresponding type of space inconsistent with either low or high sculptural relief. This was new space, outside the existing categories, space the critics had either never seen before or to which they had never before been sensitized—unconscious space becoming conscious.

So Judd succeeded in producing an art that demands—that is, induces in its viewer—an intensified observation. He talked about his new kind of space only after he and a few others created it. To his mind, it had not derived from the application or realization of a theory. If we view Judd's art through the prevailing critical understanding of minimalism, or with just this name as a conceptual guide—a noun that is itself the distillate of a theory—then we fail to reach the level of experience that Judd learned to expect from his works. As a human agent, not a conceptual identity like minimalism, he had intentions. He wanted to perceive in a material object qualities specific enough to constitute the immediate relation to its physical existence. To this end, he learned to expect both wholeness and complexity. It seems that wholeness without complexity would amount to an identity, and complexity without wholeness would lack the degree of presence that holds on-the-spot human interest. Here is Judd interviewed in 1965, the year of Irwin's *Artforum* statement:

> Usually when someone says a thing is too simple they're saying that certain familiar things aren't there, and they're seeing a couple maybe that are left ... But actually there may be ... several new things to which they aren't paying attention. These may be quite complex. ... They may [also] be read all at once. This is important to most of the best work going on now. It has to have a wholeness to it that previous work didn't have, but still, within that, it's not all as simple as [people] say.[75]

Judd's conversational language, rather like Irwin's, strays into absolutes: "all at once ... a wholeness." But he qualified his more calculated statements with details of personal observation, guided by a principle he associated with Newman and others he admired: Never presume to know more about art, or anything, than any one person knows from direct experience.[76] Each of Judd's repeating, multiple-unit "stacks" of boxes that project from a wall demonstrates his point about wholeness and complexity, because no two units within such a work, even when morphologically identical, can be experientially identical. From any actual position of viewing, each unit will look and feel different from the others. It takes the simplicity of repetition to demonstrate this complexity within a culture dulled by too much art and criticism. The repeating units become alike only in ideal, schematic drawings or verbal descriptions—like in theory, unlike in sensation. The situation was complex enough when Judd projected a stack of identically fabricated boxes, but all the more complex when he varied the units. *Untitled* (1988; Figure 4) is a set of six open, horizontal boxes of clear anodized aluminum arrayed vertically. The inside back panel of each is layered with a sheet of blue Plexiglas over a sheet of black Plexiglas, creating a complex play of light and color within the simple structure. In this instance, Judd also inserted a single horizontal panel at different positions in each of the units, partially closing the openness. This affects perceived qualities of projection and depth in the structure, as well as the amount and direction of illumination that the colored Plexiglas receives.

Newman once insisted that "a straight line is an organic thing that can contain feeling."[77] He was combating the stereotyped emotional connotations of certain forms: Straight must be geometric and rational; curved must be organic and emotional. Judd chose to build rectilinear wall boxes of metal or wood; another artist might cover walls with mud, as did Richard Long, whose art Judd collected. To regard the one as a sublimation of the other and the other as the desublimation of the one is to fall prey to cultural stereotypes and a formal ideology of seeing. Judd was only peripherally party to what Krauss called "minimalism's industrial metaphor—its con-

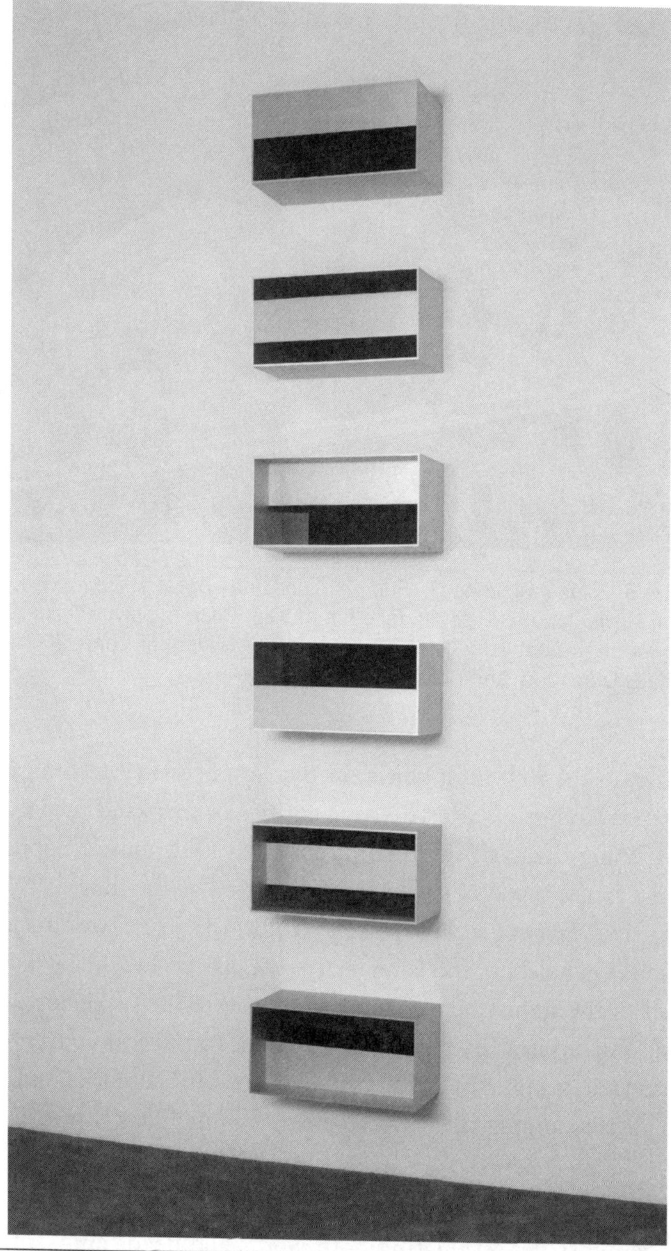

Figure 4 Donald Judd, Untitled, 1988. Clear anodized aluminum and blue over black Plexiglas, 6 units, each: 10 x 20 x 10 in., PaceWildenstein.

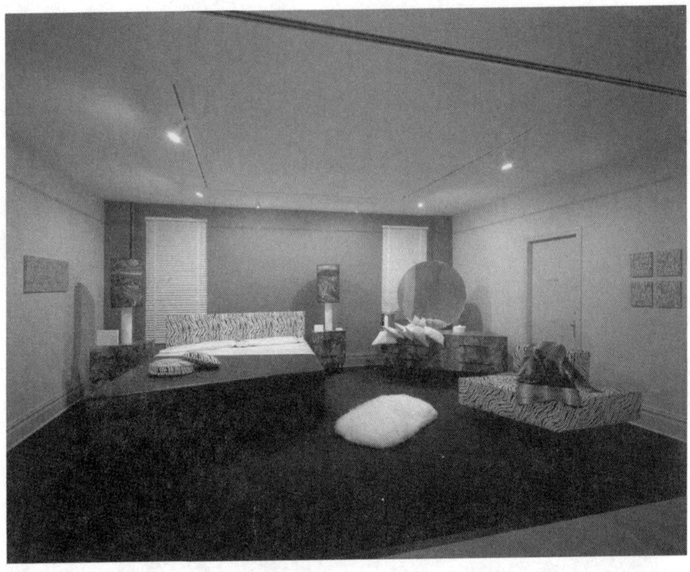

Figure 5 Claes Oldenburg, *Bedroom Ensemble 1/3*, 1963. Wood, Formica, vinyl, aluminum, paper, fake fur, muslin, Dacron, polyurethane foam, lacquer, in a room 10 x 17 x 21 ft., National Gallery of Canada, Ottawa. © Claes Oldenburg and Coosje van Bruggen.

viction in the well-built object, its display of rational tectonics and material strength."[78] Restrictive identities of this kind fit only too well or hardly at all. Judd admired Claes Oldenburg's floppy ice cream cones, made of stuffed fabric, as well as the illogically illusionistic *Bedroom Ensemble* of 1963 (Figure 5), just as, for his usual reasons—wholeness and complexity—he appreciated his own rigid boxes.[79] The industrial metaphor, tempting as it is, applies to his work only arbitrarily, reflecting the chance historical convergence of a certain number of critics who happened to share this interpretive identity among themselves, self-sustaining like a rumor.

Modernism from bad to worse

Academic critics, evaluating both words and deeds and sensitive to semiotic difference, often fail pragmatically. They ignore the gulf separating what visual artists do from what critical writers do. Judd made the box, and the critics gave him minimalism and its "industrial metaphor" in return—an exchange of incommensurables.[80] The conflation of the two, the object and the concept, is not inherent in the language and need not be an issue. Although problems with the term *minimalism* are becoming ever more evident, problems with the more encompassing term *modernism* are proportionately greater. Critics have acquired the habit of using the phrase *modernist art* without making it evident whether their reference is to the class of objects and actions that we identify as modernist or to the conceptual abstraction designated as *modernist art* or, worse, *modernism*, or still worse, *high modernism*. I say worse and still worse, because modernism and its heights constitute such a broad critical abstraction. I suppose that if I were a modernist, I would want to be judged a high one rather than a low one. Well, maybe not. Either way, the distinction would hardly affect what a pragmatically oriented artist was doing. Perhaps *high modernism* was initially a designation used with irony, an allusion to the art-historical pretense of a High Renaissance. If this irony was once present, it has gradually withered.

No single writer is to blame for the incursion of a silly terminology. These things happen. The situation is nevertheless aggravated by increasingly generalized use of a problematic identity, the type of writing that eliminates much of the conceptual flexibility in terms such as *modernism* and *modernist*. Again, I invoke Krauss because she became the most prominent of late twentieth-century theorists of modernism in the visual arts, at least within the academic world—just as Greenberg was the most prominent among mid-century theorists, despite being neither theorist nor academic.[81] Like many others, Krauss has often fallen into hypostatizing modernism, using the concept as if it had its own force of agency and teleological destiny, as in the statement, "modernist visuality wants nothing more than to be the display of reason."[82] She associates modernism with what Greenberg would have regarded as a premodern mentality: a fixation on rationality (the second of his three evolutionary stages), as opposed to a fixation on materiality (his third stage, that of the industrialized economy and its scientistic culture). This arbitrary category shift causes Krauss to see either postmodernism or antimodernism where Greenberg, less agonistically, would have seen variants of modernism—whether in the physicality of surrealist automatism, which he slighted, or in the physicality of Pollock, which he stressed. By imputing to Greenberg a perspective that he himself associated with a classical past, not a modernist present, Krauss exaggerated their critical difference. Doing so, she strayed from a base but noble principle that she worked to apply elsewhere: "to remain with the *real presence* of things, 'thinking' by means of this obstinate fact rather than with the abstractions provided by words or concepts."[83] Or, as stated in the text of Georges Bataille to which Krauss refers this issue: to attend to the "inexpressible *real presence* [of a thing] and to reject as puerile absurdities certain attempts at symbolic interpretation ... [substituting instead] natural forms for the abstractions currently used by philosophers."[84]

The situation is complicated. Krauss was writing about modernist desire from within a meditative discourse and was witnessing her own intellectual development.[85] Perhaps her address to "modernist visuality" can be considered as an element of a retrospective thought experiment—part confessional, part advocacy—part past, part future—a bidirectional projection. Her articulation of the desire felt by "modernist visuality" is found within *The Optical Unconscious* (1993) in a section that passes in and out of reverie. Poetic license is in force in the extremes of abstraction that characterize some of the sentences. For a reader, these abstractions become the material reality, effects that become causes. The rhetoric is provocative, which satisfies the writer's want and perhaps a reader's—but not modernism's. A conceptual abstraction like modernism or visuality can have no desire, save metonymically, when something of the writer-agent's desire for a decisive order of concepts is projected onto it. "Modernist visuality *wants*": It seeks or desires its condition of self-evident logic. Elsewhere Krauss referred to "the primacy that modernist art gave to pure visuality."[86] I have no precise sense of what "pure visuality" or pure anything might be. Krauss presented this instance of the pure as no approximation but rather as an autonomous, pure "pure," as if it were to inhabit an animistic world where absolutist concepts do as they will. She transformed the critical invention known as modernism into an active agent, begging the questions that might have been addressed to those who would speak for the concept, questions that would require an explanation of the political and ethical motivations for endorsing its practices at past moments of faith— questions that would temporalize modernism so that it would no longer appear as good or bad, one or the other, with no room for doubt between. If modernism must be animated, we would do well to allow it its share of mundane self-differing, just like any other force of volitional agency. In self-difference, we see modernism as its ironic double, known otherwise as postmodernism.

Have I taken the critic's rhetorical figuration of modernism— "modernist visuality wants"—too literally? If so, it is a sobering, cautionary exercise, for a reader is hard pressed to discern whose modernism is being described or characterized. This type of problem is endemic. I try to avoid it by attending to agency, but not always successfully. Krauss's prominence has led me to her writing as an exemplary case, a cultural paradigm. Her dissatisfaction appears to be with critics who championed modernism, those who sometimes disappear behind the conceptual abstraction, the word. She did not complain of modernist artists, such as Cézanne, or Pablo Picasso, or Pollock, although her writing often elides the artists and their artworks with their critics and the critics' concepts—all different entities. Her modernist critic of record is usually Greenberg, who is only one of many plausibly associated with so-called modernist values. She often works to undermine Greenberg's assessments by locating in his favored artists evidence

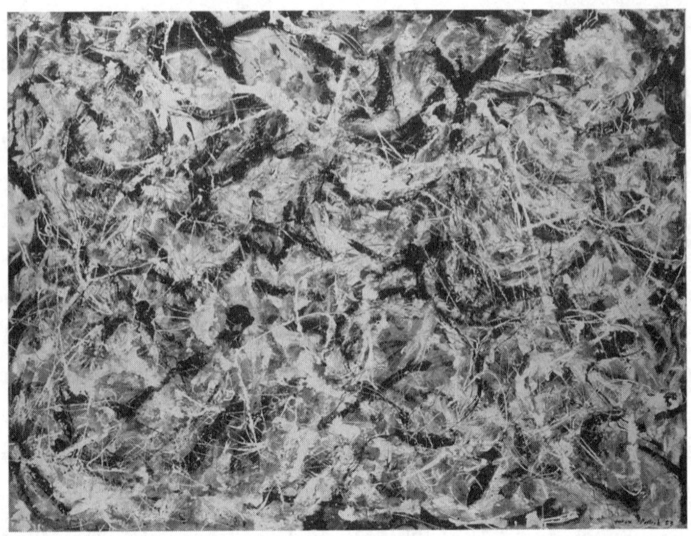

Figure 6 Jackson Pollock, *Greyed Rainbow*, 1953. Oil on canvas, 72 x 96 3/8 in., Gift of Society for Contemporary American Art, 1955.494. The Art Institute of Chicago. © The Art Institute of Chicago. © 2007 The Pollock-Krasner Foundation / Artists Rights Society (ARS), New York.

of the opposite of whatever it is that she takes Greenberg to have approved. In Pollock, then, she finds materiality instead of opticality (Figure 6).

This is an arbitrary judgment on Krauss's part, of course, not because Pollock's pictorial art lacks materiality, but because every painting has its proper materiality, and we are free to dwell on its presence. Whether or not a person imagines the material consistency and touch of a painting, usually the most immediate physical sensation it generates is visual. Such opticality is not inconsistent with the materiality of paint and canvas, nor does it prevent a viewer from relating to how the work has been made and the physical effort of the artist. What some critics have called opticality and visuality can be the most material factor of a painting with regard to its reception—what Greenberg might have called the *tangible datum* of seeing (more on this term in Part II). The conceptual opposition of opticality to materiality is misleading in relation to the medium of painting, which is a mode of tactile production designed to be consumed primarily, even exclusively, by sight. Studio practices that are laborious, time-consuming, and dirty often result in work accessible to the most direct vision. Painting is tangible and intangible, tactile and visual, material and optical—the site of qualities that logic regards as oppositional, so that if painting is tangible, it should not also be intangible. But experience follows no logic.

Does one materiality render another irrelevant? Pollock's materiality is of a certain in-your-face sort that Krauss identifies with the horizontality of its production, associated metaphorically with baseness, the ground, detritus, a primeval muckiness, excrement. Pollock worked on the floor and used the wall with its vertical orientation for purposes of display. In the case of smaller paintings and drawings, he worked on a table, as artists and other fabricators so often do; but Krauss emphasizes the horizontality of the floor for the sake of the category, passing to floor- and foot-oriented imagery in the work of Andy Warhol and the Gutaï gesture painter Kazuo Shiraga.[87] The mechanics and pragmatics of the human body ensure that things large in relation to it are usually created on a floor and things small in relation to the body are usually created on a table. Working against a wall, a person can go either large or small. But metaphorically, horizontal work is base and material; vertical work on a wall or (if smaller) at an easel is elevated and optical. Our language offers us this horizontal-vertical opposition as a way of ordering varieties of experience. Like Piet Mondrian, we shun the diagonal, gravitating to orthogonals, caught up in identifying structural dichotomies and absolute divisions, even when evoking the kind of physical existence or "real presence" that—we hope, we doubt—will assist us in resisting concepts. Is it the agonistic cultural environment, an academic ideology of agon, that compels us to argue in this oppositional manner?

Rather than claim that "modernist visuality wants" something, it would be useful to return modernism to the art called modernist, which, like other modes of art, is not an agent in itself, but figures or represents a form of agency as an ideal entertained by its producers. If autonomy has something to do with modernism, perhaps modernist art—like a certain form of fast thinking—creates the feeling of autonomy in the human subject who practices modernist techniques. Feeling free is somewhere between being free (in many senses, an impossibility) and representing or identifying yourself as free (nothing at all like being free). The activity creates the character who practices the activity. The work of art can then be associated with a social ideal, presumably beneficial, at least to someone. Two questions follow: Why would the artists and critics called modernist have an interest in projecting or creating an effect of autonomy? And what figuring process is actually in operation—how is it to be done? Questions of this nature extend beyond the personal disputes and rivalries (Krauss versus Greenberg) that seem to have motivated so much of the art criticism of the past half century.[88] The conditions of intellectual exchange may have been better in the years before.

II. EXISTENTIAL DOUBT

Although historical narratives almost always proceed in a forward chronological direction, the great majority of us would probably admit that we write history in the reverse, choosing to explore issues relevant to our present time. The selection is arbitrary; but to a person who believes in the pervasive force of ideology, it may, to the contrary, seem necessary and imposed. Does a pervasive ideology extend everywhere, affecting everything? Will there be any exceptions, any exclusions? Sometimes an individual—consciously, with self-certainty—doubts what "everyone"—as if unconsciously—believes. Should I doubt the absoluteness of the identity *everyone*? For each of us, *everyone* usually refers to everybody else, as when you want what "everyone" has—a certain fashionable commodity, for example. Perhaps the unsettling notion of unconscious motivation is what should be doubted. Then "everyone"—not only oneself—would be released from living among the benighted, fated to remain unaware of what they do.

These considerations introduce slippage between the arbitrary (a world of free judgment, willful change, luck) and the determined (a world of compulsive judgment, imposition, necessity). A family of terms overused in critical writing is *obsess, obsessive, obsession*—connoting compulsiveness. When an artist repeats an image—Cézanne's mountain, Mondrian's orthogonals, de Kooning's woman, Ad Reinhardt's blackness, Robert Ryman's whiteness—the act is likely to be psychologically typed as obsessive. The prevalence of this category indicates a bias toward concluding that others' judgments are either externally compelled or internally compulsive, neither freely arbitrary nor as open to change as not. Choosing to identify the other's choice as compelled by an obsession, the critic—as if at greater liberty than everyone else—gains the ideological upper hand. Invoking obsessiveness is analogous to ascribing a lack of consciousness to a recognized creative achievement.[89]

Walter Benjamin, one of the twentieth century's great critics of compulsive causation and narrative continuity, theorized the matter of writing history in the reverse direction. He argued that moments of historical crisis often come to be acknowledged only long after the fact, when the consequences of the crisis have been played out and have left an inescapable impression on the consciousness and forms of life of the majority of people. Only then does the critic or historian have an incentive to seek out the past historical crisis as a way of explaining the present situation that has become everyone's immediate concern. What had been ignored or unacknowledged for decades begins to look like the prophecy or the sleepwalking dream of the future, the very future that has appeared as the historian's inevitable present. Writing in the late 1930s, Benjamin put the matter in terms of technological changes and their unforeseen aftermath, which may itself have reflected the needs and sensitivities his generation had developed, given how extensively the technologies of his era had been altering warfare, communications, transportation, the domestic environment, and each individual's sense of technical skill and professional expertise. Just as we take stock of the difference in perception that a sudden switch from the postal service to electronic mail brings, Benjamin regarded the dial telephone as it replaced the old model that required cranking. Bear in mind that if Benjamin, who died in 1940, had lived a more typical lifespan, he would have been active into the late twentieth century, overlapping with my generation and with younger ones as well. He would have encountered touch-tone dialing and perhaps mobile.

Here is Benjamin on the techno-prophetic nature of art:

> It has always been one of the most essential functions of art to engender a demand for which the hour of full satisfaction is yet to come. The history of every art form has critical moments of striving toward effects that can only be freely realized with a changed technical standard, that is, in the context of a new art form. The excesses and crudeness associated with art in this type of situation ... emerge from the richest historical concentration of forces.[90]

This and other passages from Benjamin have caused me to consider that critics not only identify the origins of the present situation in a prophetic past moment, but often assume the role of prophet themselves, advising their society as to what ought to happen in its near future or what ought to be done about what is happening at the moment. Benjamin reminded his readers of the 1930s that a proper criticism has prognostic value, although, to the extent that critical writing is itself an art, it cannot be clear whether such value would be immediately apparent to a writer's contemporaries. (Do we claim to understand Benjamin only now?)

In any case, criticism, like art, addresses the problem of cultural failings and remedies, sometimes by exemplifying an attitude presumed to be beneficial for everyone (for some, it might be expressions of heightened doubt; for others, expressions of heightened belief). Benjamin's commentary on sociohistorical prophecy resembles certain passages of writing in Newman and Greenberg, statements composed around 1946-47, less than a decade after Benjamin's own. He was writing just as the course of events linked to World War II accelerated; they were writing in the wake of the same catastrophe, relieved by the Allied victory yet disturbed at the state of American society in the aftermath. Just as I have been drawn to Newman and Greenberg by their sensitivity to history and attempts to grapple with it critically, so I have also been led beyond them to de Kooning, who dismissed critical projections of every kind. His own dealings with Newman and Greenberg were complicated; and, as things turned out, both grew as dismissive of his art as he was of the ambition of their ideas. Joined by their mutual contrariness, these three figures of the New York art world demonstrated social, communicative self-difference.

Prophecy (Newman)

Around 1947, Newman jotted a note that recalls Benjamin: "Every art epoch, like every age, has its romantic dream age"—its prophetic dream after the fact.[91] Every culture chooses a moment in the past to explain the nature of its present successes and failures, its gains and losses. I have suggested that the timing of Newman's thoughts tended to be specific. During the war and the immediate postwar years of the late 1940s, he reacted to the destructive technologies of the Holocaust (blamed on the Europeans) and the atomic bomb (blamed on the Americans). He believed that art could have been something of a remedy in both instances if people had attended to what serious artists do.[92] Instead, both Europeans and Americans had become accustomed to relying on the instruments of the scientists and the intellectual constructions of the philosophers, whose discipline was another kind of science, one overstocked with abstract identity:

The more we study the forces that have been motivating Hitler, Mussolini, and Hirohito, the more it becomes plain that they live and act by pseudo-science, racism, intrinsic destiny, the progress of mankind—and most false of all—the "science" of history, with its [Hegelian] synthetics, etc. It is therefore astounding to realize that those who stand against these murderous fanatics are likewise equipped with falsehood … the claptrap of Marxian "science" of history. And [no better] are the other lukewarm phoneys who believe in political science, with its [concepts of] sovereignty, nationalism, imperialism, and capitalism, who are convinced the world can be run by a science of "checks and balances." The science of history is the curse of the world … Hegel's "science" of history and all his widespread spawn of historical interpretations have about as effectively delineated history [as did Greek astrology]. And if any book should have been burnt in our time, it should have been his.[93]

This philosophical science of history had had an unfortunate result, which was not its prophecy per se but its overt projection into the future, dictating actions in advance of the events that might conceivably justify them. A "science of history"—coupled with more belief than doubt—is a self-fulfilling prophecy.

Newman held a certain belief: The high status science attained during his lifetime was infecting art, especially abstract art, much of which had adopted analytical methods, applied to cold, geometric compositions. Within this context, he praised his surrealist contemporaries for breaking with the prevailing attitude: "Surrealism taught that ideas can be not only fruitful but important to art. [It] reviv[ed] subject matter"—initially at least, a type of subject matter outside the realm of the foreseeable.[94]

Science in general was not Newman's adversary; in fact, he was keeping current with a number of scientific disciplines, including geology, botany, and paleontology. It was the "science" of art that disturbed him, art in its scientific guise of formalism. Formalism had emptied avant-garde painting of its content, the "subject matter" that surrealism "revived" by imposing psychologically disturbing images and provoking thought—its beneficial contribution. Newman had little else good to report about European surrealism, which weighed on him because a number of its leaders resided in his native New York during the war years.[95] His appreciation of surrealism came embedded in an otherwise biting critique, most likely composed during spring 1945, when photographs of the German concentration camps first became available. Around that time, Newman was making colored abstract drawings of a relatively modest size, with odd squiggles and dry, scratchy marks. To his contemporaries, such works must have appeared unusually casual, even amateurish and uncoordinated, as if the artist were merely experimenting with various graphic qualities, arbitrarily. To put the situation positively, we might imagine Newman's art in a Benjaminian manner: It had serious meaning, but the meaning was prophetic; as a result, no one realized it was there. Newman's drawings neither lent themselves to formal analysis, nor translated into the kind of rhythmical, calligraphic gesture then acknowledged as artistic "handwriting." This is why Judd appreciated Newman's efforts so deeply: His was an art without the identifying signs of "art." Yet the early Newman was not without resemblance to accredited modern styles. Because of its vague biomorphism, along with its informal look of automatism, comparison could be made to certain works of the surrealists. Later, when Newman became a recognized figure and needed to be placed within history, critics commonly projected surrealism as his source, choosing a known quantity to domesticate his wildness.[96]

Given his stance toward surrealism, on balance negative, Newman is unlikely to have intended any link between that movement and his own practice. It may be that he and the Europeans simply shared a source in the imagery of botanical and biological illustration to be found in scientific texts.[97] It was not unusual for artists to draw on scientific taxonomies to evade artistic clichés, even when they resented the scientistic attitude they witnessed in the professions around them. Newman could accept the surrealists' biomorphic allusions to laboratory science and still reject their Freudianism as pseudoscience.[98] As for the element of automatism in surrealist art, he adapted it to his purposes. He was willing to follow what the materials in hand seemed to want to do: "How it went, that's how it was," he later said of his drawing and painting during the 1940s, as if in this exploratory work, he did little more than allow his lines and colors to fall into place—the places they wanted.[99] This material desire is analogous to the physical process of water seeking its level, not the conceptualized desire of "modernist visuality wants." Newman's "how it went" avoided the preconceived formulas of geometric abstraction along with those of conventional figure painting, landscape, and still life. To some extent, he infantilized himself, lending an animistic spirit and motivation to inanimate entities and material stuff. As so often, a statement from Peirce is relevant: "No one questions that, when a sound is heard by a child, he thinks, not of himself as hearing, but of the bell or other object as sounding."[100] The bell sounds because it wants to sound. If the bell sounded for Newman, not because he was listening for it but simply because it did, then his experience of its aesthetic would extend "beyond what he *knows* he can do," as Greenberg once characterized his art.[101]

Although Newman soon removed his own facilitating devices—the biomorphic forms, the casualness, and much of the tentativeness—he never abandoned his sense of "that's how it was." Not knowing that it would turn out as it did, he initiated a series of radically abstract paintings—radical in being devoid of identifiable outside reference, whether to things observed in nature, orders and systems conceived in theory, or feelings commonly experienced in life. A work he created in January 1948 on his forty-third birthday was the inaugural statement (Figure 7).

He later titled it *Onement I*. Such titles do establish references, but Newman chose them after the fact, sometimes long after, according to qualities in the work or the situation of its production.[102] As he told the story of *Onement I*, it seems more to the point to say that it created him rather than the other way around. By no means a product of his intended action, the painting, he claimed, changed his life.

A less passive understanding would be that Newman allowed and even encouraged *Onement I* to effect the change. He did so by acknowledging this painting as his beginning from the very beginning, as if no "romantic dream age" had preceded it. Yet much of what he had already accomplished approached the spareness and directness, the defining qualities, of *Onement I*. This causes the retrospective historian to wonder whether Newman failed to recognize the prophetic nature of his earlier production. How should we regard a work like *Two Edges* (Figure 8), which he completed less than a month before his self-proclaimed breakthrough with *Onement I*, and which shares the use of masking tape and a textured effect on its painted edges? Like *Onement I*, *Two Edges* disposes these material elements within a vertical format without significant horizontal counterforce. *Two Edges* and *Onement I* appear equally devoid of naturalism and other thematic references.

Newman thought differently. He distinguished the two paintings fundamentally, while nevertheless retaining *Two Edges* as a valid work. Something about *Onement I* seems to have stopped him in his tracks, making his engagement with this particular painting unique. It may have been the relationship of its two hues: Symmetrical bands of a deep, brownish red flank a narrow band of an intense orange-red, painted over a strip of masking tape affixed to the center line of the canvas. This arrangement fell into place with unexpected force at a specific moment in the construction of the painting—an instance of "how it went, that's how it was." Newman was using the tape as a test strip, so, technically, the work was incomplete. It nevertheless imposed itself on its

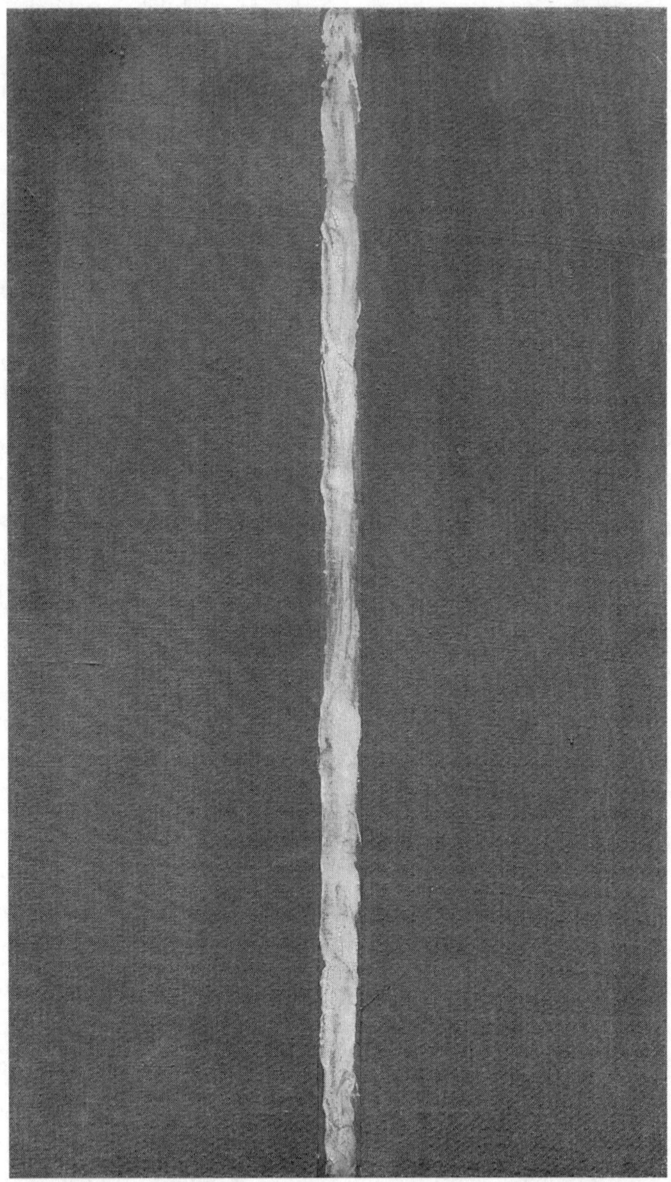

Figure 7 Barnett Newman, *Onement I*, 1948. Oil on canvas and oil on masking tape, 27 ¼ x 16 ¼ in., Museum of Modern Art, New York.© 2007 Barnett Newman Foundation / Artists Rights Society (ARS), New York.

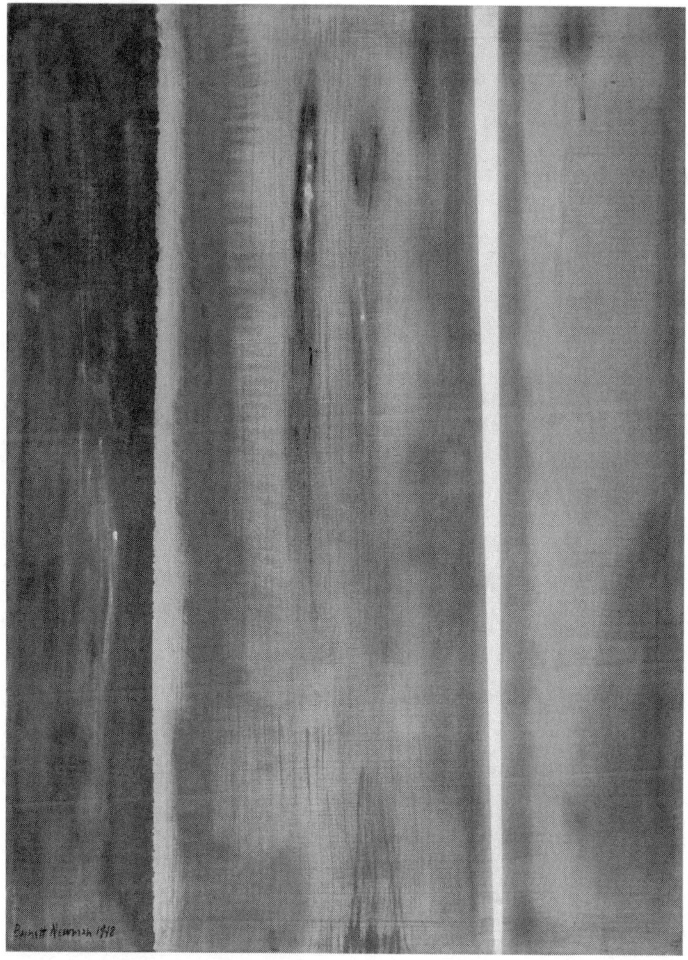

Figure 8   Barnett Newman, *Two Edges*, 1948. Oil and egg tempera on canvas, 48 x 36 in., Museum of Modern Art, New York. © 2007 Barnett Newman Foundation / Artists Rights Society (ARS), New York.

creator as finished. Announcing prophecy and fulfillment simultaneously, *Onement I* determined a distinct chronological period within the artist's development: his final period. Newman recognized that this was the beginning of his own end. His future had entered his present.

The experience showed him that all his previous work, including *Two Edges* and other accomplished paintings of the late 1940s, failed to attain the level of directness for which he should have been striving. With *Onement I* in front of him, he could see that the tapering vertical band in *Two Edges* did more than give the impression of light streaking through the painting—a metaphorical description he sometimes applied, and which might pertain to the band in *Onement I* as well. Rather, the vertical streak in *Two Edges* illuminated an entire atmosphere, as if the light in this painting might also be observed in nature.[103] In this naturalistic, representational capacity, *Two Edges* could have derived from the stock of the world's clichéd imagery, even if without its creator's conscious knowledge. *Onement I* was different, and only with its appearance did Newman understand where he had wanted to go: "Suddenly in this particular painting, *Onement*, I realized that I had filled the surface … I did not make an arbitrary, abstract decision."[104] Newman understood that if he had a fixed method of making art, every result would be "arbitrary" and "abstract," a consequence of following a set of rules and procedures, a logic. Instead, *Onement I* presented him with an immediate, organic imperative. It was emotional, not rational—it was feeling.

During Newman's formative years of the 1930s and 1940s, surrealism and abstraction were the two art movements recognized as advanced, despite their tendency to negate each other.[105] Both could lay claim to avant-garde status in two senses: Each was new, and each presented a challenge to the bourgeois cultural order—as not all new things did, for the bourgeoisie itself was relatively new. Abstract art removed the secure intellectual and emotional ground that representational reference provided. In contrast, surrealism overflowed with referential material, which should have been reassuring; but it evoked disturbing, nightmarish situations and obscene acts in which the typical viewer could find neither comfort nor refuge.

Newman was an anarchist with no desire to join one party just to defeat its rival. He objected to the rational science of abstraction that he thought he saw in Mondrian, yet this did not mean that he would accept a surrealist style of attack on the social order. He judged that by 1945 and probably much earlier, surrealism was no longer responding to compelling social and political conditions. His critique of the movement began: "It is natural that surrealism died with the advent of war. For surrealism is dead. Its leaders [in painting,] Ernst and Tanguy, continue, but their work has now become a continuous performance."[106] The parade of paintings by Max Ernst and Yves Tanguy through the decades demonstrates what Newman meant by *continuous performance*, a term indicating that a movie shown in a theater would keep playing, screening after screening, as if the entire program were a film loop. It was irrelevant whether the viewing audience for surrealism entered at the beginning (the 1920s and 1930s), the middle (the war years), or the end (the late 1940s). From before to after, there was no significant change. Surrealism lacked input from the reality of its own historical experience.[107]

Newman's critique continued: "There can be no question that the objections raised to the movement are valid. Its use of old-fashioned perspective, its high realism, its preoccupation with the dream, we now know are not the final answer or the perfect formula for artistic expression."[108] Newman's emphasis should be located in the word *now*, for he was writing in 1945. He had good cause to be appalled by the surrealist "preoccupation with the dream." Dreams can come true. And then what do you do? A person cannot keep dreaming on and on, like a continuous cinematic performance, oblivious to the new reality. With the publication of photographs of the Nazi death camps, a truth had become undeniable, therefore unbearable. Newman struggled to change his art in response to what he described as a conversion of terror into tragedy. Terror is a state of fearing the unknown; tragedy is comprehending what has already happened. What people had feared, what they had dreamed as their worst nightmares – their personal surrealist romance—had tragically become their only reality, a phantasmatic but living obscenity.

Here, Newman got to the heart of the practice of artistic avant-gardism as he knew it. The surrealist avant-garde pretentiously believed that it was ahead of its own period, even before knowing what its period was—before knowing where, or in what, its time would end. Newman wrote:

> The surrealists' work was in the nature of prophecy. For the horror they created and the shock they built up were not merely the dreams of crazy men; they were prophetic tableaux of what the world was to see as reality. They showed us the horror of war; and if men had not laughed at the surrealists, if they had understood them, the war might never have been. No painting [is better surrealism] than the photographs of German atrocities. ... All new painting when begun is in the nature of prophecy.[109]

Newman's point came laden with irony and pessimism. The surrealists' practice did little to force others to take its prophecy of horror and tragedy seriously. Because the import of its imagery was not properly understood—apparently even by surrealists—the imagery gave no effective warning.[110] Conceived as a subversion of existing identities, it nevertheless operated as a parallel identity rather than as a physical existence, a class of many rather than a class of one bearing a specific historical message—so it seemed, in effect, to Newman. There is a second, more general irony to note, which lurks behind the first: The modern avant-garde typically fails to deal with the reality it creates. As self-different as it may be, it neglects self-criticism. This is why the example of *One-ment I* is so significant. Newman claimed that he had intuited the meaning of this painting even if no others had done so. From his intuition came a moral obligation to communicate the meaning his work revealed to him, to present it in as many forms as possible while avoiding converting it to doxa. As a writer, he would need to transfer the physical existence of his painting to an analogous physicality of language. It may be significant that not long before, around 1945, he had been composing poetry.[111]

Newman's prescience did not endear him to those who, preferring their own explanations, assumed an avant-garde role as critics. Like Newman in his response to surrealism, but usually lacking his irony, many critics argued that artist-heroes who change visual culture attain prophetic truths in ignorance (recall statements by Schapiro and Rubin in this regard). Only those in a position to comprehend the social and historical context perceive the prophecy. Artists themselves are likely to be alienated from society. As culture's beneficent paranoids, they neither intend nor recognize what others know as their real accomplishments. Their acts and "dreams of crazy men" work to good effect, with history eventually "proving" that what such artists thought they were doing was not what they were "really" doing. The concept of history itself, with its eventualities and outcomes oriented ironically toward the future, provides antagonistic criticism with a purpose. As the present changes, history is ever in need of rewriting, so that it might predict whatever comes to pass. By their statements, critics establish themselves as hyperaware, if not omniscient, relating to the artist as a kind of intellectual adversary. The situation may be healthy; it may be unhealthy. But surely it involves critical arrogance—to arrogate is to usurp the proper claim of another.

When Newman stated that the realities created by surrealism were not merely "the dreams of crazy men," he implicitly recognized a paranoid distinction: The conventional "continuous-performance" surrealist was sufficiently aware of conditions to be acting in bad faith, while a different type of artist with greater sincerity but less control might be generating a more radical art without recognizing its—the artist's own—future. In Newman's experience with *Onement I*, the prophetic object of *his* future, it became necessary for the painter to cede conscious control of the painting. He was not someone who would be at ease doing this; in

Greenberg's estimation, Newman shared with Clyfford Still and Mark Rothko "a want of humility that was singular even among artists. ... [He] was an egomaniac."[112] Conditions, as this "egomaniac" perceived them, either forced him or freed him to abandon his ego. It was an atypically paranoid moment in Newman's development, when painting spoke not for him but to him.[113] Unlike his surrealist contemporaries with their controlled images of psychological alienation, Newman yielded control to his painting. It was an intuitive act of faith in the midst of his early doubts. Stopping before he had finished in the way that had become customary, he seized his future as it broke upon him.

Projection (de Kooning)

> Behind the so-called curtain which is supposed to conceal the inner world, there is nothing to be seen unless *we* go behind it ourselves, as much in order that we may see, as that there may be something behind there which can be seen.

> —G. W. F. Hegel, 1807[114]

Greenberg shared with Newman a distrust of surrealist intentions and sensitivities (and a distrust of Hegel), but he was keen on the developmental aspects of abstraction in ways that Newman never would be. Despite Newman's contrariness, Greenberg eventually became his advocate, viewing his art as an advance beyond other forms of abstraction.[115] For two or three years during the late 1940s, however, de Kooning played the avant-garde role for Greenberg, although decidedly second to the more extreme Pollock. Greenberg approved of de Kooning as long as he could see him as the creator of uncompromised abstractions, such as *Painting* (1948; Figure 9), of which he said at the time: "The emotion in that picture reminds me of all emotion. ... You can't specify what the emotion is but are profoundly stirred nevertheless."[116] This kind of remark either evasively mystifies or cleverly avoids the trap of assigning self-differing meaning, an identity, to what

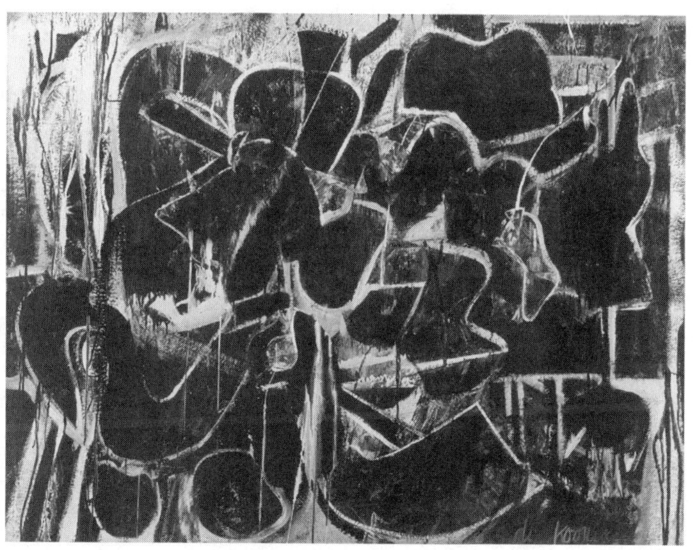

Figure 9 Willem de Kooning, *Painting*, 1948. Enamel and oil on canvas, 42 5/8 x 56 1/8 in., Museum of Modern Art, New York. © 2007 The Willem de Kooning Foundation / Artists Rights Society (ARS), New York.

already has its proper physical existence, right there to be appreciated. Whatever the case, Greenberg gradually weakened his initial support, ultimately claiming that de Kooning had been "at his best" in the early 1940s, not during but before the sequence of particularly ambitious abstractions from *Painting*, to *Attic* (1949), to *Excavation* (1950). And Greenberg concluded, "He's gotten worse since 1950."[117] De Kooning, it seemed, committed an irredeemable error in June 1950 when he turned to concentrate on a series of representational works around the theme of Woman. Greenberg had no aesthetic objection to representational imagery and in fact preferred it, but his experience showed him (he claimed) that the truly ambitious art of his time—like Pollock's, and somewhat later, Newman's—was abstract: "I think it is one of the *tragedies* of our time that great painting has to do without a 'recognizable' subject matter."[118] By the latter half of the decade,

Newman had displaced both Pollock (who died in 1956) and de Kooning as Greenberg's favored abstractionist.

Whichever way a critic was inclined, de Kooning's personality complicated matters because it was subject to contrary assessments. To many viewers, his energetic expressionist style, in both abstract and representational imagery, connoted anger and violence; yet he liked to present himself as a very ordinary type who not only identified with the common man but also joked around a lot. Perhaps he was adept at representing the conventional signs of psychic disturbance while nevertheless of a different temperament and fully in control of his effects, as Newman believed the surrealists were. Or, as the painter of Woman, de Kooning may have been reflecting—some would think he did it consciously, others unconsciously—a rampant misogyny that American society on the whole preserved in repression rather than acting to suppress and eliminate. If we take de Kooning at his word a decade later in 1964, it seems that, inadvertently, his personal choices facilitated every conceivable interpretation:

> "In a way, I feel the *Women* of the '50s were a failure. I see the horror in them now, but I didn't mean it. I wanted them to be funny and not to look sad and down-trodden like the women in the paintings of the '30s, so I made them satiric and monstrous, like sibyls."

After the Women came urban and suburban "landscapes," but these—lacking a central frontal figure—looked like abstract art. De Kooning's assessment of the loosest of his broad-brushed abstractions of the late 1950s, works such as *Montauk Highway* (1958; Figure 10), also opened onto diverse critical application, for he linked this type of imagery to early failures at representation: "I was never good at landscape as a young man. ... You have to find a substitute or imitation to really see the real thing. ... All the images inside [me] are from nature anyway."[119] As he had explained to Thomas Hess in 1953, it was all the same (all

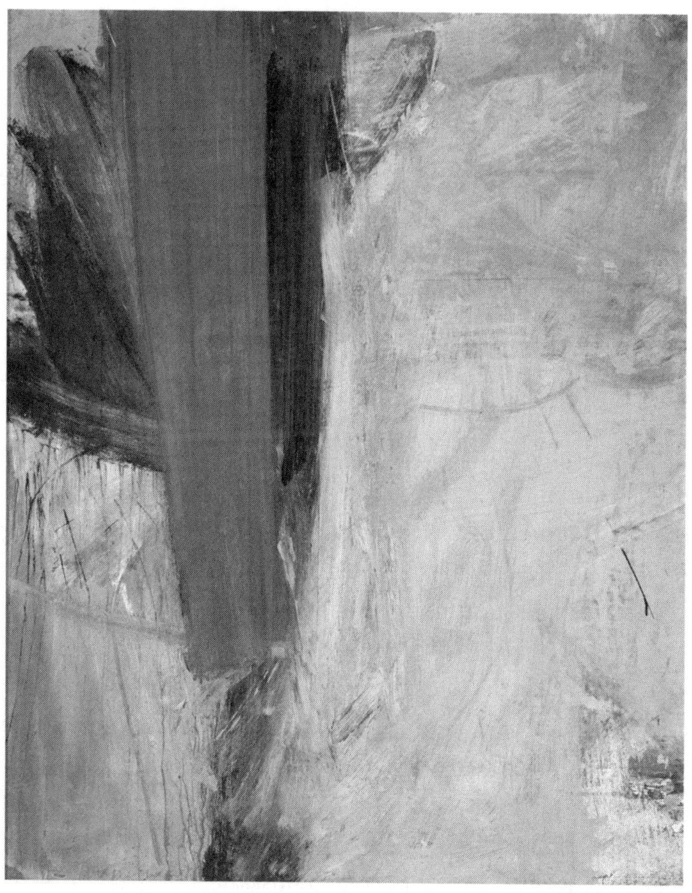

Figure 10 Willem de Kooning, *Montauk Highway*, 1958. Oil on canvas, 59 x 48 in., Los Angeles County Museum of Art. © 2007 The Willem de Kooning Foundation / Artists Rights Society (ARS), New York.

self-differing) as far as he was concerned—Woman, landscape, abstraction: "The landscape is in the Woman, and there is Woman in the landscapes."[120]

On his part, Greenberg attempted to explain innovative trends in art broadly enough to provide historical and social contextualization. The "inside" of de Kooning contained little of interest for him; what mattered was the overt work and its reception. To understand the latter, however, required knowing something of the "inside" of postwar American society, its collective psychology and system of values. When Greenberg reviewed de Kooning's abstractions in 1948, he undermined in advance the potential complaint that abstract artists of this ilk lacked a traditional painter's skills. De Kooning was resisting the comforts of his hand for the sake of a higher feeling: "Emotion that demands singular, original expression tends to be censored out by a really great [technical] facility, for facility has a stubbornness of its own and is loath to abandon easy satisfactions. ... There is a deliberate renunciation of will in so far as it makes itself felt as skill."[121] Greenberg implied that de Kooning should be credited for having struggled through a conflict of will over the way things were—"easy satisfactions" of a material kind—and the way they might be—"original expression" of an emotional kind. It was typical of him to set up this kind of critical opposition.

Not long before, in 1946, he had dealt with three roughly analogous cases, although they were well-established figures from an earlier era: Cézanne, Vincent van Gogh, and Henri "Le Douanier" Rousseau. In their different ways, they too seemed to surmount technical inhibition, but not so willfully as a later figure like de Kooning.[122] With the formal merits of the older modernists having already been demonstrated by specialists of an earlier generation, Greenberg accepted the challenge of accounting for these three painters' recent public acceptance, especially Rousseau's. In Benjaminian fashion, he would discern of what social condition the three pioneering modernists had become the tacitly acknowledged prophets. De Kooning arrived as proof of the retrospective prediction—a postwar master whose release of pictorial emotion dominated a display of technical skill that would have been all too easy for him to feature. In his account of Rousseau and other revered early modernists, Greenberg prefigured de Kooning's coupling of high emotional impact with eccentric, seemingly deficient technique. With his explanation of de Kooning, he effectively converted his view of Rousseau into critical prophecy. This may amount to no more than saying that Greenberg's writing had its own momentum and developed its own thematics, regardless of whether the artists he discussed, both nineteenth- and twentieth-century figures, would have agreed with the appraisal and accepted its implicit parallels. What Newman did in self-consciously probing the meaning of *Onement I,* Greenberg did for those who would never have made such pointed historical inquiries into themselves. For better or worse, this is critical arrogance.

In 1953, when de Kooning showed his new Woman series rather than new abstractions, Greenberg remained for a while in the painter's camp, agreeing to compose an appreciative introduction for the exhibition. But not long after, in 1955, he went public with his disappointment: "I happen to find de Kooning's *Women* pictures inferior by and large to his previous work, but that's an *ad hoc* judgment that has nothing to do with anybody else's figure paintings."[123] He was tacitly retracting statements he had made not only in 1948, in response to the artist's first one-person show, but also for the show of 1953. In 1948, Greenberg stressed de Kooning's identity as "an outright 'abstract' painter" who used black as a strategy ("refined himself down to black"); this was particularly effective in the case of a painter with a "lesser gift as a colorist."[124] To the contrary, in 1953, he described de Kooning as an underrated "colorist" who also "wants in the end to recover a distinct image of the human figure, yet without sacrificing anything of abstract painting's decorative and physical force."[125] This phrasing constitutes the critic's attempt to make the most of an unfortunate turn of events. With regard to aspects of de Kooning being "underrated," the critic might as well have been criticizing himself, but was not.

Underlying Greenberg's evaluations was his sense of a cultural war being fought between those who confront the taste of a philistine public and those who appease that taste ("original expression" versus "easy satisfactions"). Around 1950, figuration appealed to the philistines, while abstraction confounded them. Greenberg knew, however, that an artist could appease bad taste and yet make a progressive aesthetic advance: Rousseau had done this. Arising from this perverse cultural situation was the craziness, the paranoia, that Greenberg discerned not only in Rousseau, but also in Cézanne and Van Gogh. These representational painters lived before the advent of abstraction; for them, the matter of choosing a subject might have been complicated in a personal sense but was unproblematic within the culture at large. It was simply expected. Greenberg believed that in de Kooning's case, as opposed to Rousseau's, there was a genuine choice to be made and a consequent possibility of moral failing. Having struggled over abstraction, de Kooning appeared to have taken the easy way out by his return to the human figure. A reporter for *Time* was on the spot in April 1953: "Some pained partisans of abstract art pointed out that de Kooning was attempting to ride two horses (representation and abstraction) at once, and thought he failed."[126] Greenberg's judgment seems to have been that de Kooning fared no better than Newman believed the surrealists had: By the early 1950s, he consciously, not unconsciously, was giving the public what it already knew and wanted—historically, the wrong choice.

Just as Newman could appreciate surrealism up to a point, Greenberg saw some good in de Kooning. After all, with respect to form, the Woman hardly offered what the public wanted. In 1955 Greenberg credited de Kooning with being the only one at that moment to advance the formal discoveries of cubism. Nevertheless, the apparent praise was double-edged. De Kooning's "late cubist" rigors of form, Greenberg suggested, would "reassure" the knowledgeable public that his "savage dissections" of the human figure still belonged to a tradition with a viable structural logic. In fact, within the context of this characterization, it seems that what becomes savagely dissected is not a body but a picture—

dissected in the analytical sense that cubist practice tore apart the conventional signs of pictorial unity (such as linear perspective) and replaced them with new, seemingly fragmented and therefore paradoxical, unifying structures. Despite this analytical, compositional "savagery," on balance de Kooning served the conservative end of taste by holding to the past rather than projecting the future: "If de Kooning's art has found a readier acceptance than most other forms of abstract expressionism, it is because his need to include the past [his humanistic figuration] as well as forestall the future [by maintaining cubist practices] reassures most of us. And in any case, he remains a late Cubist."[127]

Today it may seem irritating, or at least odd, for a critic to refer to an artist's "savage dissections" of what appears as a woman's body, without immediately appending commentary on psychoanalytic or gender factors (see *Woman I*, 1950–52; Figure 11). We expect these considerations. Perhaps we cannot help but join certain critics of the time in regarding de Kooning's art as figured through an age of misogynist sexism in America, linked in turn to the hypermasculinity of Cold-War posturing.[128] The example of de Kooning then becomes one generalized sign among many—prophetic, but too commonplace to deserve credit as prophecy. If a male artist appears to be "dissecting" a female body, we ask whether the motivation would have been fascination and desire or anxiety and hostility—obvious interpretive choices. The question that follows is whether the psychological pathology would belong only to this individual (perhaps consciously) or to the entire society (perhaps unconsciously).

Many critics at the time spoke of de Kooning's picture of Woman as if it had come alive like a pagan idol. They could not resist the personification. With psychological projections of their own fantasy, they fetishized the Woman even if de Kooning himself did not. Fetishization was not the only obvious interpretive possibility in relation to the social context. De Kooning's cartoonish Woman could be seen as a parodic critique of American

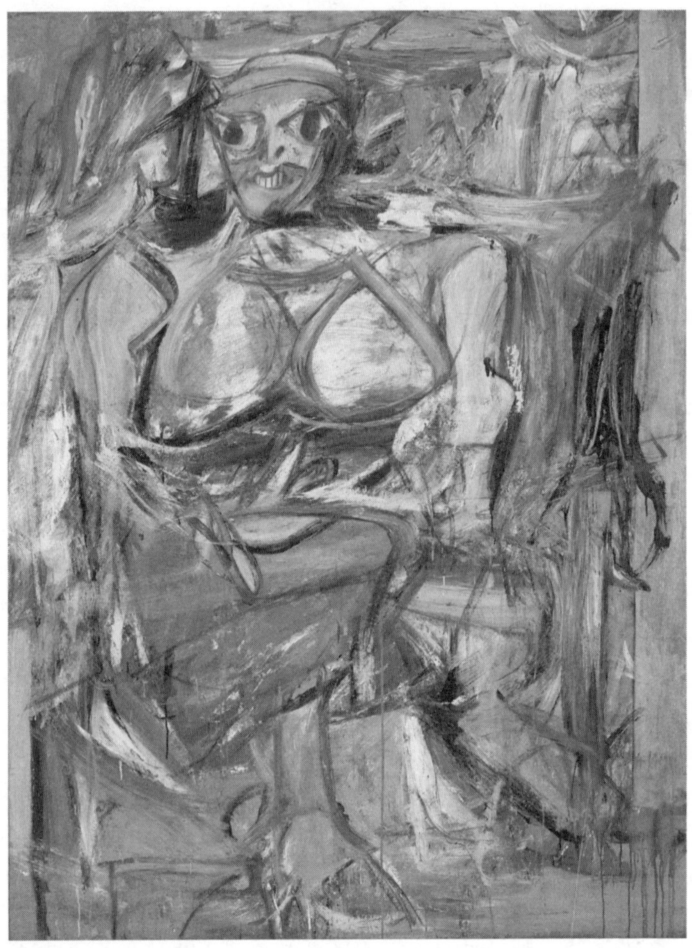

Figure 11   Willem de Kooning, *Woman I*, 1950-52. Oil on canvas, 75 7/8 x 58 in., Museum of Modern Art, New York. © 2007 The Willem de Kooning Foundation / Artists Rights Society (ARS), New York.

postwar conformity, with its advertising image of the all-American girl: part pin-up, part cheerleader, part housewife, part mother. This was the view of Hess and also of Elaine de Kooning, more intimately informed and more sympathetic critics of de Kooning than Greenberg was.[129]

Interpretations of the figure of Woman, whichever way they went, hardly interested Greenberg. He directed his analysis to the immediate materiality of de Kooning's painting rather than to the sexuality and pop-culture references of its subject. Like a good cubist, his de Kooning "dissected" form and composition, but left untouched the imaginary social body with which most viewers, male or female, were identifying. When Greenberg commented on late cubist form in 1955, he was implicitly resisting opinions like that of James Fitzsimmons, who projected the "savage dissections" onto specific anatomical parts. Fitzsimmons took representation seriously: Each picture was as alive as a real person, certainly so in his animated critical narratives. When he discovered three conspicuous dabs of red paint on the torso of *Woman III* (1952-53; Figure 12), he called them "three bloody stab wounds on the chest."[130] He gives no indication of considering whether de Kooning had added the three red marks to enliven that part of the surface—an artist's animating, painterly rhetoric. It is hard to tell, and easy enough to forget the paint, as Fitzsimmons did, converting its deposits into punctures in the "skin" of the canvas: "Look, de Kooning is wounding her with blood." Those were Fitzsimmons's words as recalled by Grace Hartigan, who disagreed: "The violence is in the paint. De Kooning's women are very loving. ... I have done a lot of painting in which I use teeth and it has nothing to do with wanting to bite anybody."[131]

Though Fitzsimmons was more or less a fan of de Kooning's art, he never hesitated to express specific reservations: "De Kooning is an obsessive [that word!] painter and in this instance [a Woman shown in 1954], unable, it would seem, to lay down his palette knife, he almost worried the life out of the poor girl with it."[132] Did Fitzsimmons himself "obsessively" entertain violent misogynist fantasies? More concerned with psychoanalytic speculation (both Freud and Jung) than with what he called "academic criticism"—"I am not a formalist," he said—Fitzsimmons aimed to write "at the level of feeling." "Whatever I write will be

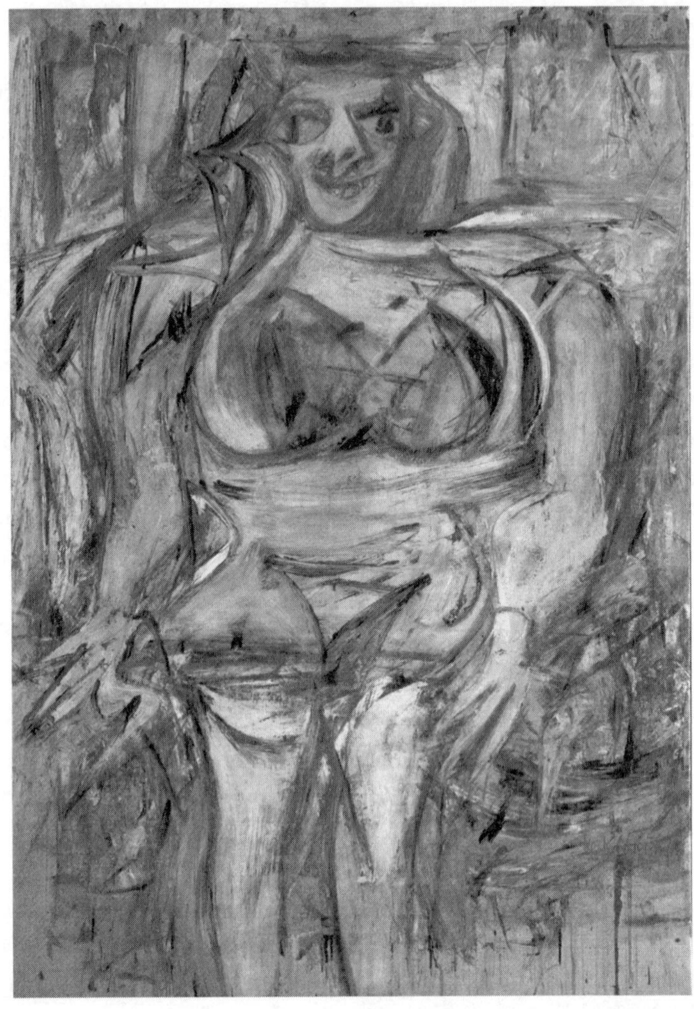

Figure 12   Willem de Kooning, *Woman III*, 1952-53. Oil on canvas, 68 x 48 ½ in., private collection. © 2007 The Willem de Kooning Foundation / Artists Rights Society (ARS), New York.

about myself," he confessed to readers in 1958. The value of these feelings? They "will have value, if any, only because I too am a human being and a fairly average one, so that what I will have to say about these paintings may also hold for others."[133] We must all feel the wounds—if we are "average" enough. Sidney Geist, another reviewer, apparently was: "In a gesture that parallels a sexual act, [de Kooning] has vented himself with violence on the canvas which is the body of this woman."[134]

Fitzsimmons indicated that the implications of de Kooning's image of Woman for society were, or should be, frightening: "I have heard her described as the American woman of the future. ... This female personification of all that is unacceptable, perverse and infantile in ourselves, also personifies all that is still undeveloped ... It is to the unconscious (and to the American unconscious in particular, I fear) that [de Kooning's] *Woman* appeals." The critic's projection served to render de Kooning prophetic. Distancing himself from Greenberg's approach, Fitzsimmons added: "It is exceedingly difficult to evaluate these paintings on a formal aesthetic basis."[135]

Fitzsimmons's problem was twofold. First, by conventional standards de Kooning's mode of formal composition not only seemed obsessive—would *excessive* be the more tempered term?—but it also verged on incoherence, though incoherence in itself would not invalidate it. In fact, Greenberg had already observed an element of incoherence in 1948.[136] Second, de Kooning's representations conveyed a psychological and physical "horror," to use Fitzsimmons's word, that added significantly to the confusion.[137] Newman, on his part, had referred to the "horror" of war as surrealist painters imagined it, because this is where he saw the pressing political issue of the day. He would never have described a picture of a woman as a horror. World War II was a horror, and the Cold War also—not Woman. For Newman, Woman would be no more than a poor choice of subject matter, as irrelevant to wartime or to the postwar political context as landscape and still life. It was Greenberg who was better positioned to understand the unease Fitzsimmons experienced, for the terms of his criticism allowed him to explain de Kooning's art as an unfortunate aesthetic compromise between form and subject matter.

Eventually, Greenberg gave the condition of de Kooning's art a special designation, "homeless representation," which he defined as "plastic and descriptive painterliness ... applied to abstract ends, but which continues to suggest representational ones."[138] This formulation implies that the figure of Woman interferes with the abstract material form of the painting, rather than the reverse.

In 1958, Greenberg was at work revising his favorite reviews and essays for what in 1961 became *Art and Culture*, the first collection of his writings. He took his account of de Kooning's "late cubist" composition and made it more cutting this time around, identifying the painter's "reassuring" traditionalism as little more than a sop for those who "still find Pollock incomprehensible."[139] His opinion of de Kooning was hardening. Like Newman in his confrontation with surrealism, Greenberg confronted de Kooning with his failure to pursue his advances, to realize his own prophecy.

De Kooning had a defense. He was expressing his independence of the value being put on abstraction, which he believed to be no more than a critical fashion. He refused to take a side in this war waged on behalf of an avant-garde in which he had no faith. He was merely being a painter, pursuing the course he chose to pursue, as he suggested in 1951: "If you paint your whole life, you take that for granted, and after a while all kinds of painting become just painting for you—abstract or otherwise."[140] De Kooning would never confuse the painting of a woman with a real woman nor the act of painting a woman with generalized feelings about women. He regarded his representational painting in terms of the experience of making it, eliminating much of the difference between abstraction and representation. This approach allied him with those who valued the expression of sensory experience through an engagement with the physicality of materials, no matter what the artistic subject.[141] Eventually, this would include Irwin and Judd, despite their lack of interest in de Kooning himself and his somewhat paradoxical, corporeal mimeticism.[142] A politics inhered in their collective position, with sociologists like

Mills citing the material experience of art as an antidote to the philistine consumerism and repressive conformity that character-ized contemporary American life in the post-Cold-War era.[143]

If Greenberg perceived a meretricious impulse in de Koon-ing's use of the human figure, others questioned his material sincerity when he worked in what looked like a purely abstract mode, as in *Montauk Highway*. De Kooning kept switching his imagery, a move he claimed as a demonstration of his continuing independence. Yet, by the late 1950s, critics and younger painters were arguing that his newer works, both abstractions and figures, lacked the intensity of his earlier ones. It was a complaint analo-gous to what Newman had said about Ernst and Tanguy, and indeed, Newman also said it about de Kooning in 1961, although in a guarded manner.[144]

In all likelihood de Kooning knew that Newman and others were carping about his technical tricks, the very devices that he used both to restrain his facility and to challenge it. His knowl-edge of their critique suggests a context for remarks he made in 1959 within the space of two or three months, alluding not only to works like *Montauk Highway* but also to figure paintings like *Woman I*. First, he told a reporter: "I'm not trying to be a vir-tuoso, but I have to [paint] fast."[145] It seems that for de Kooning, speed in painting was analogous to what speed in thinking would represent for Judd. Then, for a filmed interview, he returned to the issue with a different rhetoric: "When I'm falling, I'm doing all right: when I'm slipping, I say, 'Hey, this is very interesting.' It's when I'm standing upright that bothers me. I'm not doing so good. I'm stiff, you know."[146] De Kooning was aiming for speed—painting, as he said, "fast." He was seeking a self-induced lack of balance—"falling," "slipping." Both features of technique ensured that his painting remained spontaneous, inventive, and, for him, a creative adventure. Through it all, he wanted to avoid virtuosity: "I'm not trying to be a virtuoso ..."

Unlike Newman, however, de Kooning *was* a virtuoso, which necessarily affected the practice of his art. He possessed remarkable motor skills and an unsurpassed knowledge of painter's materials. His capacity for controlling his hand became a feature of his validation, not with the general public and the journalists, but within sophisticated circles of artists, dealers, and collectors. To speak of de Kooning's skill was analogous to the critical cliché of pointing out that Picasso drew with conventional accuracy when it suited him. Wary of virtuosity, de Kooning subjected his control to self-control, as Greenberg noted from the beginning. He modified his brushes so that they were particularly hard to handle—anything to make the situation more difficult and unpredictable—drawing with eyes closed, with the left hand, with both hands simultaneously.[147]

Despite de Kooning's exercise of manual control, his erratic pattern of change in both technique and subject matter might be viewed as anxious indecision. He had a tendency to bury representation under apparent abstraction only to release it with a vengeance. *Excavation* (Figure 13), finished in 1950 as an abstraction, began as a composition of two or three women.[148] De Kooning went to work on *Woman I* immediately after completing it, as if to reverse the direction he had been taking, which itself had been a reversal. His statements gave his critics ample cause to question him on these matters, because he second-guessed himself in public. At the time of his 1959 exhibition of abstractions, which included *Montauk Highway*, he remarked to his friendly critic Hess: "You know, I think I might want to do some Women now."[149] This was another in a long series of reversals. Should we conclude that de Kooning's art amounted to his repeated indulgence in his changing whims—an art with neither strategy, nor program, nor purpose? Or does history show that he suffered sincere confusion as to where his art ought to have been going— strategizing but to little avail? Nothing he did or said resolved the situation for his critics. His ambivalence prevented most of them

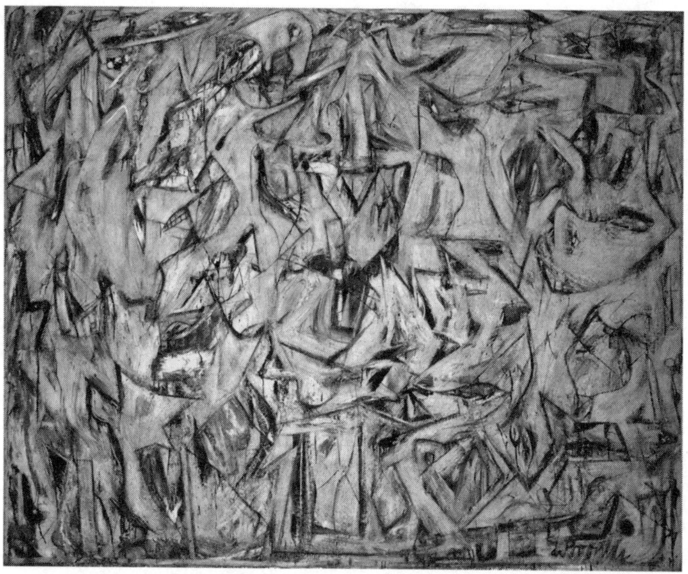

Figure 13 Willem de Kooning, *Excavation*, 1950. Oil on canvas, 81 1/4 x 101 3/8 in., Mr. and Mrs. Frank G. Logan Purchase Prize Fund; gift of Mr. and Mrs. Noah Goldowsky and Edgar Kaufmann, Jr., 1952.1. The Art Institute of Chicago. © The Art Institute of Chicago. © 2007 The Willem de Kooning Foundation / Artists Rights Society (ARS), New York.

from confronting his art directly, because—no matter whether they chose to laud or condemn him—his next move was likely to embarrass the judgment. To this day there has been relatively little interest among academic critics in addressing the work of this major artist. First Pollock, and then Newman, have received considerably more attention. De Kooning's persistent use of the image of Woman, whether overt or submerged, has made matters still more difficult, for such an art becomes a tempting target for anyone concerned to demonstrate the extremes of American misogynism and its supplemental psychological aberrations (see the likes of Fitzsimmons and Geist among other early writers). Yet the biographical facts and the witness accounts fail to support this line of interpretation, save when it becomes generalized and heavy-handed, converting this exceptional artist into a man merely typical of his generation. Turning and shifting from abstraction to representation without ever stabilizing, de Kooning's art disabled every good-faith critical projection. Appropriately, he once told an interviewer, "I can change overnight."[150]

* * *

I think Cubism went backwards from Cézanne [by] laying it out beforehand. You are not supposed to see it, you are supposed to feel it. … Cézanne said that every brushstroke has its own perspective[,] its own point of view.

—Willem de Kooning, 1971[151]

De Kooning had a father, or grandfather, in Cézanne—an anti-impressionist faithful to impressionism, an inspiration to abstraction who insisted that he merely represented nature. Cézanne was as contrary as de Kooning. And neither painter tolerated intellectual pretense. Late in life, exasperated by the ideas younger artists were applying to him and wary of being carried away with words himself, Cézanne exclaimed: "No more theories! Let's paint."[152] Somewhat bemused, de Kooning said it less directly to Emile de Antonio in 1970: "I don't think artists have particularly bright ideas." Yet he accepted Cézanne's artist-grown ideas, in agreement with his own notion that thinking too abstractly brings a painter to distraction. De Antonio asked de Kooning in return: If artists have no bright ideas, "what *do* they have?" The answer: "I guess they're talented painting things."[153]

By consensus, de Kooning demonstrated the most complex array of skills among those of his peers who were "talented painting things." Once this became the general opinion, critics set about to classify his complicated style, testing it against the rigors of a cubist paradigm. "Late Cubist" was Greenberg's verdict in 1955.[154] As de Kooning was "late," so Cézanne had been "early."

Twentieth-century critics projected his variant of impressionist style as cubism's precursor. From de Kooning's typically contrary position, dissimilar things often appeared similar—a thumb
could become a thigh, or perhaps a nose. By the same token, he
converted back into difference the stylistic similarities discerned
by others. In his view, Cézanne was no cubist. Concerning his
own imputed link to cubism, he introduced a distinguishing factor: The cubists started from a concept, an identity, a "bright idea";
they pursued their art through it, "laying it out beforehand." This
was just the type of determinate practice that a "postmodernist"
and multi-directional de Kooning, like Cézanne, resisted. Lodg-
ing this complaint with Harold Rosenberg in 1971, de Kooning
kept its target vague, neglecting to specify which cubists and
whose theories were culpable. It would be odd for him not to
have regarded Picasso as cubist, yet this was a cubist who avoided
theory and whose imagery hardly arrived in predictable order. De
Kooning admired Picasso's inventive genius, manifested in works
he had contemplated during his formative years in New York,
especially *Guernica*.[155] He was suitably on record for placing the
historical phenomenon of cubism in a favorable light in a talk he
gave in 1951 at the Museum of Modern Art, where *Guernica* was
then housed.[156]

Perhaps the motivation for de Kooning's anti-cubism of 1971
derived from a grudge. His critic Greenberg, despite his initial
enthusiasm in 1948 and certain lasting points of appreciation,
had long been categorizing his art in a demeaning manner. In
1962, new writing by Greenberg compounded the slights of the
1950s. He attacked de Kooning's staunch ally Rosenberg for mis-
conceiving abstract expressionism as action painting in which
"everything lay in the doing, nothing in the making."[157] Here,
"doing" expressed Rosenberg's existentialist orientation, whereas
"making" expressed Greenberg's own pragmatic orientation. It
was at this point that he identified de Kooning with "homeless
representation" and the ambivalence of "large facet planes [that]

seem to grope for ... a model in nature."[158] In view of Greenberg's accumulated remarks, de Kooning had more than sufficient cause to assert that he was "really much more influenced by Cézanne than by the Cubists."[159] His statement of 1971 put the lie to recent Greenbergian history and did so with Rosenberg, Greenberg's antagonist, as interlocutor and witness. Cézanne had become de Kooning's moral choice, even if not the most convincing family relation in terms of painting technique.[160]

Cézanne set the precedent for putting feeling before seeing, sensation before conceptualization. Because he had refused to be guided by theoretical identities, he was always risking failure. To de Kooning, this was admirable. He had once suggested that Cézanne was compelled to give "the finishing touches to Impressionism" (that is, to terminate it) because it constituted a style, an order. "Order, to me, is to be ordered about," de Kooning confessed. A style, a concept, a theory, a "bright idea"—each was constraining. Only by rejecting style, de Kooning argued, was Cézanne able to come "face to face with his 'little sensation.'"[161] Sensation directed his art and the life his art consumed.

De Kooning sought the same situation. In the 1971 interview, Rosenberg epitomized de Kooning's attitude as moving from "Don't think, look!" to "Don't look, paint!"[162] In the spirit of Cézanne, each of his lines or brushstrokes was felt, not conceived, at the moment of its appearance. Each mark took "its own point of view"—paint did the looking—as the painter applied the stroke and simultaneously responded to it. De Kooning regarded multiple points of view as entirely proper and desirable; his distinctive marks translated into a multiplicity of effects and feelings. This was a Cézannean brand of multiplicity, not the cubist variety. Its operation required no transcendent principles of form, space, and perspective: no unifying theory, no identity. Accordingly, de Kooning tolerated a remarkable degree of disjunction across his painting surface—not stab wounds fixed in their anatomical place, just disjunctive marks of red. More than merely tolerating it, he found this disjointedness stimulating. Though he was known for being reluctant to finish paintings and have them leave his active consideration, his fragmented practice did not conform to what we usually consider indecision. His signs of compositional ambivalence, ambiguity, and simple doubt derived from choices; they were willfully arbitrary.

Was there an element of prophecy in de Kooning's vision? Fitzsimmons had associated the Woman with a dark future; or rather, he projected the image into that future, already invested with his belief. If de Kooning was the all-seeing prophet for middle-class America, the painter himself neglected to seize on the fact. This was not because—like the surrealists in Newman's view—psychoanalytic pretensions and fantasies blinded him to the real-world implications of his insight. De Kooning belonged to the here and now; his identification with average Americans and their ambivalence toward the finer ends of professional art making appears to have been genuine. In 1951, having already struggled over *Woman I* for almost a year, he exhibited a group of his previous abstractions, remarking: "I haven't felt ready for exhibitions, and I'm not particularly happy about this one. I'm still working out of doubt."[163]

Doubt (Cézanne)

If we were not already aware of de Kooning's affinity for Cézanne—as he expressed it in 1971—we would nevertheless have recourse to a metonymic connection via the word *doubt*. It was one of the simple terms that de Kooning favored: *doubt* rather than *ambiguity*.[164] The link to Cézanne is circumstantial and arbitrary: Maurice Merleau-Ponty. His essay with its memorable title, "La doute de Cézanne" (Cézanne's doubt), enjoyed immense transatlantic and cross-disciplinary popularity. In its wake, it became harder than ever not to believe that Cézanne doubted. The essay appeared in France in 1945—the final year of the war—and a translation arrived quickly in 1946 in *Partisan Review*, the journal for which Greenberg wrote much of his early criticism. Within the

American context, Merleau-Ponty became the relatively laconic artist's authoritative spokesperson, especially among those who wanted more than the surface facts of his case. Merleau-Ponty's statement began, "He needed one hundred working sessions for a still life, one hundred and fifty sittings for a portrait. What we call his work was, for him, only an essay, an approach to painting"—intimations of obsessiveness.[165]

Parallels are apparent: Both Cézanne and de Kooning kept laboring over particular images; both failed to bring their highly eccentric pictorial orders to any traditional resolution; both had trouble finishing. "Will I reach the goal I've sought so much and so long pursued," Cézanne wrote to Emile Bernard about a month before he died; "I'm working from nature as always, and I think I'm making some slow progress."[166] Here the analogies break down: de Kooning too might have referred to "slow progress," but not in such a general way; his slowness applied only to his indecision over specific works, such as *Asheville* of 1948, an abstraction on which he spent an entire summer, and *Woman I*, which required at least two and a half years.[167] De Kooning had no belief in progress. His aim was to change, not to advance; he would change even if it meant reversal. When he said, "I can change overnight," he was referring beyond individual paintings to his general way of working and beyond that to his general conduct.[168] The appearance of doubt arose as a feature of his attitude toward just about everything.[169] As I have stated, de Kooning's doubt was probably genuine, but it may also have been a projection, a pose. Sometimes we realize that our quirks and failings work to our advantage, and we feel free to indulge and even exaggerate them. An admiring acquaintance reported that Cézanne behaved strangely in order to keep people from interacting with him; it protected his working time.[170] So his personal effect on others was conscious and cultivated. But was this the case with the effect of his art?

Merleau-Ponty's meditation on Cézanne suffers from anachronism. Interpreting the painter and the painter's doubt, he was

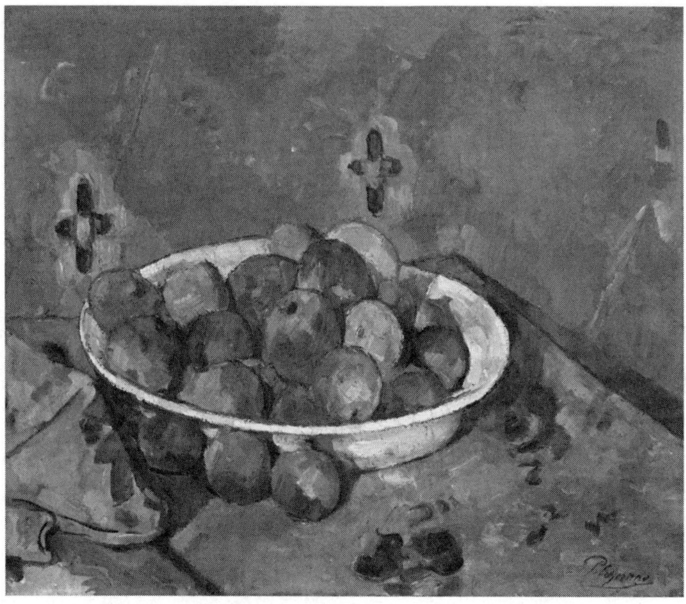

Figure 14 Paul Cézanne, *Le plat de pommes*, c. 1877. Oil on canvas, 18 x 21 1/2 in., Gift of Kate L. Brewster, 1949.512. The Art Institute of Chicago. © The Art Institute of Chicago.

actually approaching the position of de Kooning, his own true contemporary.[171] Unaware of de Kooning but in some respects much like him, Merleau-Ponty believed that finality and certitude were false desires that blunted the sensation of life. He defined the successful picture as one that "makes movement [or life] visible by its internal discordance."[172] The description fits the instability in figurative (that is, representational) painting by either Cézanne (Figure 14) or de Kooning. As a phenomenologist, Merleau-Ponty wished to counter interpretations that derived the meaning of a work from a given ideology or an artist's programmed psychological state—from life regarded as if formed outside one's immersion in and responses to the flux of perception.[173] Among those who preceded him in this endeavor was a near-contemporary of Cézanne, the aesthetician Paul Souriau. In his study of movement (1889), he noted that critics often took academic painters to task for the artificiality of their figures' gestures. The complaint was valid because these artists relied on preconceived models and standardized compositions, depicting only "those postures we adopt to express our feelings to show them on the outside." This was emotional expression after the fact of the feeling—a kind of self-differing. Souriau associated it with miming.[174] He continued, "Truly expressive postures are those that do not set about to express anything, but are unconsciously determined by a deeply felt emotion."[175] This insight—uttered today, it would seem like a Freudian cliché—raises a troubling possibility: Subtle movements that actually reflect a subject's emotional state appear to represent nothing in particular. They constitute a kind of tacit expression because they follow no stock thematic structure, as if to form a language devoid of iterative wording. It is expression without identity. As Greenberg had said of de Kooning's *Painting*: "You can't specify what the emotion is but are profoundly stirred nevertheless."[176] The deep meaning of a felt sensation remains undisclosed somewhere between the lines consciously chosen to represent a related feeling "on the outside"—a fictive feeling proximate to, but not in contact with, the real one. Reliable meaning—without pose, without a multivalenced identity—would lie in the little bits of meaningless excess between one conventional element of expression and another. The problem is that the real feeling and its meaning would never be articulated outside their immediate situation, outside the material medium of their generative expression. The medium, thought to facilitate a transfer of information, to send it forth, would instead be holding it back.

If the conditions of modern life were painful for Cézanne, his medium- and material-bound art was notable in demonstrating its own painfully unresolved condition for others to see. Cézanne's art became a kind of prophecy broadly acknowledged not only by twentieth-century commentators like Merleau-Ponty but also by his near-contemporaries, the younger generation of painters and writers around Paul Gauguin, who became involved with his work during the 1880s, 1890s, and into the new century. Cézanne died in 1906. Several months later, Gauguin's literary collaborator Charles Morice composed a modernist lament: "We hardly dare say that Cézanne lived; he [only] painted. … His is *an art of separation* … painting estranged from the course of life, painting with the [sole] aim of painting … This separation [amounts to] a tacit protest."[177] Morice believed that scientism, materialism, and technocratic efficiency were deadening all spiritual life. The situation tempted artists to abandon the decaying remains of humanistic principle and withdraw into pure sensory experience. Just as a poet might withdraw into words and their material sound, a painter would withdraw into paint and its material look. Cézanne's life amounted to the work of painting—as Merleau-Ponty recounted, "he needed one hundred working sessions for a still life"—because he had no life other than this. For him, life and a still life occupied the same time and space, moved and emoted in tandem, with the vicissitudes of Cézanne's soul being displaced by the strokes of his brush.[178] He had purged his life of all social and "moral values," for which, as Morice put it, he substituted "color values."[179] In lieu of intellectual and ethical abstractions, the painter produced color abstractions—or physical existence: paint, color, a look.[180]

Cézanne did not lack political, religious, or philosophical beliefs but appeared resigned to the fact that theoretical and ideological concerns could no longer guide his or any other artistic practice. The technique of painting—isolated from its representational content, abstracted, and linked only to the sensing hand of the artist—became the means of a "tacit protest." To the observant critic, it signaled the corruption of the intellectual and moral bases of modern society, a loss of integration and harmony. Morice had been developing this general theme in a series of exhibition reviews. In 1905, just over a year in advance of his summation of Cézanne's career, he addressed the problem of self-differing: "I see a lack of lovingness in daily life, etched on the contorted, hardened faces of my contemporaries. This is a consequence of the fragmentation and atomization that not only separates one person from another, but beyond that, divides each of us internally and divorces our feeling from our thinking."[181] The concern that Morice addressed was self-differing in its social and psychological guises, as opposed to its semiotic and linguistic forms. Later, Judd would engage the psychological divide—"That's the division between thought and feeling. You have to [think and feel] all at once"—whereas poststructuralist critics like de Man would be involved with the linguistic divide (the identity and self-difference of the *I*).[182] In 1907, Morice confined himself to acknowledging the impenetrable mystery of Cézanne, who seemed to indicate both the external social problem and a rather sad, internal solution. The critic asked, "Was [Cézanne's protest] fully conscious? I don't know."[183] We should credit Morice for his pragmatic doubt: He understood how unlikely it was that he would successfully differentiate conscious from unconscious motivation in another person. Recall Wittgenstein: "Imagine that someone unconscious … were to say 'I am conscious'—should we respond 'He ought to know'?"[184]

History has its own dubious moments and their ambiguous causal entailments. It remains uncertain whether the example of Cézanne contributed to de Kooning's attitude of doubt and the *indeterminateness* of his imagery, which was Greenberg's way of describing the de Kooning look in 1948.[185] In 1971, when de Kooning told Rosenberg that Cézanne had been his great influence, he may have been defending himself from Greenberg's claim that cubism was the relevant precedent. De Kooning shaped his understanding of the art practices of the past as a way of dealing with his more vital relationship to the art criticism of the present. Doing so, he anticipated the critical strategy that Krauss pursued not long after, when, during the 1970s, she molded many of her views on a Greenbergian template turned inside-out so that they would contradict points of interpretation her former mentor had long sought to establish. This was local academic politics. Ironically for de Kooning, this meant that Krauss would need to focus on Pollock, just as Greenberg had done, and to neglect de Kooning, just as Greenberg had done—a quirk of history.

Whether or not de Kooning, during his formative years of the 1930s, paid more attention to Cézanne than to cubism and Picasso—in fact, this is doubtful—he was Cézanne's heir in instability. When he looked at Mondrian's abstract art, famous for its dynamic sense of balance, what he liked were the flashes of light that appeared where the black lines crossed—a shaky optical illusion. And de Kooning is the one who said, "When I'm falling, I'm doing all right." The thought would have seemed very strange to Cézanne—to enjoy the falling, which for him would only bring frustration.

"I think I'm making some slow progress": This was all Cézanne could say for himself in 1906, although he may have been ironic, since he tended to be self-deprecating one week and arrogant the next. As in the case of de Kooning—"after a while all kinds of painting become just painting for you"—the way Cézanne made his choices was not theoretical but material, through the medium of paint. Materiality interferes with representation, the modernists claim, because it limits what an artist can do and sometimes even imagine doing. Two years after Cézanne's death, the neoimpressionist painter Henri-Edmond Cross, a master of structured technical procedure, recorded a particularly problematic note in his diary: "The materials allow a certain thought and not others. ... Consciousness is limited to what the material allows."[186] Here, then, is a plausible cause of Cézanne's doubt and insecurity: The technical limitations of his medium—the range of color he could use, the degree of refinement of his brushstrokes—kept him from reaching his straightforward goal, whether or not he ever realized, as critics of Morice's generation did, that the paint, not some mental or visual failing, was the source of the difficulty.[187] Living in a different world, de Kooning could accept the notion that "material complexity" negates all "doctrinal logic" (the words belong to his, and later Newman's, critical ally Hess).[188] Physical existence supercedes the conceptual order that would claim to contain it. Richard Wollheim stated the operative principle: "That things are simpler than they are is something that theory asks us to imagine: to imagine, *not to believe*. … So long as we continue to think about [things] in the fullness of their empirical detail, [they] will always seem very different."[189]

Greenberg had another way of expressing this modernist realization: "What matters is not what one believes but what happens to one."[190] For his part, Newman wrote: "Just as I affect the canvas, so does the canvas affect me."[191] Or, "How it went, that's how it was." All of them—de Kooning, Greenberg, Newman, and Merleau-Ponty as well—were comfortable in a world where the specifics of experience would overrule the logical generalizations of theory. This is very much a late modernist theme, aligned with Judd's pragmatic sense of "local history," with categories ventured only "after the fact … made from what is happening."[192] And it is aligned as well with Bataille's notion of excess, invoked by Krauss.[193] A frustrated Cézanne had anticipated the mid twentieth-century position, not as a point of principle, but as his last resort—these words previously quoted, in a different context—"Time presses. No more theories! Let's paint."[194] Adopting this attitude of sensory immersion under duress, he could not perceive its end, nor, consequently, understand his own beginning. Yet he became famous for having said: "I remain the primitive of the way I discovered."[195] Here there is doubt once again, for when he said this, he may have been feeding back to his interlocutor Bernard ideas that Bernard had already presented to him. This was one of Cézanne's ways of fending off further questioning. Another was to disappear from view; on his visits to Paris, acquaintances sighted his evasive figure only "by chance."[196] As we know, acting strangely was still another of the strategies to which he resorted—reliable in all situations.

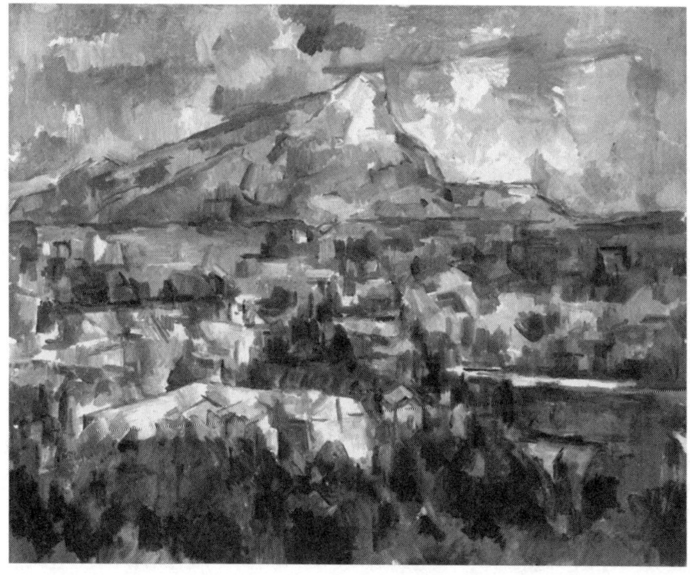

Figure 15 Paul Cézanne, *Mont Sainte-Victoire*, 1902-04. Oil on canvas, 27 1/2 x 35 1/4 in., Philadelphia Museum of Art, Elkins coll., E1936-1-1.

True to his nineteenth-century context, Cézanne wanted no more than to render his experience of nature (Figure 15). As he attempted to bring his painted image closer to nature—whether still life, landscape, portrait, or nude—he kept adding more strokes of color. Some additions were adjustments to existing passages; others were tantamount to erasures or maskings, which obliterated much that was already painted. His actions amounted to a holding operation, keeping pace with sensation without succeeding in getting the jump on it. As the artist painted, the image kept changing. Cézanne should have expected this result for at least two reasons: First, he knew that he was remarkably sensitive to the slightest shift in his portrait models and to nuances in the Provençal light; second, he must have understood that no technique of the hand could be completely adequate to visual representation.[197] When painted, the image acquired a tactile sense as much as a visual one. Although Cézanne's hand worked to represent his eye's observations of evanescent light and color, it did so in a particularly corporeal manner, as if eye and hand were operating through different mediums each with its specific characteristics and capacities. This may account for the strange patterns of brushmarks that appear in Cézannes dense paintings. He indulged his hand in rhythms that seemed natural and comfortable to it—given painting's physicality, not nature's.

From our perspective, Cézanne was acting properly. He may have doubted his success because his material construction of nature, the result of his painting technique, did not match the cultural construction he accepted as a context for his work—"those [conventional] postures we adopt to express our feelings," according to Souriau. Culture, art education, and even the science of aesthetics told Cézanne how things ought to look as opposed to how things actually felt. Culture determined what counted as progress in art. Cézanne the radical painter lost the argument with Cézanne the conservative critic of culture. When a new generation began to appreciate and imitate him, he failed to return their admiration.[198] Either Merleau-Ponty or de Kooning could have provided Cézanne with a cultural construction sufficiently different to shock him out of his conservative mind-set. Had he ever entered their world as they projected themselves back into his, he would have had a different set of values to guide his self-assessment. His fate was to maintain a pictorial paradigm inappropriate to the practice he was developing through his felt experience—his "sensation," as he used to call it.[199] He experienced self-differing in extremis.

Tension between the prevailing cultural forms and one's personal sensation generates paranoid anxiety. Famously, Picasso claimed to perceive such anxiety in Cézanne's painting.[200] Making his case for a state stronger than mere doubt, Merleau-Ponty referred to Cézanne's "schizoid temperament" in two different passages: "There is a rapport between Cézanne's schizoid temperament [*constitution schizoïde*] and his work because the work reveals a metaphysical sense of the disease: a way of seeing the world reduced to the totality of frozen appearances, with all expressive values suspended." Merleau-Ponty listed a number of Cézanne's peculiarities, as he understood them from reading the witness accounts recorded toward the end of the painter's life, when he had become famous enough to generate such things. Morice's reviews are not among those cited, but Merleau-Ponty approached the same conclusion: "This loss of flexible human contact; this inability to master new situations; this flight into established habits ... all these symptoms permit one to speak of a morbid constitution and more precisely ... of schizophrenia [*une schizoïdie*]. ... [The elements of Cézanne's psychology] represent a flight from the human world, the alienation of his humanity."[201] As Morice had summarized in a pun: Where others perceived moral values, Cézanne saw color values.

Paranoia (Rousseau)

> We live in the museums, the theatres, the concert halls, amidst the sensations of art: There we gradually lose the sense of real life; our sensibility increasingly requires purely aesthetic feelings. At the same time, real life each day loses a bit more of its [individual] character.
>
> —Maurice Denis, 1905[202]

> [People are] sick with sophistication and conventionality, their sensibilities atrophied and their imaginations dead [within a] devitalized environment. Rousseau may not be a great artist ... but he is greatly significant in that he measures very exactly the dividedness of our civilization, our schismatic culture.
>
> —Herbert Read, 1944[203]

> The middle class in this country ... is now surging toward culture under the pressure of anxiety, high taxes, and a shrinking industrial frontier. All this expresses itself in a market demand

for cultural goods that are up to date and yet not too hard to consume. ... The serious and ambitious artist ... is tempted—most often unconsciously—to meet this demand by softening, sweetening, and simplifying his product. ... [Yet] the public still wants something that has the smell of high art.

—Clement Greenberg, 1946[204]

As the statements from Maurice Denis (French), Herbert Read (British), and Greenberg (American) indicate, critics relate art to their societies as well as to the artists they propose to psych out. During the first decades of the twentieth century, writers commonly classed Cézanne and Rousseau (Figure 16) together as societal outsiders. In the case of Rousseau, Read reversed the usual psychological dynamic between artist and public. It was not the naïve painter whose eccentricity alienated him from the culture; it was the culture—having lost all depth of aesthetic feeling, having lost its spiritual center—that alienated itself from the artist.

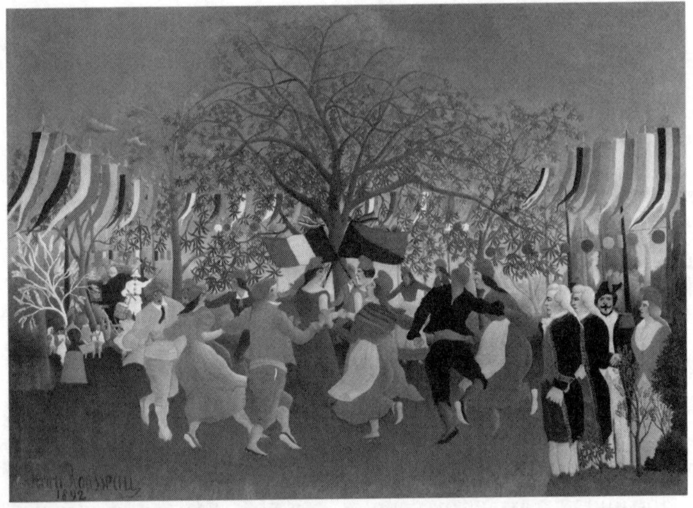

Figure 16   Henri Rousseau, *A Centennial of Independence*, 1892. Oil on canvas. 44 x 61 7/8 in., The J. Paul Getty Museum, Los Angeles.

Just as Cézanne and de Kooning shared the word *doubt*, so Cézanne and Rousseau shared the descriptor *primitive*. Cézanne had called himself the "primitive" of his way. Rousseau appeared primitive in other, not unrelated, respects—primitive both as a naïve mentality and as a *maître populaire*, a seemingly self-taught, working-class hero. Cézanne sometimes behaved vulgarly, but he was hardly common, having been raised in wealth and privileged by his education. Rousseau, Read wrote, "is essentially a people's painter, in a sense in which one would never apply that condescending phrase to Cézanne."[205] We might say that comparisons between Cézanne and Rousseau were themselves a bit schizophrenic: While acknowledging the difference in social class as the basis of an aesthetic difference, they projected the two painters on closely parallel routes to modernist canonization.

Robert Delaunay, writing in 1913, provides a striking example, which, coincidentally, includes the factor of Cézanne's doubt:

> Feelings [*sensibilités*] ... out-perform methods [*moyens*]. Cézanne was always searching for his method: Did he not write that he never brought his pictures to realization? Cézanne's doubts ... his bruised feelings ... Rousseau [is entirely different]—what a liberated vision, what a working man ... more forceful, less wavering, less bourgeois than Cézanne. ... Rousseau, painter of the people. ... Cézanne, a troubled bourgeois. ... Two completely distinct types in this heroic era of modern painting. Two primitives of this great movement.[206]

According to Delaunay, Rousseau occupied a polar position on a psychological scale invoked by critics and by the artists themselves: "With Rousseau, there is no theory, no rhetoric. Everything is feeling and sense of style."[207] In 1909, Arsène Alexandre contrasted him to typical painters who "thought things out": "The good Douanier Rousseau, he alone, would be incapable of [consciously] wanting the result he achieved ... [or] of deriving things from a calculated system."[208] It was as if Rousseau had always followed instinctively the pragmatic advice Cézanne ultimately offered: "No more theories! Let's paint." Yet two of Cézanne's early devotees were significant hold-outs in the wave of enthusiasm building for Rousseau. In 1905, Bernard referred to an unfortunate divide between Paul Signac, a neoimpressionist "who thinks too much," and Rousseau – no better – "whose intellect is only embryonic."[209] Denis was equally dismissive: "Rousseau's genius doesn't interest [serious] painters. It's a question for psychologists or the business of collectors."[210]

Born in 1844, Rousseau was only five years younger than Cézanne. It took some time, but when public acceptance came to his art, it extended remarkably broadly; for Cézanne, this was less the case. Rousseau gained as much favor with the untutored public as with sophisticated critics and curators. Because nearly all classes of society responded to his pictures, their presence effectively narrowed the gaps between one cultural level and another. This could be threatening to critical hierarchies and identities. Always quick to catch on, Gauguin joked about it—"After all, [a Rousseau] is no more stupid than a Bouguereau"—bringing the revered academic master down to the low level of the plebian worker.[211] The problem intensified. In 1938, the American critic Henry McBride wondered whether Rousseau's naïve manner "heralded the end of aristocracy and aristocratic art." McBride's worry—in the near future there might "be no aristocracy to purchase the naiveté"—would soon be shared by Greenberg.[212] Both intuited that people want—naturally enough—what they lack: Those with sophistication crave whatever is naïve. This quirk of class distinction might account for some of Rousseau's popularity, but no more than a fraction, for the majority of the public was far less sophisticated as viewers of modern art than the elite aristocracy of critics. From McBride's perspective, as from Greenberg's, public understanding was already closely aligned to Rousseau's level of popular art. The tragic difference was that the people who constituted this public were hardly naïve at all, for they had acquired middle-class culture. Their new culture was materialistic—and it was crude.

In 1923, fifteen years before McBride wrote, the French critic Gustave Kahn, who had witnessed the Rousseau phenomenon from its late nineteenth-century beginnings, noted with some amazement that Rousseau's manner was now "dogma" for every young artist. Kahn remembered that it was Camille Pissarro, first in perceiving genius in Cézanne, who, in 1886, had also been the first to perceive it in Rousseau. This coincidental fact bore a certain appropriateness, because, at least in Kahn's opinion, Rousseau's career had initially benefited from his being criticized for the same kind of crudeness attributed to Cézanne's style of impressionism. Although the two were entirely different social types, avant-garde writers instinctively, and perhaps indiscriminately, defended both of these outsiders from attacks by cultural conservatives. In addition, Kahn recalled that many of the older, technically sophisticated painters had been "particularly charmed by the sight of a work in which feeling replaces technical skill."[213] This, of course, is what Greenberg was to suggest in a more complicated way about the situation of de Kooning in 1948. (In Elkins's terms, the hostility of conservative viewers toward the early modernists would have resulted because neither Cézanne nor Rousseau exhibited techniques sufficiently conventional, though for very different reasons, the former having bypassed the niceties, the latter never having developed them.)

Pissarro responded to naïve art because he perceived its "feeling," and this was Gauguin's response also. He sent a note to Pissarro in July 1884 to report on two groups of paintings he had just viewed—new works by Claude Monet and by Cézanne. Gauguin complained of excessively showy technique on the part of the former, but praised the latter for "purity"—that dangerous notion—here referring to directness, restraint, and the blunt physicality of the brushwork, lacking any embellishment.[214] There was no pose in it, no allusion to an "outside." Guillaume Apollinaire later attributed a similar purity to Rousseau's art, describing it as "without mannerism, without method, without system"; it had been guided instead by abundant "feeling."[215] Perhaps this is what Pissarro himself imagined in 1892 when he advised his son Lucien to attend to "*free* sensations, relieved of everything other than their own feeling."[216] Kahn recalled that during the years that Pissarro and Rousseau were at work and exhibiting in Paris, there had been a number of amateurish painters, soon to be forgotten though briefly admired for the "direct expression of their strange feelings." Endowed with a certain talent—rather than skill—they nevertheless lacked full awareness of what they were accomplishing: another case of the "unconscious" artist.[217]

There were always those who admired Rousseau's art for a certain cultivated expertise, however hard to define and analyze; but most persisted in characterizing him as naïve and unaware.[218] In 1938, the catalogue text for an exhibition of so-called popular painting and modern primitives, first organized in France and then sponsored by the Museum of Modern Art in New York, introduced Rousseau as a painter who had made "more use of heart and impulse than of mind and will, attaining 'naïvely' the objective toward which [cubists and other postimpressionists] were reaching intellectually."[219] As presented in this context, Rousseau's art was without self-consciousness, without strategy, without theory, even without culture. The American Max Weber, who befriended Rousseau in Paris, recalled: "To walk into his studio was like walking into a vineyard—fresh, no debates—here it was art without words. … No mention of religion, no mention of politics. … Rousseau [was] an example of *aesthetic* piety."[220]

For many supporters of modern art, this view of a know-nothing master became increasingly untenable; they refused to accept that a painter acknowledged as a major modernist could have been "primitive," lacking all cultural refinements and predispositions, even simple-minded. In 1942, the Museum of Modern Art and the Art Institute of Chicago cosponsored an exhibition devoted

solely to Rousseau. Its curatorial team made their radical intention
explicit: "Throughout, the object has been to show Rousseau not as
a 'naïve' eccentric but as an artist significant in his own right—one
of the great painters of his generation."[221] A sympathetic reviewer
verified that the exhibition took a formalist stance: "[For] Rousseau, a painting [was] primarily an organization of pictorial elements that has its validity independent of any necessity to copy
'nature' academically, scientifically or conventionally."[222]

When faced with an array of dogmatic statements of conservative cultural accomplishment, left-leaning or socially liberal nineteenth-century critics (the likes of Thoré and Paul Mantz) called
on artists to submit themselves to nature as naively as possible,
in order to reach a more personal level of expression, otherwise
suppressed.[223] Now, when presented with the apparently natural or naïve self of Rousseau, twentieth-century American critics attributed to it cultural powers equal to figures they regarded
as self-consciously revolutionary, such as Pissarro, Monet, and
Gauguin. They granted to Rousseau the professional status that
had escaped him during his lifetime, when, by all accounts, he
aspired to recognition by academic authorities with whom he
shared systematic studio techniques but not their proper results
(Figure 17).[224] Rousseau had wanted to be mainstream. His unintended countercultural success may not seem strange today, for
the mythology of the primitive and the naïve—with all its lasting
ironies—has been a feature of modern culture from the beginnings of its modernist self-consciousness. Historical and theoretical studies have been directed at primitivism in the arts long
enough to put us at ease with the revisionist argument that modernism institutionalized and rendered anodyne its own strategies
for cultural liberation, primitivism being one of them. Tacitly at
least, we understand how self-differing modernist practice always
was.

The revisionist account is in fact such an old one that even
during the 1930s critics were likely to regard with suspicion any

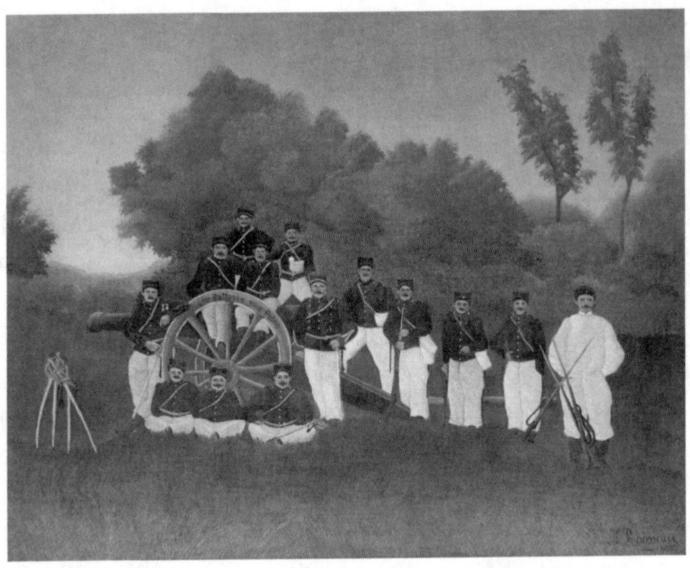

Figure 17   17. Henri Rousseau, *Artillerymen*, c. 1893–95. Oil on canvas, 31 1/8 x 39 in., Solomon R. Guggenheim Museum, Gift, Solomon R. Guggenheim.

primitivist look in a work of art. Along such lines, one reviewer complained that some of the art exhibited with Rousseau's in 1938 "betrayed a deliberateness of intention, a [self-]conscious utilizing of the primitive formula."[225] A true primitivism should, of course, escape self-consciousness and, to an unusual extent, all the distracting troubles linked to self-difference. A second reviewer ranked among "the best" of the exhibiting painters precisely those so-called primitives that the first discredited.[226] If we were to take at face value the range of response to exhibitions of primitivistic art during the early twentieth century, we would be led through a paranoid maze, uncertain who was genuine and who was posing, that is, who might be affecting a feeling "on the outside," consciously indulging in self-difference and taking advantage of it—like using an innocent word to lie. Making the artist's acquaintance might be no help at all since any person's attempt to articulate feelings experienced from the inside of consciousness begs failure. As Peirce wrote, "Feeling [is] completely veiled from introspection, for the very reason that it is our immediate consciousness."[227] The critical viewer of a naïve art is left to decide, to guess, what might really be what: true primitive or false primitive, naturally naïve or culturally manipulative. It seems that only the thoroughly nonnaïve, those under the spell of a fully developed culture, would be in a position to attribute naturalness to another. They would sense the greatest difference. McBride stated in 1930 that "it was [Rousseau's] total lack of so-called 'culture' … that enabled him in his pictures to set forth so unhesitatingly the figment of his dreams."[228] Correspondingly, Read emphasized that this was an artist who never acquired style: "I would rather call Rousseau a *natural* painter."[229] The language and logic of these two sophisticated critics is relatively direct, but the cultural history from which their judgments derive amounts to an unfathomable mass of myth and lore deposited by human society from its beginnings and still continuing. The terms are extraordinarily general: nature, culture, the natural. When people or things are "natural," are they part of nature or partaking of culture? It would help to consider the terms other than oppositionally, as Peirce would regard belief and doubt. This can be done.

Greenberg's most developed response to Rousseau, offered slightly later than the statements by McBride and Read, introduced a twist. He became uncomfortable with the two-sided recognition of "primitive" aesthetic accomplishment. The majority of commentators were invoking Rousseau's childlike capacity for the purest self-expression, which successfully rivaled the self-conscious achievements of avant-garde abstraction.[230] This group stressed that Rousseau's formal design entered his art "unconsciously." Here is a representative statement from 1938: "The primitive quality of [Rousseau's type of] painting is a result of the artist's unconsciously abstract attitude. … [With primitive artists,] colors are more elementary and vivid than they appear to the eye [and] the detail is sharpened in a strikingly unillusionistic manner."[231] Primitivism was being linked to flat, unmodulated color and a neglect of naturalistic spatial illusion, which was an achievement of culture. In this respect, primitivist representation approached abstraction—not of a conceptual kind but of a perceptual kind. A second group had begun to describe Rousseau's manipulation of precisely the same elements of formal, even abstract, design as a fully conscious, controlled procedure. In his case—and this is what is peculiar—the opposing critical judgments were both positive. The unconscious Rousseau was admired; the conscious Rousseau was admired. Greenberg took the critical stance of asking why this artist was faring so well before so diverse a board of aesthetic evaluators.

In 1946, the Museum of Modern Art reissued its Rousseau exhibition catalogue, strengthening its institutional commitment to the painter's elevated status. The interpretive essay by Daniel Catton Rich emphasized Rousseau's conscious side. By this account, Rousseau was all the more clearly acknowledged as a model for the sophisticated use of modernist form. For the new edition, Rich appended his assessment of the effect of the exhibition: It had countered the more common view of "essayists who admire the 'primitive'" in Rousseau, and it had worked to "diminish critical faith in this easy explanation of his art."[232] This is the event that provoked a response from Greenberg, as he resumed the "unconscious" side of the debate with a new set of considerations. He argued that Rousseau's remarkable formal qualities were unconscious products not because he was a cultural "primitive," but because he was alienated; on this point, his position was antithetical to Read's, yet directed at the same end. The problem was psychological: Rousseau's mental state was out of sync with the rhythms of his society and its culture. Alienation—eccentricity taken too far—had always been regarded as the dark side of artistic creativity. It was not the curious acceptance of Rousseau that Greenberg needed to explain, but its unusual extent.

Recognition in 1946 could only have become so universal if the painter were touching the normative soul of Greenberg's contemporary society—the conventional types, not merely a minority of alienated types.[233] A more specific question emerged: Why did the mentality of this nineteenth-century French outsider connect so well with postwar taste in America?

The answer lay in the formalism of Rousseau's painting, but not in the way that the museum curators had imagined; it was not a matter of mastery acknowledged. Greenberg's argument was more searching than theirs, and far more cynical, to the extent that even now most readers miss the gist of it. This is its twist, unexpected in retrospect, given how many times writings of this sort seem to have been misread: Greenberg argued that Rousseau's art satisfied an unvoiced, but profound, cultural demand. He linked Rousseau to an existential pressure very much like the one Morice believed had affected Cézanne. Yet Rousseau "was far from the knowingness that would have led someone to become a primitive deliberately."[234] Because this artist seemed so naïve, childlike, and clueless, it would have been unusually risky for Greenberg to suggest causation; a person of such temperament might never feel pressures as others do. Connections and parallels might be articulated but would have to be regarded as no more than accidents of history—accidents that occur not in the course of real events but in composing their fictive story.

When setting the context for Greenberg's attitude toward de Kooning, I mentioned that Rousseau's story inspired the critic to link him with two other modernist pioneers, Cézanne and Van Gogh (Figure 18). The three painters had cluelessness in common; their most culturally significant results arrived unintended. They also shared what Greenberg regarded as "derangement," and he identified a ready precedent for this brand of alienation: "Just as Rimbaud had to give birth to modern poetry by deliberately cultivating the 'derangement' of his senses, so those who made the leap from Impressionism to that which came after [were] pushed

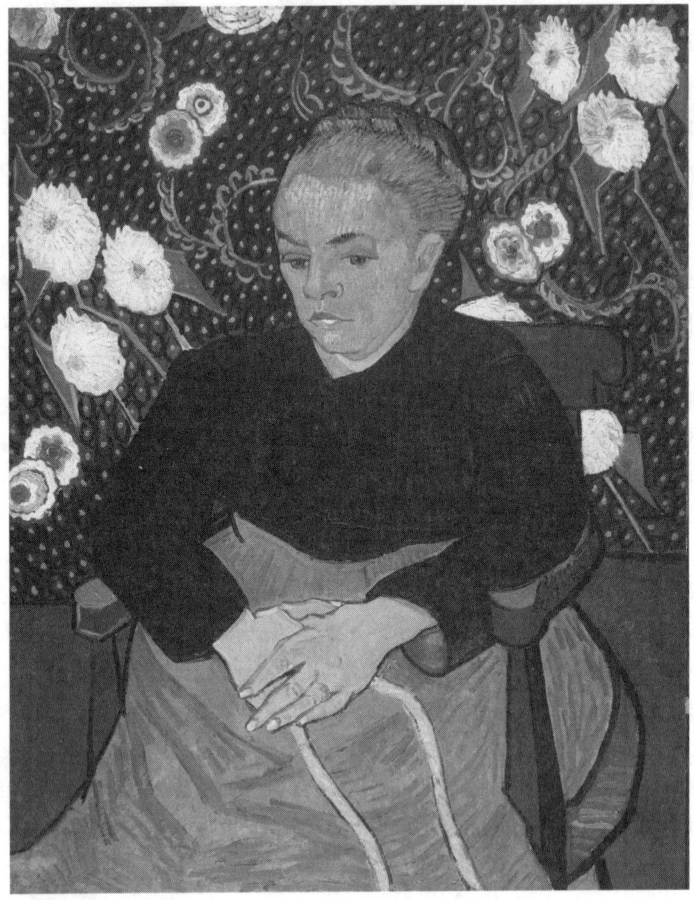

Figure 18   18. Vincent van Gogh, *Madame Roulin Rocking the Cradle (La Berceuse)*. 29 January 1889, o/c, 36 1/2 x 29 1/8 in., Helen Birch Bartlett Memorial Collection, 1926.200. The Art Institute of Chicago. © The Art Institute of Chicago.

by mental impulses so strong and so disconnected from the actual environment that they had to be those of psychotics."[235] Greenberg may have chosen words such as *psychotic* and *deranged* to pique his reader, who would be either intrigued or provoked to disagree. In fixing on *derangement* as a term, he was encouraged by a passage from Rimbaud's "Lettres du voyant" of 1871, concerning the "reasoned disordering [or disorientation] of all the senses."[236] The key word is *dérèglement*. Etymologically, both the English *derangement* and the French *dérèglement* suggest the demise of the given, conventional order—indeed, a disordering. But in Rimbaud's case, the lack of order or regularity was willed ("reasoned"), even though it threatened to lead the artist-poet into sensory situations he would no longer control. By featuring the word *derangement* as an alternative to *disordering*, Greenberg put a psychoanalytic spin on his cultural interpretation, indicating that the case of the three modernist painters was different from Rimbaud's. They arrived at their penetrating view of modern experience without being fully conscious of aiming to do so. Just as Greenberg labeled Rousseau "deranged," he referred to Cézanne as an "extreme eccentric" who was "a little balmy," and alluded to "madness" in Van Gogh as well. None of the three painters could regulate his own deregulation. Whereas Rimbaud "cultivated" his derangement, the painters became "psychotic." A psychotic fails to coordinate ends and means. Rousseau, although desiring to paint like a conventional academic, developed and retained the style of a primitive.

Greenberg perceived that the situation held an advantage— not for the deranged painters, but for history. He linked the social and cultural conditions of recent modernity to industrialism and to a materialist or positivist mentality, arguing that Rimbaud's escapist poetic effects—"transcendent exceptions and aberrated states"—amounted to pointless fantasy.[237] Rimbaud had been dreaming for the sake of the dream, oblivious to history and prophecy. At just about the same moment, Newman was saying much the same about the surrealism of Ernst and Tanguy. As dreamy as Rousseau's imagery might be, however, Greenberg exempted it from this very basic level of critique.

Rousseau versus Rimbaud: In his naiveté the painter met a cultural demand that the poet could never satisfy with his sophisticated manipulation of signs and modes of conduct, for Rimbaud's form originated, as it were, "on the outside." Before

Greenberg wrote on Rousseau, he composed a brief review of the Whitney Museum Annual for 1946. I took an excerpt as one of the epigraphs for this section, which I now telegraph: "The middle class in this country [suffer] the pressure of anxiety. [They demand] cultural goods that are up to date and yet not too hard to consume. [An artist might respond by] softening, sweetening, and simplifying his product. The public still wants something [resembling] high art."[238] And here, five months later, is Greenberg addressing the problem of Rousseau: "His flat, direct, almost crass colors, contours, and modeling gave to many painters the first real impression they ever got of what life, reduced to solely empirical considerations and without the deception (but also protection) of faith in anything, looks like in art."[239]

Rousseau's qualities seemed destined to appeal to anyone immersed in modernity—his was an art "not too hard to consume." Yet it was neither "soft" nor "sweet." "Crass" is not "sweet." Greenberg understood that this type of painting had come to represent the empiricist mentality, flattened emotion, and coarsened sensation that modern social and material conditions had for decades been inducing not only in artists (in Cézanne, as Morice argued) but also in the broad public, in Europe as well as in America. At the psychosocial base of it all was "the conscious or unconscious positivism that forms the core of the bourgeois-industrialist ethos."[240] Artists were the canaries in modernity's mines: hypersensitive creatures signaling the modernist syndrome in advance of the general population. Crassness does not preclude being easy to grasp, as Rousseau's art certainly was in its general appearance. As such, it presented no moral ambiguity to a bourgeois society and its unaccommodating culture, neither of which showed much tolerance for ambiguity. It came across as simple—sometimes even approaching "sweet" in its charming way—though this may have been far from the painter's intention. Greenberg recognized that Rousseau's primitivism was a ready palliative for nonspecific middle-class anxiety during the transition from World War to

Cold War. Two decades earlier the American populist writer Clarence Bulliet aptly stated that Rousseau developed "from nowhere, unless [from] out of the 'subconscious' of Art."[241] In this sense, the painter was unconsciously prophetic, his art bursting into the social consciousness in the decade or so after his death, as Kahn had recorded at the time.

Greenberg's sense of Rousseau would explain why this painter in particular became the dogma of a more calculating, younger generation. Recognizing that "positivist" abstraction in painting had nineteenth-century roots in Cézanne, Gauguin, and the French symbolists, his analysis of the situation included this proviso: "It did not matter that the individual artist was a professing Catholic or a mystic or an anti-Dreyfusard"—some believed that Cézanne was all three—"in spite of himself, his art spoke positivism or materialism: its essence lay in the immediate sensation, and it operated under the most drastic possible reduction of the visual act."[242] Lending tacit support to Greenberg's view, Weber stated at the time of Rousseau's 1942 retrospective, "[His work] does not shock, it does not baffle. It defines itself in its own pure and simple language of art. There are no perplexing geometric problems to solve, nor ... does one find a thousand plastic intricacies or complications to unravel."[243] This was an art to be enjoyed. Having stressed the societal link between such formal directness and a bourgeois life devoid "of faith in anything," Greenberg alluded to the simple "poetry" of Rousseau's aesthetic appeal. Yet the appeal itself was not so simple, for the critic withdrew the allusion as soon as he introduced it: "I doubt whether that poetry is the main thing." Indeed, "we should be careful not to over-rate him," Greenberg advised. As a modernist innovator, Rousseau could not rival his more accomplished partners in paranoia, Cézanne and Van Gogh. But this aesthetic hierarchy of quality—this too was not "the main thing."[244]

What modernist story, finally, was Greenberg telling through Rousseau? The following passage from his 1946 review prefigures the terms he soon would apply to postwar American modernism. Here is the flatness, the picture plane, the centrality of medium, the object-based physicality—the familiar components of a formula for successful art production that later critics would consider rigid and constraining. It all appears as Greenberg describes the accident of Rousseau's encounter with his materialistic foundation and contrasts it to the calculated encounter of Matisse and Picasso:

> That which modern art asserts in principle—the superiority of the medium over whatever it figures: thus the inviolable flatness of the picture plane; the ineluctable shapedness of the canvas, panel, or paper; the palpability of oil pigment, the fluidity of water and ink—this expresses our society's growing impotence to organize experience in any other terms than those of the concrete sensation, immediate return, tangible datum. ... Such relatively cold, hard heads as Matisse and Picasso ... needed mental cases [like Rousseau] to show them the way, to cut through to the ultimate truth of life as it is lived at present.[245]

According to Greenberg, Matisse and Picasso (Figures 19, 20) moved rationally toward boldness and simplicity in order to relate their art to a properly modern quality of experience. Greenberg views these two modernist masters of the twentieth century as having conceptualized the genuinely intuitive practices of Rousseau, Cézanne, and Van Gogh (and others)—those who drifted loose within their cultural environment due to psychological alienation. They achieved through mental illness and a certain introversion a level of creative freedom that a nineteenth-century naturalist painter may once have sought down an ordinary forest path. But the modernist avant-garde adulterated Rousseau's childlike, even simplistic directness. As Greenberg understood the situation, the "cold, hard heads"—Matisse and Picasso, conscious of their avant-garde identity—remained somewhat aloof and separated from the conditions that their art professed to

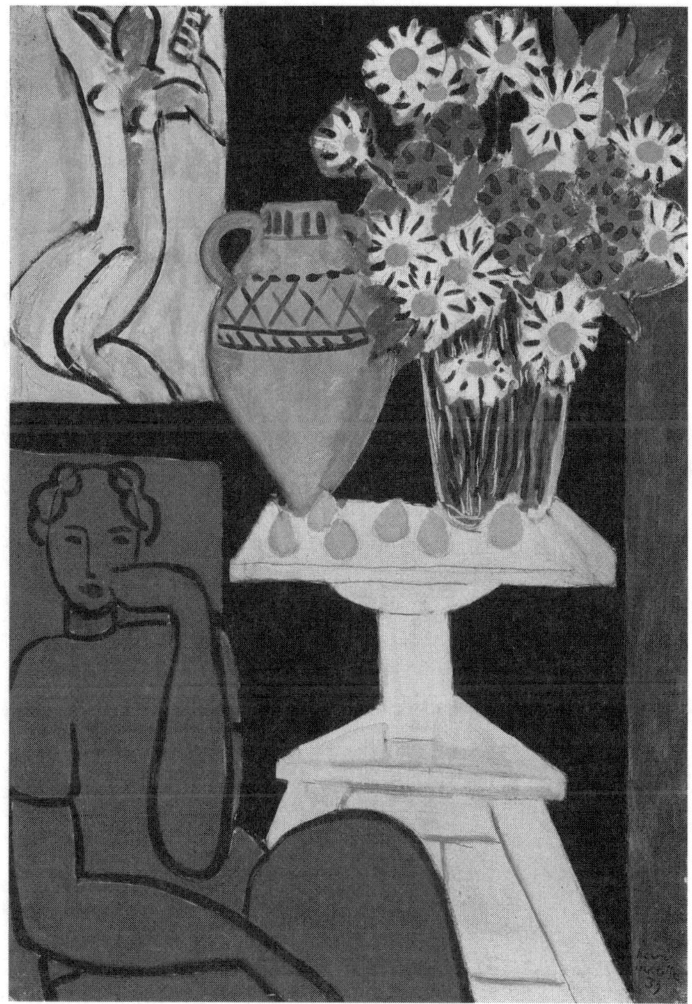

Figure 19   Henri Matisse, *Daisies (Les marguerites)*, 16 July 1939. Oil on canvas, 35 3/8 x 28 1/8 in., Gift of Helen Pauling Donnelley in memory of her parents, Mary Fredericka and Edward George Pauling, 1983.206. The Art Institute of Chicago. Photo: © The Art Institute of Chicago. © 2007 Succession H. Matisse, Paris / Artists Rights Society (ARS), New York.

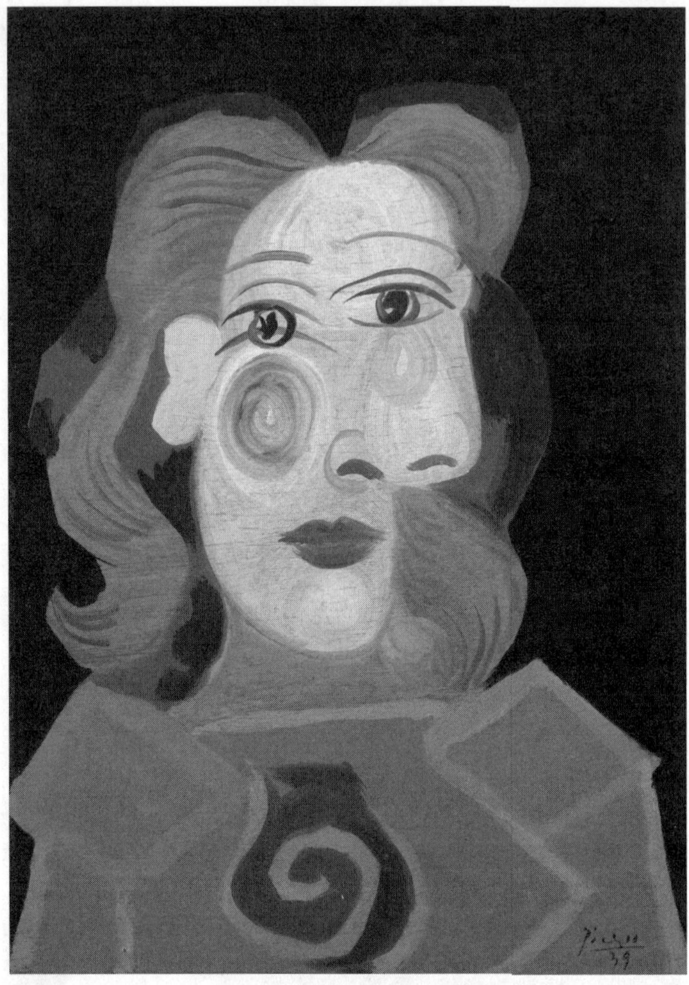

Figure 20   20. Pablo Picasso, *Head of a Woman (Dora Maar)*, 28 March 1939. Oil on wood, 23 9/16 x 17 3/4 inches. Solomon R. Guggenheim Museum, NY, Thannhauser Collection. © 2007 Estate of Pablo Picasso / Artists Rights Society (ARS), New York.

address. Their separation was of a different order from Rousseau's or Cézanne's alienation.

Greenberg regarded Rousseau as a lesser artist but a more sympathetic personality. He argued that the Douanier succeeded inadvertently by offering tangible value to a society that lacked faith in intangible value, its antithesis. Somewhat later the critic isolated what he called "the discomfort of our civilization." It was the inability to "believ[e] what we feel," that is, a failure to think and feel at once.[246] To coordinate feeling and thinking would reduce the effect of one of the coarser, more troubling forms of self-difference. This separation of reason and belief from emotion and feeling had been a theme of some of Cézanne's early critics and, as we know, was later to become central to Judd's criticism.[247] To have faith in responsive, emotional, and intuitive feeling would be to accept the value of an intangible phenomenon or psychological state, converting it into something tangible, acknowledging its empirical validity. The divide between tangible and intangible was at times just as pernicious as that between feeling and thinking. Greenberg implied that instead of trusting their own feelings, postwar Americans were performing the simplest possible acts of reasoning with the simplest sets of material facts available to them. They passed directly from sensation to reason, rather than from sensation to feeling and intuition, and then to reason and belief. The intuitive-emotional factor dropped out, what Peirce had regarded as "a single feeling of greater intensity ... the *sensuous* element of thought."[248] The thinking process of postwar Americans was as reduced and short-circuited as the art they liked, but such a double reduction could hardly be expected to lead to a "primitive" or naïve sense of naturalness. Perhaps crassness and crudeness were all that came of it.

What was Greenberg's version of the connection to feeling? How would postwar, conformist Americans come to feel something, as if against their acculturated nature? Rousseau offered the public what it craved: in Greenberg's words, "concrete sensation, immediate return, tangible datum." The only way to shock a materialistic culture out of its restrictive cultural identity was through a radically homeopathic appeal to its materialism. As Greenberg noted, Rousseau's "flat, direct, almost crass colors" succeeded in seizing the public's attention. This, the public could feel—therefore, a modernist quality an artist could use. The American abstract art just then beginning to gain critical recognition was also "flat, direct, almost crass." But it added an edge by removing the mitigating distraction of Rousseau's, or Cézanne's, or Van Gogh's representational subject matter. New York School artists such as Pollock and Newman responded to the materialistic need of their philistine culture with such force that what might have provided pleasure could only generate pain. Public tolerance was being tested with this paranoid aesthetic amalgam, pleasure-pain. Here was red, but no flower—the sweep of a curve, but no flesh.

* * *

To my knowledge, Greenberg's analysis of the Rousseau effect and its implications for the situation of the new abstract art in American culture has been cited only once by someone other than myself.[249] The reference appears in one of Greenberg's last interviews, conducted in 1991 by the British critic Peter Fuller. Fuller used elements of the Rousseau review to demonstrate that Greenberg advocated reducing pictorial effects to material and optical flatness. There are two intriguing problems with Fuller's presentation. First, it is actually not Greenberg who was converting flatness into a value; but, according to his argument, this was the established result of the ideological workings of modern culture. Greenberg was merely calling attention to an existing condition that he believed should have been apparent to anyone through self-reflection. He had no need to advocate flatness as an aesthetic because the aesthetic in question was already in place—actually, somewhat to his dismay. Second, Fuller misquoted Greenberg in a very telling way. Instead of referring to "concrete sensation, immediate return, tangible datum," he referred to "concrete sensation, immediate return, and intangible data."[250] *In*-tangible dat-*a*. In this form, the series of terms no longer exhibits consistency. The substance of Rousseau's art, its "tangible datum," has gone into cyberspace as "intangible data." What was singular and concrete has become multiple and dematerialized.

Why this mistake? It would not have been malicious, for Fuller admired Greenberg. Among many plausible explanations, two take the lead: Either Fuller, from the very beginning, unwittingly misquoted the words, or faulty transcription of an audiotape introduced the error. In either case, the passage would have been edited and proofed in production. Yet the error remained. Was *intangible data* such an expected or familiar phrase that several people failed to note it did not follow? However many were involved in reviewing the text, the mistake slid by them, despite the utter lack of logic. As it turns out, it slid by Greenberg as well, who received the copy once it was published and sent back a list of its several errors, which did not include "intangible data."[251] I can guess why: In proofreading, if there are two errors close on the page, the first tends to distract from the second, which then goes unnoticed. This was the case with Fuller's interview. In place of the Greenbergian "inviolable flatness of the picture plane," his text had the absurd "inviolable flatness of the picture frame." Greenberg spotted this one but not "intangible data," just below it.

Still, why did Fuller or another editor not notice that the passage had lost its sense? Perhaps for them, it had acquired a better sense. Like others of the time, Fuller would have been conditioned, through the repeated statements of fellow critics and scholars, to believe that Greenberg had long been promoting "opticality" in art, that he wanted painters to develop dematerialized effects of color at the expense of the materiality of the canvas support and the physicality of its applied pigments. This "opticality" would also supplant the virtual materiality associated with traditional illusionism, the kind of pictorial effect that had once been perceived as establishing "tactile values."[252] If a pure dematerialization could be achieved—with "intangible data" replacing the "tangible datum"—this would correspond to what Krauss and others identified as a specifically Greenbergian aesthetic of advanced formalist abstraction. Krauss called it "color field or opticality." Writing even later than Fuller—the quoted phrase is from 1999—she argued that Greenberg's sense of the opticality of line and color sent all elements of form "beyond the physicality of their material substance."[253] In her understanding of Greenberg, as in Fuller's, it seems that the formal structure of a painting has no recourse but to become "intangible data." Whereas Krauss had long been battling what she regarded as the Greenberg doctrine, Fuller was relatively sympathetic; yet both prejudicially inverted his position, whether with malice or mere carelessness. Together, and with the collusion of other writers as well, they produced a paranoid version of Greenberg's sensibility.

Fuller followed his reference to "concrete sensation, immediate return and intangible data" by motivating Greenberg: "In essence this is what you really wanted from art." Because he garbled the quotation, I cannot determine whether Fuller at that moment was referring to the presumed benefit of *concrete sensation* (materiality, physicality) or its antithesis, *intangible data* (opticality, dematerialization). In any event, Greenberg characteristically resisted being motivated; he replied that this—whatever it was—was never what he personally desired from art; it was merely what the best art was offering. "No," he insisted as he had on many other occasions, "I said that's the way the best art comes about. ... I can't choose what to like and not like. My prejudice is towards realistic art ... but I'm forced, compelled to like abstract art in this time."[254] Why? Because it was "the best." Apparently, the best is what affects a viewer's senses most immediately, concretely, and compellingly.

If we are honest, we acknowledge "the best art" not according to our theoretical or even emotional prejudice but by its impact. It might as well be called the "tangible datum." We acknowledge the physical existence as opposed to a predetermined identity. We feel it and have to believe what we feel.

* * *

If an exaggerated materialism in art had long been accommodating an acknowledged social or psychic need (the desire to confront one's modernity), perhaps that same materialism now serves a lingering doubt. I refer to the doubt that we as individuals can be fully represented by an ideologically constructed self—the postmodernist self of acquired meaning, of conformity, of fashion, of all our familiar social, political, and gender identities. Having raised so much suspicion over claims of naiveté in the past, we are now beset by doubt that comes from the other side. Claims for the ubiquitous efficacy of cultural forces may be creating a more pernicious mythology than speculation on the putatively absolute value of aesthetic immediacy and naturalness.

This doubt leaves us hanging. To acknowledge it does not entail being convinced of the real existence of the natural self that certain artists may be continuing to seek as a liberating alternative to culture—Rousseau being but one of a number of suggestive paradigms. Our doubt merely indicates how deeply dissatisfying it is to believe that there can be no natural self and no physical existence at all—no source of sensation that might escape the generalizing sameness of our various cultural identities. To occupy multiple identities and to experience self-difference does not eliminate the problem of being limited to the degree of sameness that every identity entails. James wrote, "The principle that the mind can mean the Same is true of its [cultural] meanings, but not necessarily of aught besides."[255] To classify yourself as this or that social type is hardly edifying. Believing that all experience is cultural, we relegate our thoughts, emotions, and sensations to depersonalized social forces, reducing the entirety of experience to a set of variants within an ideological order. To put it another way, the names of feelings are not the feelings.

And yet, this immediacy is not my usual reality, nor is it my indoctrination, for I tend to accept that I live, like others, under conditions of mundane self-differing.[256] I see the point in claiming that a person does not have a feeling without already having a concept or a model for that feeling, that specific emotions are identities learned "on the outside." Still, there is also something that might be called emotionality—the sensation of feelings that have no names. This is the quality that Greenberg attributed to de Kooning's art in 1948, as if true emotion could take no form other than such a nonform: "The emotion in that picture reminds me of all emotion. … You can't specify what the emotion is but are profoundly stirred nevertheless."[257] How profoundly? Was this Greenberg's temporary indulgence in what Newman called "a romantic dream age"? Whatever the case, it would be worthwhile to ponder the fact of feelings of emotionality—to dwell on and in them for a time—without converting the feelings to categories, identities, and names.

Rousseau's admirers believed that his art captured sensations outside the named categories and generalities associated with the bourgeois cultural self. Neither traditional nor avant-garde, his painting never threatened to surpass the achievements of modern culture but operated underneath its censorship at a relatively low level. Yet it had high impact, and—like the American pop art of the 1960s—"everyone" liked it. It pursued sensation through accentuated materiality, the tangible datum—a form of experience to which the culture was predisposed. For a significant number of twentieth-century viewers, Rousseau convincingly projected a natural self, oblivious to the cultural divide of tangible sensation and intangible belief. His art was nonironic. Either it had no codes of which a viewer had to be informed, or its codes were so general that their operation did not matter. Viewers found that they could accept the experiential value of Rousseau's art while doubting the relevance of its cultural attachments: doubting not only the mythology of the primitive but also, eventually, the twentieth-century critical theory that debunked the claims primitivism made to human origins and cultural innocence. "Unconsciously," Rousseau became a demythologizer of both the myth and its antimyth.

He still appears innocent to us: "Rousseau the illusionist, whose own jungles scared him."[258] Unlike de Kooning or even Cézanne, he tends not to attract critics who would expose potential ideological evils—sexism, racism, colonialism. He may be an impossible target, hiding nothing so there is nothing to unmask. We treat him as if he and his art were too naïve to be an effective ideological agent; and yet, those who are naïve, who entertain no doubt, ought to be the most effective of agents. His art attracts a modern sensorium so fundamentally—"everyone" takes a dose of aesthetic pleasure in it—that it makes no difference whether the artist, like nature, knew what he (it) was doing, or not. There ought to be an ideological lesson in this, something to believe in.

Beyond their European context, Rousseau, Cézanne, and Van Gogh inadvertently produced art for a mid-century America they could never have foreseen—an art direct in its materialism and requiring no imaginative projection of moral, religious, or psychological values. Greenberg, a mid-century American, accepted this as a fact of history. Did he approve? No more than Newman approved of the fact that during the years of the war terrifying fantasies became a tragic reality that no one could wish away. As much of a fatalist as Newman, Greenberg did not expect conditions to be other than as they were. "Modern art," he wrote, "like modern literature and modern life, has lost much ... I cannot help regretting what has been lost. The regret is futile."[259] Like Cézanne in his doubt, postwar Americans experienced what Greenberg called a long-standing and ever widening "gap between poetic practice and actual knowledge." "This schizophrenia," as the critic called it 1950, amounted to an inability to—I quote it a second time—"believ[e] what we feel."[260] Here was the prophetic truth of Rousseau's art. It mirrored the reduced, disjunctive terms of life in its most modern phase: "life," as Greenberg wrote, "without the deception (but also protection) of faith in anything."[261]

Greenberg was no surrealist. He was facing what he took to be reality, not a projective fantasy; he spoke, for example, of de Kooning's materiality, not of de Kooning's Woman. It was not "derangement" that made Rousseau's case exemplary for Greenberg, nor the fact that the painter's questionable mental condition hardly prevented him from achieving significant art; this fact was historical accident. Rather, the remarkable irony was that the public, sophisticates and philistines alike, were accepting Rousseau's art so enthusiastically. This reception, Greenberg realized, was hardly accidental. We already know why. It was because Rousseau's art offered the public what it craved: "concrete sensation, immediate return, tangible datum." I have no assurance that Greenberg actually learned anything from observing this bit of cultural history and perceiving Rousseau as prophetic. More likely, he used the Rousseau phenomenon to demonstrate what he already believed about American life, identifying historical facts arbitrarily to suit what he needed to say about social issues. He too was capable of working in reverse.

At the very least, what Greenberg wrote about Rousseau's craziness helps explain why, a decade later, he would regard de Kooning's "savage dissections" as cuts in the material paint, canvas, or paper, not in the corporeal Woman. Viewing contemporary art in this way was, in Greenberg's terms, simply to accept the historical fact of a materialist mentality, the condition that avant-garde artists had to confront rather than wish away—or, through projection and other defenses, evade. To recognize the prophetic beginning in Rousseau's paranoid paintings was to understand one's own fated end. The New York painters whom Greenberg sometimes disputed but mostly admired, such as Newman, and those he sometimes admired but mostly disputed, such as de Kooning, were willing to face the reality of modernity and its tragedies. They were also prepared to beat American conformists at their materialist game. For them, the postwar twentieth century was no time for dreaming.

Hegelianism without the happy ending

I cannot say what I think.

—G. W. F. Hegel, 1817-30, as rephrased by Paul de Man, 1982[262]

If we eliminate the religious fundamentalists (a huge subtraction), the modernist twentieth century was an age of theories of indeterminacy, a great many of them—from the physical and phenomenological sciences of the earlier decades to the linguistic poststructuralism of the later decades. From some perspective outside ourselves, it might appear that we have more ideological concord on this matter of indeterminacy than we have difference. But such sameness is damaging to academic and critical egos. Disagreements often arise merely because those who think alike refuse to acknowledge the commonality of their beliefs and attitudes, and self-difference appears on a communal scale. Anxious over catching the right intellectual fashion, each critic nevertheless seeks distinction. We fail to recognize the general recognition. Perhaps the academic consciousness must await a historical jolt, something like the "changed technical standard" to which Benjamin referred, which would induce a new way of enjoining academic argument. As Cézanne realized, a new means of looking is worth more than yet another theory of looking. I would be satisfied if we would stop conflating the history of the criticism and theory of art with the history of making art.

Newman knew that his pragmatic understanding and control of his art was limited: "How it went, that's how it was," he said. Already well accomplished, de Kooning believed he was "still working out of doubt." Greenberg held the unsettling conviction that the inaugural masters of modern art were alienated psychotics who could not have known what they were doing. Their achievements were arbitrary accidents of history, apparent only to critics and sometimes not even to them. With regard to Cézanne, he wrote, "His expressed theory contradicted his practice … he kept on trying to rescue the conventions that his Impressionist vision compelled him to undermine."[263] Acknowledging such accident— fortunate for history, unfortunate for Cézanne—Greenberg never claimed for himself the power of predicting what would count as artistic value in the future.[264] His firm judgments concerned only the present. As for de Kooning, he was satisfied, even fulfilled, by working at the edge of insecurity: "When I'm falling, I'm doing all right." We might take his attitude as representative of a late form of Rimbaud-like intentional derangement, but de Kooning would certainly have resented this degree of generalization and theorization of what he merely felt. Judd, usually critical of de Kooning, would agree on a very basic, antitheoretical observation: "A lot of things look alike, but they're not necessarily very much alike."[265] Given their tendency to generalize, art critics should consider Judd's point. Their analyses so often depend on metaphorical description, which can cause any two things to look alike—two identities converging on their theoretical sameness.

In a world regarded as packed with indeterminacy, unstable relationships, and paranoid, self-differing identities, some space does remain for certainty. I noted that Newman had been moved by seeing photographs of the liberated concentration camps in 1945. These images represented a breaking point in humanity and human history. They confirmed him in his growing belief that the old ways of making art—everything from naïve flower painting to sophisticated surrealist fantasies—were ineffective and irrelevant exercises, no adequate acknowledgment of the break that all should have been witnessing, a gap so wide in human behavior. A bit of historical documentation, some journalists' photographs with accompanying reports that appeared in the *New York Times* and elsewhere, provided him with a new baseline reference for his painting and critical writing. April 16, 1945: "More than 20,000 nondescript prisoners [at Buchenwald], many of them barely living [were] all that remained of the normal complement of 80,000."[266] Because Newman recognized this historical turn in his own time, he was disinclined to seek a crisis point in the past or to theorize the break as opposed to doing something directly in response. He nevertheless had his own kind of doubt, resulting from his realization that he would be unable to predict in full the consequences of any action he might take. Although the painting *Onement I* showed him the kind of thing he needed to do (what to make), it did not convert him into the prophet of himself. It represented not an absolute beginning but a new beginning, not a culmination but an opening, not an indicator of the future but just an indicator—like a feeling, an emotion with no name.[267] Newman's fate was to be forced into the future by this break, left to his arbitrary decisions, acting in a conceptual void as much as within a pervasive cultural context. Like his political situation in the postwar environment of the late 1940s, his aesthetic and ethical situation in the studio was forced in the sense that it could only be perceived as arbitrary, having no justification in rational principles as he understood them—not even in a principle of self-interest.

Some years later, in 1955, a particularly low point in his shaky professional career, Newman painted one of his most ambitious works, *Uriel*. I have already remarked on the circumstances of the area of pale greenish-blue at the left of this painting, which occupies about three quarters of its eighteen-foot width. When asked to explain his purpose, Newman answered: "I wanted to see how far I could stretch it before it broke."[268] With *Uriel*, he made a point of operating without a guideline. Forcing his art beyond what he knew he could do, he would see what happened, feel how it felt. This had been the situation of *Onement I*, though in that case, more definitively unintended. Should we say, then, that *Uriel* made its point to Newman, rather than assigning full responsibility to Newman for making his point by means of *Uriel*? His open-ended explanation represented an afterthought rather than any conscious program. Like the *want* in "modernist visuality wants," Newman's *want* in "wanted to see how far" could be realized and understood only after his act of pictorial judgment, in response to a demand that he reveal his aesthetic program. His "to see how far" amounted to a nonprogram, an unintended demonstration that whenever left to explore its own devices, painting proceeds, or should proceed, "without any strict plans."[269] It would nevertheless do Newman and *Uriel* a critical injustice to claim that this is what painting "wants," for painting, as a mode of modernist visuality or otherwise, has no plans of its own. Its suggestion of its own motivating cause is an effect of its appearance—at a certain moment, under certain conditions, to a certain observer. The value of a painter's "stretching" of color, Newman's creative experimentation, is allegorical: Such action becomes exemplary and therefore other-oriented, self-differing. It is a material instance of self-difference in advance of still other instances. The others come with the artist's own critical explanation, perhaps ironic, and the commentary eventually offered by interested parties at a personal and cultural distance.

Like any of Newman's paintings, *Uriel* represented the human capacity to make an ethical decision despite having little information to guide it in the process or support it in its result. With much to fear in the world because so much was tragically unknowable, Newman believed that people should never fear their free judgment. It could only be arbitrary, neither right nor wrong and no third identity either.

2

SEMINAR[*]

James Elkins: Your talk reminded me of a debate that Panofsky had with George Boas, about what Panofsky called *atomization*. Boas wanted to insist on the particularity of every artwork, a position that would result in a collapse of historical categories and judgments; against that Panofsky posited an equally unhelpful extreme, which can be called *monism:* the doctrine that art is a single enterprise. I think in philosophy Panofsky's atoms are called *perfect particulars* or *abstract particulars*. They entail the idea, which is inimical to historical writing, that "properties are just as much … particulars as the things that have them."[1]

---

[*] *This seminar was conducted April 29, 2004.* James Elkins, History of Art, University College Cork; Francis Halsall, History of Art, University College Cork; Simon Knowles, History of Art, University College Cork; Margaret MacNamidhe, Government of Ireland Postdoctoral Fellow, University College Dublin; Tony O'Connor, Philosophy, University College Cork; Laura Rascaroli, Italian Department, University College Cork.

You were talking in different ways about these same unattractive options, and so I am led to wonder how far your four categories [prophecy, projection, doubt, paranoia] might coalesce into one, or multiply into more, and what internal principles might regulate those possibilities.

Richard Shiff: The danger would be that my four attitudes might slide into particularity—

JE: —so that instead of four categories you would end up with a humoralism gone berserk, with dozens of humors, or on the other hand with a kind of monism, although it would presumably not be a collapsing of historical periods but of attitudes.

RS: The four I was thinking about for these lectures, and have been thinking about for several years, are genuinely arbitrary: They produced each other. If I wasn't able to get the four down to three, or up to five, it's only because it didn't work out that way. I wasn't aiming for any particular number. Four is plenty; ten might have been unwieldy. I didn't do this systematically and don't have a memory of what came from what. I know that one of them, probably projection, came after the others; prophecy may have been the first because I have long been fascinated by some sentences out of Walter Benjamin. So it's interpretation all the way, not a code or a logic. In the work of many of my postmodernist colleagues, I see overgeneralization that's masquerading as theory; I see unacknowledged absolutism and utopianism, invocations of internal logics and inherent demands—all this, even when the topic is subjectivity or cultural difference. I don't think things can be so certain, so I often seek out particularities and failure points within the general systems. It's a corrective, perhaps a moderating gesture on my part.

JE: In the faculty reading groups leading up to your visits, we spent quite a long while on your distinction among the artistic, the critical, and the historical, as they are made at the end of the essay "Flexible Time."[2] The artistic perspective entails, for example, that "the evolution of classical art proceeds from an original indexical moment," "the spontaneous discovery of representation in the tracing of a shadow," for example, up to the "initiation of a tradition of imitative skill," exemplified by apprenticeship: "as skill gradually increases, authentic expression decreases." The critical perspective is self-doubting: Such writers "focus on the play of artistic means, those specific techniques that modernists devise to bring art back into contact with indexical 'reality,' with the phenomenological immediacy of the subject's engagement with objects. A critical concentration on techniques and procedures often leads to recognition of representational distance even where unexpected and unwanted." The third perspective, the historical, is described in part this way: "Whenever modernists see their art as having a determinate history, modernist indexicality loses its privilege and becomes a representational practice like any other; the indexical ceases to appear as indisputable physical evidence of self-expression and begins to operate more as a linguistic sign"—those "indicating certain interests."

So among the things we were discussing is that there is a certain way of understanding painting whose self-description would correspond with the artistic perspective. The critical perspective, especially when you describe it in terms of irony, the study of indexicality, and a rethinking of history, corresponds very well with what art historians do—

RS: —in our age anyway—

JE: —including several of us. This makes the historical perspective especially interesting and problematic.

RS: It is almost empty.

JE: Exactly. If an historian believes that the objects of study are linguistic signs, then the objects are not taken at their value, and that, it seems to me, is a very rare condition. Your example in "Flexible Time" is John O'Brian in his capacity as editor of Greenberg's papers; my example, in another context, is Caroline Jones, who sometimes writes from a tremendous historical distance from her subject, which is also Greenberg.[3]

RS: The artist-critic-historian distinction is a way of getting around saying who is a modernist and who isn't, or who is political and who is formal (isn't everyone some of each?). A shift in methodological perspective can shake us out of methodological habits and absolutism. Historians who specialize in periods other than modern might ask, "What are you doing? Is this criticism? It isn't history. You went and visited the artist and asked some questions, so where's the history?" So I thought it was important to try to define an attitude that would correspond with what people would accept as history, whether or not this is what historians are actually doing; and I think in our time there aren't very many historians. Academic historians don't do history in the strict sense. They do criticism, they do interpretation; they aren't chroniclers, and they don't allow themselves to be as objective as they could be. This happens because we put so much value on interpretation, subjectivity, and attitude. I have no problem with this convergence of history and criticism. But when we nevertheless pretend to criticize our contemporaries objectively, we end up using the critical perspective as a sledgehammer. I think this is dishonest, because either we aren't operating in the open, critical spirit we profess or we're adopting the same degree of inflexible denial of subjectivity that we're attributing to others.

JE: It seemed to us that the third perspective, the historical, is not only rare but fascinating, and so it presents itself as the final term in a dialectic—although I appreciate the fact that you present all three modes as coexisting possibilities. It seemed to us that they are actually a logical progression and that a person who wrote from the third perspective might not ever go back or ever want to.

RS: I don't think that the historical attitude represents the end of the line. Even though the history category is nearly empty, it's there because there are people like myself who are acknowledged to be historians. We still have the profession, and therefore we have the category, and we may as well see what goes in it, except maybe nothing properly goes in it.

JE: It seems that almost nothing of our own work goes in it—

RS: Well, certain aspects of our work probably belong in that category, even if not the whole. There are times when I am being very dry about what I am doing, but in the end I'm not dry: I feel I can't get away with just presenting the facts, let's say. To present them may be regarded by my profession as having done very little. Maybe a pure historian could write a dictionary, although it's surprising what you find in dictionaries, which are so deeply interpretive.

One of the things that made me think of the three perspectives was seeing academics having arguments with one another, and one accusing the other of being some kind of positivist, when there are no positivists. It's ridiculous, and you shouldn't have to defend yourself against that charge, because people today are so unlikely to be guilty. There ought to be more genuine sources of disagreement. Almost by definition—you couldn't have gotten an academic job if you were a positivist—

JE: —at least not in a humanities department—

RS: —certainly not. There is a sentence in "Flexible Time" that refers to the historical perspective as one you can fake:

You can assume that pose, although you don't believe in it. You can use it to defend yourself: If someone objects to your claims, you can say, "Look, I went to this archive, and that archive, and that's the way it was." You can then make it look as if you had done no interpretation at all. In this case, against the grain, you end up using positivism as a kind of defence, not a crime.

This reminds me of a wonderful five pages or so in Kleist about how we form thoughts while speaking: It concerns things you say because you're not yet at the end of a coherent thought, and you need more time to think, so you introduce some stuff that is meaningless. Your interlocutor has to wait a little, while you continue talking.[4] Research sometimes amounts to this kind of holding position. Once it's in the record, meaningless research assumes its default position, which is to be meaningful if only because it's now in the record, like the delaying filler within a thought.

JE: This is one of my definitions of the talk that goes on in studio art critiques, often because the speakers are trying to be as complex as possible.[5]

Margaret MacNamidhe: I wanted to ask a question that relates to your attempt to wrest art historians from their superior position. As you say in "Flexible Time," the jury is in that the subject is embodied, yet art historians pay lip service to the notion: not least because of art historians' certainty that, as you put it in "Realism of Low Resolution," all is "cultural construction"—our "current prejudice, our doxa."[6] For example, you mentioned Judd's use of the release of a new variation on space, and the way it was immediately understood as part of a metacritical narrative, as Krauss's modernist visuality.

So I am wondering about the nature of the changes we need to make as art historians in regard to concepts you're introducing, in keeping with modernist notions of the subjective embodiment of vision, but fending off the self-enhancing reciprocity which rather smugly uncovers the very conventional constructions, specifically of iconicity, lurking within the successive stages of modernism. I am interested in how this aspiration to a changed rhetorical or narrative form works, specifically in regard to your point last night that our treatment of earlier periods seems more arbitrary than our response to things and people in our own world.

RS: So what can be done?

MM: Yes, in relation to current practices of art history …

RS: What I've been thinking recently in terms of icon and index, or artist, critic, historian, or prophecy, projection, doubt, paranoia (I hope I'm not going in twos, threes, and fours) is oriented toward particular cases. The concepts then tend to come from specific situations in which I'm trying to puzzle things out. The artist, critic, historian schema is very useful, I think, in figuring out what was going on between Paul Gauguin and Paul Cézanne, because Cézanne is really a hard-core artist type. That's why he is so inflexible. He's full of irony, and there is even irony in his art, but that does not make him a critic: He had a kind of faith in his own art that just is not characteristic of the critical mind. Gauguin, on the other hand, is the supreme critic. He practices art as if it is criticism. He's intellectually restless. The artist types are probably less common than the critic types, at least among those we now consider to be major artists.

JE: Their uncommonness might also be a defining characteristic of modernism.

RS: Yes, in that modernism may favor critical types. Anyway, what I have been trying to do in answering specific questions

I became interested in, and then moving toward certain theoretical constructions that could help me, and even in producing essays that I think of as being theoretically oriented, is just looking for devices that will work, as opposed to committing to a theory and then applying it helter-skelter, whether it produces useful results or not. Many revisionist accounts of earlier modernist art result in telling us what we already know, only in a new vocabulary. I suppose it makes us feel virtuous because we have the illusion of having changed something. It's just the illusion of change. But you get somewhere working more openly and pragmatically: You don't get the art-historical kind of answers, and you don't get the art answers. I think you do get a certain kind of critic's answer. The procedure is willful and arbitrary because it matches critical terms that come from elsewhere with specific media of production. You have to keep switching the terms, given the kind of art in question.

JE: Yesterday we were talking about C. S. Peirce, and your adoption of two thirds of the triad—icon and index, without symbol—to work with the problem of photography and painting. I mentioned Peirce's tendency to multiply, so that three signs become ten, which become sixty-six, which become 59,049.[7] I take your point about the pragmatic reason for adopting two thirds of Peirce's basic triad, but that would be different from what happens with the triad artist-critic-historian, because they form a logical sequence, with each leading on to the next. The allure of the third perspective, the historical, is that it is a kind of conceptually pristine state: not only positivist, as you say, but also somehow outside of history, looking back and down on it from a tremendous distance. When the subject is modern art—a history that we still live in and through—the third position cannot be occupied without sacrificing plausibility, yet it can neither be ignored nor rescinded: Once you're there, you cannot go back. In that sense a pragmatically oriented historian, intent on a specific problem, cannot discard it as the third term in Peirce's triad can be omitted or subsumed into the other two.

RS: I don't know. A little doubt can cause you to retreat—or maybe advance—from historical certitude. And there are probably ways to argue that the artistic perspective is just as impossible as the historical one.

JE: You would need to have no ironic distance on the project of painting.

RS: Yes, you won't find people like that. In the last paragraph of "Flexible Time," I say that it's impossible to find pure examples of any of the three perspectives.

JE: You break the penultimate paragraph and say that there are no pure states, and you say the same in the final paragraph. In our faculty discussions of this in the past weeks, I think some of us found those paragraphs problematic after the apparent succession of ideas in the preceding three perspectives.

RS: Bear in mind that I associated my conclusion with the critical position—my critical position—which allowed me to entertain this perspective of doubt.[8] Whether you are troubled more by the doubt or by the sense of succession that may have preceded it (a sense I myself don't dwell on, although I can perceive it just as you can) may depend on how affirming or disaffirming you find instances of apparent succession or entailment to begin with. You have to begin somewhere, so I did. I presented my terms in a certain order, which is what the medium of discursive writing usually does. There are cases where the usual discursive mode is altered—by James Joyce, for example, or by Jacques Derrida, though not in all of his writings—but you risk affectation to achieve whatever you gain this way. For my purposes, I suppose I've retained the feel of entailment, yet I'd rather not think that the critic position necessarily follows the artist position. It's just that our inherited mythologies of creativity play out better if we think through the differential order in this sequence: artist, critic, historian. We could nevertheless be born into a condition of doubt and seek the intimate faith of the artist position as relief from our own initial intellectual insecurity. Or we could move toward history, generating distance as a remedy. These attitudes characterize not only those who exemplify them but also those who may favor or desire them. Once the alternatives have been identified, they may well correlate with an existing sense of historical periodization.

You could write a history with the index-icon factor in mind: Does it correspond with a period? With a type of art? When in history is either one dominant? The indexical seems dominant during most of the twentieth century, with a possible shift in the later decades. You could do the same with the triad artist-critic-historian. Perhaps because of my own historical situation, I think that the critical perspective is always dominant, though in some periods more so than others. In some periods I imagine there must be more of a balance. The artistic element comes into play when people take strong positions; in such cases they are not being ironic. In art criticism of the later twentieth century, somewhat paradoxically—this may amount to some sort of character flaw—many who claim the critic position are really occupying a variant of the artist position. Rhetorically they are ironic, but in fact their views are dogmatic articles of faith, often simply the faith that they must be right. The artist position includes the dogmatic position, because it is the only one open to faith, to belief so strong that you feel no need to consider contrary arguments. Many professional critics become zealots. As critics, they shouldn't be.

MM: This suggests a question about the era of the interpreter. For example, how would one deal with the question of the break between traditions? Thus, the critics of the impressionists suspected a diminution of visual iconicity in the rapidity of impressionist painting because the painting signaled a break with tradition, but on the other hand—and coming from the other direction, so to speak—the self-enhancing reciprocity of modernist art historians reveals a large admixture of visual iconicity. I would take this as an example of the historical conditioning that can make different discursive contexts difficult to compare. So my question concerns the nature of the break: Might the apparent diminution of visual iconicity, experienced as a cutting of links with tradition, not have appeared so threatening to contemporaneous critics of impressionism if it had been possible to see the intermediaries that might now be posited?

RS: What I can say is that the intermediaries were much more evident to the younger generation; and, of course, there are always several different generations active at any one historical moment. Gauguin, Vincent van Gogh, and Paul Signac, as well as a critic like Félix Fénéon, were able to explain the impressionist situation and to build on it in ways that the befuddled graduates of the École des Beaux-Arts could not. Throughout the nineteenth century, different senses of what was conventional, what was natural, what was expressive, what was an abstraction—all these notions were in play. You can reconstruct the complicated critical map with its intermediate positions by reading through the writings of the more adventurous exhibition reviewers—figures such as Théophile Thoré, Paul Mantz, and Jules-Antoine Castagnary—who had a well-developed sensitivity to historical change.

Simon Knowles: Might there be an arbitrary perspective in the view you are taking, because of the position you occupy?

RS: It may well be so. I would be satisfied if my perspective were to prove useful and commodious, that is, if it didn't exclude much. It's unfortunate that smart artists can get bad ideas from critics they think are smarter than they. When I say unfortunately I mean that without irony. This is true even of Donald Judd, who had a lot of influence as a thinking artist—he was a complainer by temperament, and in his case the complaints are valid. People invited him to speak, and collectors and museums wanted his work, but he felt that he had not had the right influence on other artists. They seemed to learn more from the commentary on Judd than from Judd himself. A major complaint was that he was the father of installation art and that he didn't want to be. He put something on the floor, and other artists started putting a whole lot of stuff on the floor.

SK: But the wrong kind of stuff.

RS: Yes, Judd's artistic statements proved useful, but the use was a bad one. There is a line in one of his essays in 1983 or 1984: He says, "Maybe we didn't talk enough." He means himself, Richard Serra, Carl Andre, Dan Flavin maybe. You say to yourself, My God, these people talked all the time; they were interviewed, they wrote essays—what is he complaining about? He's complaining about art criticism because after all, art critics talk all the time, and the artists only get to talk part of the time. He believes that his famous essay about specific objects has been misread over and over again, and I think he was right about that. He knew that commentators tend to repeat whatever a previous commentator has said. "Specific Objects" becomes canonical, but not in the way Judd wanted. He complains not because he doesn't get credit for inventing installation art but because he's failing to get credit for inventing what he actually did invent. Doing installation art is in his mind a bad idea, so he becomes the father of a bad idea, and the good idea that he had has no followers, so he can't be the father of that because his true idea has no children.

Laura Rascaroli: Does this have to with *projection,* which is a term you have used, even though it seems to me perhaps not fully articulated?

RS: Yes, it would be a case of projection. There are personality types: If you paint a landscape and say you were impelled to do it by Chuck Close's pixeled images, I think he would be curious about this. Close is a very accepting person. I think he would find it interesting that his portraits happened to spawn a landscape even if the connection made no immediate sense to him. To the contrary, Judd would accept virtually nothing as a variant, although I suppose he would accept a lot of parallels. So the artist who sees Judd's art in a way that is alien to Judd's own thinking will be projecting—at least it would seem that way to Judd. Pablo Picasso certainly saw things in Cézanne that have nothing to do with Cézanne. He is the one who abused the model Cézanne provided, being quite willful about what he drew from his predecessor's work. It's like Rosalind Krauss's way of dealing with the model of Clement Greenberg, circumventing his arguments by being *so* different that there's little left to discuss—a dismissive response rather than a constructive one, perhaps the result of projection. Greenberg used to say in conversation, "Don't motivate me," meaning "Stop projecting."

Tony O'Connor: To come back to an earlier point that Jim was making, concerning the role of plausibility, legitimation, or justification of your own position, relative to the notion of theory that you are using or perhaps trying to get away from: You mention that one of the things that might make your account plausible is that you use terms that seem appropriate to your interlocutor. But do you see as a feature of plausibility, that the accounts to be given then may vary considerably depending on to whom one is talking? For example, if you are talking to a Marxist, and the Marxist says, "You need to take economic considerations into account," or if you are talking to a Heideggerian, and he says, "You've got to talk about the manifesting and withdrawal of being"—and so forth. In your model, do you have to expect a large number of conflicts of interpretation, or even accounts that may well pass each other by, simply because the language and terms they use are quite at odds with one another?

RS: I think you do. Are you asking whether an individual person would engage in these incommensurable discourses?

TO: Yes, I am thinking of individual encounters.

RS: I think that the Marxist clearly has a point but should be recognized as a Marxist. So it works both ways. I have an inclination not to have a center: That's why I don't mind switching theorists, without any immoveable commitment aside from pragmatic considerations.

TO: Could you be persuaded, in principle, that you are wrong in some fundamental respect?

RS: You mean that this is a bad method?

TO: Either that it is a bad method or that something central that you say in regard to a painter or group of works may be wrong.

RS: Yes, I think so: I am trying to work in such a way that it is unlikely that I would be completely wrong, and that's why I try to pay attention to multiple factors, many of which would be material, having to do with the objects the artist is producing. In a certain sense, I would be wrong if it turned out that my conclusions had no application—that they were of use neither to the artist nor to other critical and historical writers. Dead ends are wrong moves. But even a dead end doesn't have to stay dead forever.

JE: I am thinking ahead to the next few years of this book series, and I imagine you may present the most formidable challenge to my request to the writers to respond to those who went before. I notice that in the essay on which part of these lectures are based you say, "Disagreement arises because those who think alike refuse to acknowledge the commonality of their beliefs and attitudes."[9] So a pure lack of disagreement, which I imagine might well happen in future books in this series, would be a pure difference …

RS: When you agree about the big things and stop arguing about them, then you can get down to the new stuff and see something that you don't already know. You would have an issue on which you would actually have to decide rather than merely continuing along the lines of an existing critical syndrome. After we dispense with what I consider petty arguments about big things, such as, "Shall we call this work modernist or postmodernist?" (this is a dead end, an unproductive differential), let's talk about something that might actually teach us something. If we debate the points of modernism and postmodernism, we're going to be debating forever. We can all observe the social conditions identified with postmodernism; the notion of some kind of break or struggle as a point of contention becomes an arbitrary debate, having no effect on the social conditions that were the concern to begin with. Arbitrariness can be generative, but not in this instance. I am serious about the arbitrary factor often being beneficial. When I turn to a random page in a book and read it without reading what comes before or after, this is when I learn the most: I am truly focused, forced to pay attention, and not distracted by trying to size up the author. I only want to be stimulated—emotionally as much as intellectually—and to use that stimulation to get me going, to make connections, and to learn something I don't already know, or maybe remember something I'd forgotten.

JE: I think for me the question is whether or not those large terms, modernism and postmodernism for example, really are agreed on. Are they a common ground, which everyone knows and which would probably be ignored in favor of new and arbitrary unopened pages of history? Or are they what guide our choices? And if they are something we can't afford to take as given, then what is the relation between your enterprises and perspectives (since there are several) and those of the speakers I have invited for the following years?

For me a good way of thinking about this is with the concept of incommensurability. I know a wonderful artist, Stephanie Brooks, who made some paintings of scales on either side of a line, like opposing scales on a slide rule. The tick marks above the line might be labeled, "Miles I have hiked" and those below, which never line up with the ones above, might be marked, "Happiness." This is what I think of when I imagine some art historians in this series, considering terms such as prophecy and projection, and wondering if they are in fact incommensurables.

RS: Art historians are cultural confreres and ought to have tacit agreement about 99 percent of the material. It's not as if we're arguing about everything. Many of the individual things we historians argue about should nevertheless not be argued, because they too are points of agreement. For example, I've heard people criticized for being too fact oriented. I've heard that so many times that it can't be a good argument: If everyone is making it, how can it be a point of disagreement? Even the positivists are complaining about positivism, just as the ideologues are complaining about ideology.

TO: Would you then want to move some of the big terms, such as *theory* and *practice,* to soften them out or mess them up?

RS: Yes.

TO: I see that, but then it makes a great deal of difference to whom you are talking. You can easily arrive at an imbalance in such conversations.

RS: You would have to try to recognize all those differences and deal with them.

JE: Maybe one way to bring a conversation about commensurability forward would be to talk about the labels we have been giving to our operative concepts. *Categories* is not really the right label for the four ideas you propose in your lectures. They are, as you said, *attitudes,* and I would want to make a strong distinction between an attitude such as *prophetic* and the expression *prophetic art:* The latter is a kind of art that might be typical of a historical period, and historical periods are not attitudes. There are in other words species and occasions of incommensurability—unlike the slide rule, which presents only one kind of mismatch.

TO: Your work, Richard, strikes me as a kind of analogue to Willem de Kooning's. It is like his representational painting, where you more or less throw a lot of things at us and say, "Find things in that." There are definite helps and aids along the way but very definite challenges as well.

RS: Yes: In a kind of intellectual way I have discovered in the past few years that I identify with both de Kooning and Newman, who incidentally did not like each other all that much. They would do anything to avoid fixity in categories; as soon as anybody would pin them down, they would just go on to something else. As an academic, I think it would be irresponsible to act that out, yet I sympathize with what they were doing as critically minded artists.

JE: I am sorry to change the subject here, but there are several other topics I would like to get on tape, partly because they are important issues in your text and partly because I would like them to be on the record for subsequent authors. The first pertains to Maurice Merleau-Ponty. We were talking the other day about the possibility that a large percentage of contemporary art historians take Merleau-Ponty as a theorist whose ideas need not be located in mid-century French intellectual history. The art historians who might be most in need of hearing that might be the ones least amenable to hearing it, because they would think they had contextualized him in various ways—by stressing his interest in Robert Delaunay or Paul Klee, or by tracing his philosophy to Edmund Husserl or other sources. To some degree it is a condition of contemporary art history that parts of Merleau-Ponty are taken as true: I have done so myself, and I read it in various places in your texts. There are some art historians, for example Michael Fried, who take Merleau-Ponty as a starting place (no matter how far from him they stray), and there is a large literature on the body and its representations that would be impossible without a more or less unconditional but untheorized acceptance of Merleau-Ponty.

This is therefore not a question but a problem: Can we describe current scholarship's dependence on Merleau-Ponty, and can we understand his exemption from historical contextualization? One way might be to parse the parts of Merleau-Ponty that are taken into contemporary historical scholarship. We might distinguish, for example, the notion that seeing is reciprocal (as Merleau-Ponty says, "I see according to" Cézanne's pictures, rather than seeing with them or merely seeing them) from the idea that seeing is embodied (an idea that is also derived from Jacques Lacan, Theodor Lipps, George Lakoff, and Johnson, and several others). Or we might look closely at the places in texts where Merleau-Ponty switches from being a figure in history, with limitations and a language peculiar perhaps to him, and becomes a source of truths about painting. Those places are where the historian, in your terms, becomes the critic.

RS: As you suggest, there are places where Merleau-Ponty is used as if his method is timeless, and other places, perhaps in some kind of expanded intellectual history, where his method is understood as specific to a moment. What happens all too often—and it happens to people who are old enough to know better—is that people acquire the three-sentence version of the major thinker, and then they use it. They acquire, say, three sentences of Hegel, and then they use them. If you're trying to pass a college exam, this may be acceptable, but when you're a full professor and you're doing this, it's regrettable. Academic life encourages it, because you seem to get points for the number of important thinkers you cite. I do tend to be very specific about quotations I take from authorities, and there's always a reason why I'm using a particular one and not some other.

TO: I think we have to approach these questions of citation in connection with a creative interpretation of what's at stake and think about it on the model of playing a musical instrument: It's possible to just play the notes, but also we need to think about phrases and how they relate to other structures in the piece.

RS: Merleau-Ponty will become a category, and once that happens—

TO: —he is dead, in a sense.

JE: At first I thought there is a place in "Cézanne's Physicality" where Merleau-Ponty moves from being a figure situated in history to being an analytic tool that helps move your argument forward. But then it occurred to me that the earlier critics, Gustave Geffroy for instance, are also taken as tools. It's an interesting sliding back and forth between historiography (taking sources as characteristic of certain decades in the reception of Cézanne) and criticism or philosophy (taking sources as partial views onto Cézanne's work).

RS: Yes, I try to find something anchored in the time of the artist—for Cézanne, it can be Geffroy's writing—and then turn the perspective around so that the wisdom or sensitivity of both artist and critic (Cézanne and Geffroy) can play a role in my thinking now. This is how to learn from the past, as opposed to recording the past. But this is rather like Merleau-Ponty's own method of seeing "according to," isn't it? And one of the things we see is that there was a lot of "Merleau-Pontyism" before there was Merleau-Ponty.

JE: I'd like to end with a question about skill, since it appears skill will be a thread in these books. I wonder if it might be helpful to take a moment to set out some of the meanings of *skill* that have already surfaced. In the conversation following my own lecture, Paul Hegarty said, "There are other things going on in skill than the ones you mention: There's modernist skill, conceptual skill." If skill is expanded in those ways, I wonder where it can end. Wouldn't a conceptual skill become continuous with conception? What would remain as its opposite? When I was talking about skill in my own text, I meant specifically naturalistic skill, the kind inculcated in academies. Hence, there are two questions: First, how much latitude would you allow the concept of skill? And second, when will a broader sense of skill lose contact with the debates about modernism's putative lack of skill (or its shame about skill, or its way, as de Kooning has, of showing off skill by closing his eyes or otherwise hobbling skill)?

RS: We tend to oppose skill to talent, or natural endowment (giftedness), or genius. I think of the Kantian notion that genius gives the rule to art—or the notion that the romantic aberration of today, the talented invention, becomes the classical norm of tomorrow, the convention to be mastered by skill. The transition from genius to skill or skill to genius is flexible and unstable. I suppose that when you move from genius to skill, it seems like a reduction, and when you move from skill to genius, it seems like an elevation, but it doesn't have to be conceived that way. When skill, or the kind of facility that comes from practice, is unusually developed—as it was in de Kooning—we are likely to attribute the results of the application of that skill as signs of creative genius. What looks like effortless genius to me might feel like the exercise of a skill to the artist at work in the studio. Still, there may be ideological reasons to suppress the more obvious exercises of skill—as de Kooning often did. And when talking about work after the fact, an artist can adopt a position of critical doubt, or historical distance, or a return to artistic engagement—the doing position and the talking position needn't manifest one and the same character. When this kind of difference occurs, the result can be a certain form of productive paranoia—perhaps uncomfortable but still productive.

JE: And finally, a question about *tacit knowledge* and *intuition.* You get the former from Michael Polanyi, for whom it is "a tool to handle what is in focus," and the latter partly from Kant, where *Anschauung* is understood as an immediate relation to an object, without concepts. These are both fundamentally nonrepresentable or nonconceptual categories—like the two sides of Brooks's misaligned slide rules. How, then, would you adjust tacit knowledge or *Anschauung* so they can work as historical knowledge? Perhaps by connecting them to concepts already in use such as *spontaneity*? So much seems to depend on this link, which—perhaps together with the unbridgeable passage from particularity to generality, atomism to monism, defines the distance from artistic practice to either something called criticism or something—I think something unapproachable—called history.

RS: One form of tacit intellectual knowledge would be those points that people within a society agree on—the culturally specific constants, whether they are good ideas or bad ideas. Certain forms of tacit knowledge arise rather mysteriously from individual practice. Somewhere Polanyi talks about surgeons and their tacit knowledge. Some artists have a lot of tacit knowledge, and in general tacit knowledge would itself have a history.

Francis Halsall: I wonder what your position on tacit knowledge is in relation to aesthetics: Is tacit knowledge a form of aesthetic knowledge? Is it an aesthetic project for you, rather than a historical one, when you attempt to find a match between your theories and what the artists have done?

RS: The feeling that an intuition gives is that it is right. Doubt and disagreement enter when it becomes of interest to explain your intuition to someone else. When language fails you, it can cause you to doubt what by intuition you also know is absolutely true. I guess the result is paranoia. Aesthetic judgments feel like intuitions, although it is not clear why that should be so: We get away with relying on our feelings in aesthetics but not in other fields. Yet try to explain aesthetic specifics (as art critics do), and there's doubt again ...

FH: I was asking the question the other way around: that tacit knowledge as a type of intuitive or fast thinking (as you call it) might actually be a type of aesthetic reflection.

RS: Well, I think in many cases yes, although there are intuitions that are more neutral than that. If you're lost, and you need to decide whether to turn right or left, that's not an aesthetic intuition: Well, maybe it is aesthetic, and you're not aware that the determining factor is aesthetic. But why do I pick the artists I do? Newman was strong and somewhat belligerent; de Kooning was more playful and would maybe have been easier to get along with. I might have just yielded to Newman, saying to him, "You talk, go right ahead; I'll be quiet." Yet Newman also liked a good argument. Cézanne is further back, and so it's harder to relate to him, but if I had known him personally, I probably would not have warmed up to him. He was too sensitive and touchy, perhaps, though he did have a real sense of humor.

FH: It's not so much the aesthetic judgment with regards to the painters.... I'd like to know to what extent there are aesthetic concerns at play in how you measure your own project, which, I would argue, constructs its discursive model in sympathy with its object.

RS: Its model being what?

FH: It seems to me that a primary motivation of your project here and in your other writings is an attempt to reconcile on the one hand a model of criticism or mode of writing and on the other the object that the model negotiates. But just what does it mean to have the logic of description be adequate to experience? Because you would like to make something—an intellectual mode, a discursive activity—match the work it engages with, which is itself perceived under the sign of aesthetics, are you ultimately, in your writings, involved in an aesthetic act?

RS: Probably ... yes.

ENDNOTES

Introduction

1. The title of this Introduction has been adapted from Shiff's work on Vija Celmins's sculpture *To Fix the Image in Memory* (1977-82). See Shiff, "Originality," in *Critical Terms for Art History*, ed. Robert S. Nelson and Shiff (Chicago: University of Chicago Press, 1996, second edition, 2003), 145-59. An army of kindly babysitters deserve to be thanked for their assistance in helping me write this introduction. Particular thanks are due to Tía and Luis in Gijón, Spain; to Penny and Maria in Cork; and to Ina and Mary in London.
2. This quote has been taken from the transcript of Shiff's University College Cork lectures, *Doubt* (date: April 29th and April 30th 2004).
3. Shiff identifies the abuses made of Barthes's work as a target in his "Handling Shocks: on the Representation of Experience in Walter Benjamin's Analogies," *Oxford Art Journal* 15 no. 2 (1992): 88–103, p. 91. On Roland Barthes see, for example (the reversible model of "writerly reading" suggested by the forty-six paragraphs that constitute his book) *The Pleasure of the Text*, translated by Miller (New York: Hill and Wang, 1975).
4. Jill Beaulieu and Mary Roberts, "On Modernism: An Interview with Shiff," *Art Monthly Australia* 81 (July 1995): 7–9.
5. Shiff, *Cézanne and the End of Impressionism: A Study of the Theory, Technique and Critical Evaluation of Modern Art* (Chicago: University of Chicago Press, 1984) This book brought together ideas from Shiff's doctoral research and his publications at that date.
6. A full bibliography on Shiff's writings aears in the present volume.
7. Shiff is currently working on a book length interpretative study of Willem de Kooning (Reaktion).
8. Shiff, "Critical Reflections," *Artforum* 34 (October 1995): 82–83, 124–25, p. 83.

9. See Shiff, "Originality" and also Shiff, "Afterword: Figuration," in Nelson and Shiff (eds.) *"Critical Terms For Art History,"* 479–85.

10. See, for example, "Shiff replies to Sidney Geist," *Art Journal* 51 (Spring 1992): 125. For Shiff's initial review of Geist's work see Shiff, "Cézanne" (Sidney Geist, Interpreting Cézanne and Mary Tompkins Lewis, Cézanne's Early Imagery), *Art Journal* 50 (Summer 1991): 82–83.

11. Shiff, "Cézanne and Poussin: How the Modern Claims the Classic," in *Cézanne & Poussin: A Symposium*, edited by Kendall (Sheffield: Sheffield Academic Press, 1993), 51–68, see p. 54.

12. Shiff, "Cézanne and Poussin," 51.

13. Shiff once paid the same compliment to Fred Orton for his work on Jasper Johns. See Shiff, "Go Figure" (Figuring Jasper Johns by Fred Orton), *Artforum Bookforum* (Summer 1995): 1, 26, 33.

14. Shiff, "Ascribing to Manet, Declaring the Author," in *Twelve Views of Manet's Bar*, edited by Bradford R.Collins (Princeton: University of Princeton Press, 1996), 1–24, quotation on p.6.

15. Shiff, "Ascribing to Manet," 18.

16. Shiff, "Ascribing to Manet," 9.

17. Shiff, "Handling Shocks," quotation on p. 91.

18. Shiff, "Handling Shocks," 91 and 98. See also Shiff, "Critical Reflections," 125.

19. Shiff, "To Move the Eyes: Impressionism, Symbolism and Well-being c.1891," in *Impressions of French Modernity: Art and Literature in France 1850–1900*, edited by Hobbs (Manchester: Manchester University Press, 1998), 190-210; see 190-1.

20. Shiff, "Radicalizing Impressionism" (T.J. Clark, The Painting of Modern Life), *New York Times*, Book Review, 3rd March 1985: 16; See Shiff, "Hermetic Zeal" (Michael Fried, Manet's Modernism), *Bookforum* (Winter 1996), 20–21, 32, 34; See Shiff, "Break Dancing" (Yve-Alain Bois, Painting as Model) *Arts Magazine* 65 (April 1991): 25–26, 29, 31, 35.

21. See Shiff, "Modest Proposals" (David Sylvester, About Modern Art), *Bookforum* (Winter 1997): 5, 51; See also Shiff, "Go Figure"; See Shiff, "Flying Colors" (Leo Steinberg, Leonardo's Incessant Last Suer) *Artforum* 39 (May 2001): 23–24; and his "Statement on Leo Steinberg" (Encounters with Rauschenberg) *Artforum* 39 (December 2000): 35.

22. Shiff, "Art History and the Nineteenth Century: Realism and Resistance," *Art Bulletin* 70 (1988): 25–48, especially . 47–48. See also Shiff, "Afterword: Figuration," p. 481.

23. See Shiff, "Critical Reflections" and Walter Benjamin, *One-way Street and other Writings* (London: Verso 1979).

24. Shiff, "Flexible Time," Art Bulletin 76 no.4 (December 1994): 583–87, quotation on p.583. These ideas are expanded on in Shiff, "Afterword: Figuration." It is instructive to read "Flexible Time" together with Rosalind Krauss's article "We Lost it at the Movies," *Art Bulletin* 76, no.4 (December 1994): 578–80. This special issue of *Art Bulletin* was titled "A Range of Critical Perspectives—the subject in/of Art History."

25. Shiff, "Originality in the Visual Arts," in *Encyclopedia of Aesthetics*, edited by Michael Kelly (New York: Oxford University Press, 1998), vol. 3, 408-14 and in the same volume Shiff, "Photography/Catechresis," 502–06.

26. Shiff, "Art History and the Nineteenth Century," 47.

27. Shiff, "Flexible Time," 584 and Shiff, "Afterword: Figuration," 482.
28. Shiff, "Handling Shocks," 88.
29. In reviewing the exhibition "Negotiating Rapture," Shiff asked "Shouldn't rapture be felt, rather than contested, adjudicated, or philosophized?" Shiff, "Review (Negotiating Rapture: The Power of Art to Transform Lives)," *Artforum* 35 (October 1996): 112–113. In reviewing George Didi-Hubermann's exhibition "L'Empreinte" (1997), Shiff took him to task for failing to use the artworks to move beyond the very binary concepts he himself had already identified as operative in Rosalind Krauss's and Yve-Alain Bois's "*L'informe*" in 1996. See Shiff, "Review (L'Empreinte)," *Artforum* 35 (Summer 1997):132-33. See also his "On Criticism Handling History," *History of the Human Sciences* 2 no. 1 (February 1989): 63–87; his "Criticism at Odds with Its Art: Prophesy, Projection, Doubt, Paranoia," *Common Knowledge* 9 no.3 (Fall 2003): 434–62; and his "About Recent Painting: A Critical Exchange Among Thierry de Duve, Lane Relyea & Shiff," ed. Lane Relyea, in Annette DiMeo Carlozzi, Negotiating Small Truths, exh.cat., Jack S. Blanton Museum of Art, Austin, 1999, 129-37.
30. Shiff, "Flexible Time," 584.
31. Shiff, "Art History and the Nineteenth Century," 47.
32. Shiff, "Art History and the Nineteenth Century," 29 (the italics are Shiff's own).
33. *Alley Oop* is oil and collage on cardboard, 23 x 18," collection of S. I. Newhouse. See Shiff, "Jasper Johns *Alley Oop*, 1958" *Artforum* 34 (March 1996): 98. See also Shiff's earlier work on these ideas in his "Constructing Physicality," *Art Journal* (Spring 1991): 42–47, and his "Cezanne's Physicality: The Politics of Touch," in *The Language of Art History*, edited by Salim Kemal and Ivan Gaskell (Cambridge University Press, 1991), 129-180.
34. Shiff, "Jasper Johns *Alley Oop*," 98.
35. Shiff, "Jasper Johns *Alley Oop*," 98.
36. Shiff, "On Criticism Handling History," 83. On the same page he astutely observes that "a history [that adjusts] competing perspectives as they interact, might be regarded as a history written from the position of the maker rather than a (passive) viewer. To write or figure such a history is to make it as a product of purposefully assembled parts. The position of the maker becomes more critical than that of the viewer; to assume this position is to acknowledge that one forms an object of attention in describing an object, perhaps transforming it."
37. Shiff, "Modest Proposals," *Bookforum* (November 1997): 5, 51.
38. Shiff, "Afterword: Figuration," 482-83, and Shiff, "Flexible Time," 584.
39. Shiff, "Handling Shocks," 83.
40. Shiff, "Handling Shocks," 98.
41. Shiff, "Handling Shocks," 83.
42. Shiff, "Afterword: Figuration," 484.
43. Shiff, "Art History and the Nineteenth Century," 47-8.
44. Shiff, "Afterword: Figuration," 482.
45. Shiff, "Handling Shocks," 91.
46. Shiff, "Handling Shocks," 91 (the italics are Shiff's own).
47. Shiff, "Handling Shocks," 98.
48. Shiff, "Handling Shocks," 98.
49. Shiff, "Handling Shocks," 98.

50. Shiff, "Critical Reflections," 83.

51. Shiff, "Critical Reflections," 83.

52. Shiff, "Lucien Freud," Artforum 35 (January 1997): 76–77; quotation on p. 77.

53. Shiff, "Lucien Freud," 77.

54. Shiff, "The Subject in Question," *Artforum* 34 (January 1996): 62–67, 99.

55. Shiff, "The Subject in Question," 62.

56. Shiff, "The Subject in Question," 67.

57. Shiff, "The Subject in Question," 67.

58. Shiff, "Review of John Rewald, The Paintings of Paul Cézanne: A Catalogue Raisonné," *Art Bulletin* 80 (June 1988): 384–89, quotation on p. 385.

59. Shiff, 'Original Copy,' *Common Knowledge* 3 (Spring 1994): 88–107, 89–92. For a reworked version of the introduction to this essay see Shiff, "Originality," 151–154.

60. Shiff, 'Original Copy,' 89.

61. Shiff, 'Best and Worst, 1995,' *Artforum* 34 (December 1995): 65, 67.

62. Shiff, "Realism of Low Resolution," *Apollo* 144 (November 1996): 3–8. This article is expanded in his "Realism of Low Resolution: Digitalisation and Modern Painting," in *Impossible Presence: Surface and Screen in the Photogenic Era*, edited by Terry Smith (University of Chicago Press, 2001), 124–56. For a development of these ideas on Close's work see also Shiff, "Allover You," *Artforum* 36 (April 1998): 92–9.

63. Walter Benjamin "The Task of the Translator" (1923), *Illuminations*, ed. Hannah Arendt, trans. Harry Zohn, (New York: Schocken Books, 1968) 69-83, p. 72–73.

64. Shiff, "Realism of Low Resolution," 5.

65. Shiff, "Through a Slow Medium," in *Chuck Close Prints: Process and Collaboration*, edited by Terrie Sultan (Princeton: Princeton University Press, 2003): 18–43 quotation on p 23.

66. Shiff, "Anamorphosis: Jasper Johns," in *Foirades/Fizzles: Echo and Allusion in the Art of Jasper Johns*, edited by James Cuno (Los Angeles: Wight Art Gallery, 1987): 147–66.

67. Freud "Some Character-Types Met with in Psychoanalytical Work" (1916), in Sigmund Freud, *Art and Literature* 14 (The Penguin Freud Library, Hammondsworth 1955) 291–319.

68. Shiff, "Jasper Johns, *Alley Oop* 1958," 89.

69. Shiff, "Performing an Aearance: On the Surface of Abstract Expressionism," in *Abstract Expressionism: The Critical Developments*, edited by Michael Auping (New York: Harry N. Abrams, for Albright-Knox Art Gallery, 1987), 94-123, quotation on p. 100.

Doubt

1. Charles Sanders Peirce, "Some Consequences of Four Incapacities" (1868), in Christian J. W. Kloesel, ed., *Writings of Charles S. Peirce: A Chronological Edition*, 6 vols. (Bloomington: Indiana University Press, 1982–2000), 2: 212. I thank James Lawrence, Charlotte Cousins, Justine Price, Michael

Schreyach, Adrian Kohn, and especially Caitlin Haskell for essential aid in research. Unless otherwise indicated, all translations are mine. A version of the second half of this book ("Existential Doubt"), now substantially expanded, appeared as "Criticism at Odds with Its Art: Prophecy, Projection, Doubt, Paranoia," *Common Knowledge* 9 (Fall 2003): 434–62.

2. C. S. Peirce, "Illustrations of the Logic of Science: Deduction, Induction, and Hypothesis," *Popular Science Monthly* 13 (May–October 1878): 481–82 (emphasis original). Peirce sometimes referred to hypothesis as "abduction." I have used the locution *come to pass*, a synonym for *happen*—"proof would come to pass as mere feeling." *Come to pass* signifies both approach and withdrawal, proximity and distance, the present as both emergent actuality and remembrance. It stretches or temporalizes the sense of something happening in the present, in just the way that we might imagine a reasoned proof being a stretched version of an intuition, or (here, more to the point) an intuition being a contracted version of a reasoned proof.

3. Charles Sanders Peirce, "Concerning the Author" (c. 1897), *Collected Papers*, ed. Charles Hartshorne, Paul Weiss, and Arthur W. Burks, 8 vols. (Cambridge, MA: Harvard University Press, 1958–1960), 1:x–xi.

4. Robert Irwin, statement in "United States Section, VIII São Paulo Bienal 1965," *Artforum* 3 (June 1965): 23 (emphasis original). At the time, Irwin was making "dot" paintings, aiming to "maximize the energy or the physicality of the situation and minimize the identity or idea or imagery of the situation"; Irwin (1976–79, interviewed by Lawrence Weschler), quoted in Lawrence Weschler, *Seeing Is Forgetting the Name of the Thing One Sees: A Life of Contemporary Artist Robert Irwin* (Berkeley: University of California Press, 1982), 90. The noticeably unsatisfactory quality of reproductions of the dot paintings of the mid-1960s, even in well-produced catalogues, lends physical support to Irwin's position; yet none is needed because his claim—in effect, that identities generalize—rests on its logic. For a reproduction, see *Untitled*, c. 1964–66, in Russell Ferguson, ed., *Robert Irwin* (Los Angeles: Museum of Contemporary Art, 1993), 107.

5. Irwin, statement in "Robert Irwin: An Interview with Alistair Mackintosh," *Art and Artists* 6 (March 1972): 24.

6. Compare Peirce, "Quale-Consciousness" (c. 1898), *Collected Papers*, 6:150, 154: "If [a state of] consciousness is to blend with [a state of] consciousness, there must be common elements. But if [one state: 'this moment as it is to me'] has nothing in itself but just itself, it is *sui generis* and is cut loose from all need of agreeing with anything. Whatever is absolutely simple must be absolutely free; for a law over it must apply to some common feature of it. And if it has no features [that is, no identities other than its self-sameness], no law can seize upon it."

7. Irwin, "United States Section, VIII São Paulo Bienal 1965," 23 (emphasis original). "[If] no change, [then] no perceptual consciousness. ... All perceptual knowing is knowing in action (change)": Robert Irwin, *Being and Circumstance: Notes Toward a Conditional Art* (San Francisco: Lapis Press, 1985), 9, 11 (emphasis eliminated).

8. See, for example, Rosalind Krauss, "Video: The Aesthetics of Narcissism," *October* 1 (Spring 1976): 50; Rosalind E. Krauss, *The Optical Unconscious* (Cambridge, MA: MIT Press, 1993), 48.

9. See, for example, Paul de Man, "The Rhetoric of Temporality" (1969), *Blindness and Insight: Essays in the Rhetoric of Contemporary Criticism* (Minneapolis: University of Minnesota Press, 1983), 187–228; and De Man's various essays collected as *The Rhetoric of Romanticism* (New York: Columbia University Press, 1984).

10. Rosalind Krauss, *"A Voyage on the North Sea": Art in the Age of the Post-Medium Condition* (New York: Thames and Hudson, 2000), 44, 47; Rosalind E. Krauss, *The Optical Unconscious* (Cambridge, Mass.: MIT Press, 1993), 98.

11. "Animals living in water do not notice if the surfaces of things which touch are wet": Aristotle, *De anima (On the Soul)*, II, xi, 423 a–b (trans. W. S. Hett), in Aristotle, *On the Soul, Parva Naturalia, On Breath* (Cambridge, Mass.: Harvard University Press, 1957), 131.

12. "Abstracts from experience": Richard Wollheim, "Response to James I. Porter," in Shadi Bartsch and Thomas Bartscherer, eds., *Erotikon: Essays on Eros, Ancient and Modern* (Chicago: University of Chicago Press, 2005), 142.

13. Peirce, "The Logic of 1873: Investigation" (c. 1873), *Collected Papers*, 7:195.

14. The problem of distinguishing originals from copies—more of an issue for theory than for practice—is analogous: see Richard Shiff, "Original Copy," *Common Knowledge* 3 (Spring 1994): 88–107.

15. "The middle [of opposite parts] is the limit of both extremes": Aristotle (?), *De animalium motu (Movement of Animals)*, ix, 702 b (trans. E. S. Forster), in Aristotle, *Parts of Animals, Movement of Animals, Progression of Animals* (Cambridge, Mass.: Harvard University Press, 1945), 471.

16. Peirce, "Chapter 1 (Enlarged Abstract)" (1872), *Writings of Charles S. Peirce*, 3:20.

17. Michael Polanyi, *Personal Knowledge: Towards a Post-Critical Philosophy* (Chicago: University of Chicago Press, 1962 [1958]), 275. Polanyi (1891–1976) is generationally the contemporary of Walter Benjamin (1892–1940), who died prematurely. During the 1960s, Irwin was either directly acqainted with Polanyi's writings or indirectly through the interest of his friend Ed Wortz; see Weschler, *Seeing Is Forgetting the Name of the Thing One Sees*, 207. For specific references to Polanyi, see Irwin, *Being and Circumstance*, 10, 24.

18. William James, "Does 'Consciousness' Exist?" *The Journal of Philosophy, Psychology and Scientific Methods* 1 (1 September 1904): 491. I was alerted to the relevance of this passage by David Raskin, "The Shiny Illusionism of Krauss and Judd," *Art Journal* 65 (Spring 2006): 21.

19. Peirce, "Questions Concerning Certain Faculties Claimed for Man" (1868), *Writings of Charles S. Peirce*, 2:201, 206–07.

20. I refer obliquely to the massive body of theoretical writing on various aspects of social subjectivity that appeared during the later twentieth century. See, for example, Jacques Lacan, *The Four Fundamental Concepts of Psycho-Analysis*, ed. Jacques-Alain Miller, trans. Alan Sheridan (New York: W. W. Norton, 1978); René Girard, *Things Hidden Since the Foundation of the World*, trans. Stephen Bann and Michael Metteer (Stanford: Stanford University Press, 1987); Paul de Man, "Sign and Symbol in Hegel's *Aesthetics*," *Critical Inquiry* 8 (Summer 1982): 761–75.

21. On Bann's Nietzschean antiquarianism, see Richard Shiff, "Something Is Happening," *Art History* 28 (November 2005): 752–82.

22. See, for example, Richard Shiff, "Mastercopy," *Iris* (Paris) 1, no. 2 (1983): 113–27; "On Criticism Handling History," *History of the Human Sciences* 2, no. 1 (1989): 63–87; "Handling Shocks: On the Representation of Experience in Walter Benjamin's Analogies," *Oxford Art Journal* 15, no. 2 (1992): 88–103; "Original Copy."

23. James Elkins, *Master Narratives and Their Discontents* (New York: Routledge, 2005), 85.

24. Stephen Bann, *Ways Around Modernism* (New York: Routledge, in press).

25. Rosalind E. Krauss, "The Crisis of the Easel Picture," in Kirk Varnedoe and Pepe Karmel, eds., *Jackson Pollock: New Approaches* (New York: The Museum of Modern Art, 1999), 155.

26. Rosalind E. Krauss, "We Lost It at the Movies," *Art Bulletin* 76 (December 1994): 579.

27. C. S. Peirce and J. Jastrow, "On Small Differences of Sensation" (1885), *Writings of Charles S. Peirce*, 5:135.

28. De Man, "Aesthetic Formalization: Kleist's *Über das Marionettentheater*" (1983), *The Rhetoric of Romanticism*, 275.

29. Krauss, "We Lost It at the Movies," 580.

30. See note 1.

31. Roland Barthes, "The Photographic Message" (1961), *Image—Music—Text*, trans. Stephen Heath (New York: Hill and Wang, 1977), 27.

32. "Was der Adel tut, ist Gesetz": Franz Kafka, "The Problem of Our Laws," trans. Willa and Edwin Muir, *Parables and Paradoxes in German and English* (New York: Schocken, 1961), 156–57.

33. Have Vivid Recollections of conversations with people who had vivid recollections of conversations with people who had immediate contact with this or that French Impressionist painter. Subjectively, this causes me to feel that Pissarro, say, or Cézanne is more real to me than Delacroix or Corot.

34. Meyer Schapiro, "Nature of Abstract Art," *Marxist Quarterly* 1 (January–March 1937): 84. See further commentary below, note 142.

35. Clement Greenberg, who figures significantly in this essay, implied late in his career that Marxists lacked such intellectual discipline: "Marxists, or quasi-Marxist critics of culture [often argue that] if so-and-so happened, and this and that happened, at this or that time, then there must be a causal connection. You reason from the state of society at a certain time to the art that was produced at that time, and make an easy equation"; Clement Greenberg, "Interview with James Faure Walker" (1978), *Clement Greenberg: Late Writings*, ed. Robert C. Morgan (Minneapolis: University of Minnesota Press, 2003), 158. Greenberg nevertheless admitted that the natural way to understand the condition of a practice or discipline (such as painting or sculpture) was to construct a relational logic for its past: "If you're going to deal with the past you have to see some logic in the way one event follows another. ... There's free choice, I'm sure, but somehow as it happens you can see some inexorabilities. And a series. It's the way to make sense of the thing"; Trish Evans and Charles Harrison, "A Conversation with Clement Greenberg in Three Parts" (1984), in *Clement Greenberg: Late Writings*, 178.

36. William Rubin, "Cézannisme and the Beginnings of Cubism," in William Rubin, ed., *Cézanne: The Late Work* (New York: Museum of Modern Art, 1977), 189.

37. Thoré-Bürger (Théophile Thoré), "Salon de 1845," *Les Salons*, 3 vols. (Brussels: Lamertin, 1893), 1:105. Thoré believed that artistic creation required reciprocity between artist and nature: nature possessed its own properly expressive qualities, but these would be evident only to an artist sufficiently sensitive to nature; and nature in turn, because of this sensitivity, would succeed in eliciting from the artist his or her feelings of individuality. Such personal feeling would not exclude impersonal, collective meaning. Allegorical content of broad social value would be likely to emerge from any particular artist's experiential union with nature. Just as often as not, however, the general, allegorical meaning would appear only after the work of creation had been completed, perceptible only to a third party committed, like a good critic, to interpretation. Thoré's commentary in 1845 implied that a painter absorbed in practice is likely to remain unaware of his or her own meaning. The notion that the most valid meaning may arise outside the conscious intention of the artist would reappear in the writings of numerous theorists, a cliché of modern criticism.

38. Friedrich Nietzsche, *The Gay Science*, trans. Walter Kaufmann (New York: Vintage, 1974 [1887]), 299–300.

39. Ludwig Wittgenstein, *Zettel*, eds. G. E. M. Anscombe and G. H. von Wright, trans. G. E. M. Anscombe (Berkeley: University of California Press, 1970), 71 (translation modified for clarity).

40. Greenberg, statement (1983) in Evans and Harrison, "A Conversation with Clement Greenberg in Three Parts," *Clement Greenberg: Late Writings*, 202. For the record, Greenberg on Peirce: "The great Charles Peirce [argued] that whatever is valued for its own sole sake, even when it's a supreme sake—like human life—has in the showdown to be understood as being valued aesthetically; in other words, anything valued as an end in itself, as something other than a means or instrument, is experienced in the aesthetic mode"—that is, in the mode of feeling (Clement Greenberg, "The State of Criticism: Art Criticism," *Parisan Review* 48, no. 1 [1981]: 42, note).

41. Donald Judd, unpublished note of 18 November 1990 (Judd Foundation, Marfa, Texas), quoted in Raskin, "The Shiny Illusionism of Krauss and Judd," 18.

42. Elkins, *Master Narratives and Their Discontents*, 101, 130–31. Self-forgetfulness is a rich notion, which assumes rarefied forms (T. W. Adorno, Brice Marden) as well as popular ones: see Richard Shiff, "Force of Myself Looking," in Gary Garrels, ed., *Plane Images: A Brice Marden Retrospective* (New York: Museum of Modern Art, 2006), 28–75. On "philosophical self-forgetting," see also de Man, "Sign and Symbol in Hegel's *Aesthetics*," 768–69.

43. Peirce, "Josiah Royce, *The Religious Aspect of Philosophy*" (c. 1885), *Collected Papers*, 8:43.

44. Bann, *Ways Around Modernism*.

45. Elkins, *Master Narratives and Their Discontents*, 106.

46. "It is disastrous to name ourselves": Willem de Kooning, statement in "Artists' Sessions at Studio 35" (23 April 1950), ed. Robert Goodnough,

Modern Artists in America, ed. Robert Motherwell and Ad Reinhardt (New York: Wittenborn, Schultz, 1951), 22.

47. Tom Ferrara, "One Giant Leap," *De Kooning: A Centennial Exhibition* (New York: Gagosian Gallery, 2004), 131. Ferrara was de Kooning's primary studio assistant during the 1980s.

48. See Richard Shiff, "'With Closed Eyes': De Kooning's Twist," *Master Drawings* 40/1 (2002): 73–88.

49. On Deleuzean thematics applied to art production, see Richard Shiff, "Manual Imagination," in Adam D. Weinberg, ed., *Terry Winters: Paintings, Drawings, Prints 1994–2004* (New Haven: Yale University Press, 2004): 18–33.

50. De Kooning (1980s), quoted in Ferrara, "One Giant Leap," 130.

51. Elkins, *Master Narratives and Their Discontents*, 89. On postmodernist practice as contemporaneous with modernist practice, see Shiff, "Mastercopy"; "On Criticism Handling History"; "Original Copy."

52. Krauss uses the phrase "internal logic" to further an argument, structuralist in character, establishing conceptual oppositions and dichotomies that pit a given identity or order against its antithesis or negation: Krauss, "The Crisis of the Easel Picture," 165.

53. Clement Greenberg, "A Critical Exchange with Fairfield Porter on '"American-Type" Painting'" (1955), in John O'Brian, ed., *Clement Greenberg: The Collected Essays and Criticism*, 4 vols. (Chicago: University of Chicago Press, 1986–1993), 3:240.

54. Greenberg, "Introduction to an Exhibition of Barnett Newman" (1958), *Collected Essays and Criticism*, 4:54.

55. Greenberg, "Sculpture in Our Time" (1958), *Collected Essays and Criticism*, 4:56.

56. Compare Greenberg's later remarks, as quoted in note 35.

57. Greenberg, "The Present Prospects of American Painting and Sculpture" (1947), *Collected Essays and Criticism*, 2:168.

58. Greenberg, "The Present Prospects of American Painting and Sculpture," 2:167–68.

59. Newman, quoted by Harold Cohen, introduction to "Barnett Newman Talks to David Sylvester," BBC radio broadcast, 17 November 1965, typescript, Barnett Newman Foundation, New York.

60. Greenberg, "The New Sculpture" (1949), *Collected Essays and Criticism*, 2:315. "Sculpture in Our Time" (see note 54) is a substantially revised version of "The New Sculpture." Greenberg often repeated his point in late interviews. "[Purity] was the motive power behind a lot of very good art of the past hundred years. But that *I* subscribe to the notion of pure art? I should say not. [Purity is] an illusion ... an idea you never achieve, an ideal"; "Interview with James Faure Walker" (1978), *Clement Greenberg: Late Writings*, 160. "I don't believe in purity at all. It acts as some kind of beacon. It's there, but it's not possible. It has no ultimate reality"; statement (1983) in Evans and Harrison, "A Conversation with Clement Greenberg in Three Parts," *Clement Greenberg: Late Writings*, 179. "[Purity in art] was perhaps a very useful fiction, but really only fiction"; "Clement Greenberg: Modernism or Barbarism" (interview by Karlheinz Lüdeking, trans. Paul Lundgren; 1994), *Clement Greenberg: Late Writings*, 227. See also Clement Greenberg, "Detached Observations," *Arts* 51 (December 1976): 88.

Greenberg had ample reason to imply that "purity" in art had been part of the lingua franca of criticism in his time, not a notion he would have claimed as his own. Two examples: "De Kooning … arrives at stimulating solutions while remaining within the field of 'pure' painting" (Howard Devree, "Individual Modern: The Work of Modigliani—De Kooning—Osver," *New York Times*, 15 April 1951, 106); "Is [Newman] proving some new theory of composition, or is he attempting to isolate the pure substance of painting?" (Stuart Preston, "Diverse New Shows: Drawings by Modigliani—Newman, Foy, Wells," *New York Times*, 29 April 1951, 6X). In parodic reaction to this critical environment, Elaine de Kooning published her "Pure Paints a Picture," *Artnews* 56 (Summer 1957): 86–87. As an example of the earlier (and common) discourse of "pure painting," see Pierre Hepp, "Sur le choix des maîtres," *L'Occident* 8 (December 1905): 264: "For the eye that has no material taste for the qualities of a tone, the fullness of a harmony, the orderly arrangement of a surface of colors, apart from every objective concern, [Cézanne's] pure painting [*pure peinture*] remains without attraction, offering indigestible food."

61. Greenberg, "The Present Prospects of American Painting and Sculpture," 2:166.

62. Greenberg, "Sculpture in Our Time," 4:55. In his earlier version of this essay, Greenberg referred to "our taste for the actual, immediate, first-hand … [Art needs to] communicate that sense of concretely felt, irreducible experience in which our sensibility finds its fundamental certainty. … The tendency toward 'purity' or absolute abstractness exists only as a tendency, an aim, not as a realization" (Greenberg, "The New Sculpture," 2:314–15).

63. Polanyi, *Personal Knowledge*, 49–131.

64. C. Wright Mills, "The Man in the Middle," *Industrial Design* 5 (November 1958): 71.

65. Irwin, "United States Section, VIII São Paulo Bienal 1965," 23.

66. Meyer Schapiro, "The Liberating Quality of Avant-garde Art," *Artnews* 56 (Summer 1957): 40–41. See further commentary below, note 142.

67. Schapiro and Newman were friends. Schapiro identified modern abstract art with "contemplativeness and communion with the work of another human being" ("The Liberating Quality of Avant-garde Art," 41). Similarly, Newman stated in 1965: "I hope that my painting has the impact of giving someone, as it did me, the feeling of … his connection to others … I think you can only feel others if you have some sense of your own being" ("Interview with David Sylvester" [1965], in John P. O'Neill, ed., *Barnett Newman: Selected Writings and Interviews* (New York: Knopf, 1990), 257–58).

68. Schapiro, "The Liberating Quality of Avant-garde Art," 38. Schapiro's attitude is similar to Harold Rosenberg's; see Rosenberg, "The American Action Painters," *Artnews* 51 (December 1952): 22–23, 48–50. Artists like Irwin and Judd made little direct use of Greenberg's notions, but shared his stress on the material aspects of art: "If you analyze the Minimalist rhetoric, it runs fairly parallel to Greenberg's thoughts" (Al Held, statement in Maurice Poirier and Jane Necol, eds., "The '60s in Abstract: 13 Statements and an Essay," *Art in America* 71 [October 1983]: 125).

69. Greenberg tended to regard postwar invocations of religiosity as insincere, ironic, and ultimately ineffective ("Religion and the Intellectuals: A Symposium" [1950], *Collected Essays and Criticism*, 3:39–42).

70. See note 2.

71. Donald Judd, "Art and Architecture" (1983), *Complete Writings 1975–1986* (Eindhoven: Van Abbemuseum, 1987), 30.

72. "If one *sees*, one cannot avoid the percept [the sensory feeling, say, greenishness]; and if one *looks*, one cannot avoid the perceptual judgment [the intuition that something significant is being sensed, the greenness of the grass]": Peirce, "Telepathy and Perception" (1903), *Collected Papers*, 7:373 (emphasis original).

73. Judd, "Abstract Expressionism" (1983), *Complete Writings 1975–1986*, 39.

74. Martin Heidegger, *The Metaphysical Foundations of Logic* (1928), trans. Michael Heim (Bloomington: Indiana University Press, 1984), 57–69; Leroy E. Loemker, ed. and trans., *Gottfried Wilhelm Leibniz: Philosophical Papers and Letters* (Dordrecht: Reidel, 1970), 291–95.

75. Donald Judd, interviewed by Bruce Hooton, 3 February 1965, unpublished transcript, Archives of American Art, Smithsonian Institution, Washington. Compare Richard Wollheim's thoughts, published just prior to Judd's interview, concerning what he may have been the first to call "Minimal Art" (using Ad Reinhardt as the prime example): "At once destructive and yet also creative, [Minimal Art] consists in the dismantling of some image that is fussier or more cluttered than the artist requires. ... The canvases of Reinhardt exhibit to an ultimate degree this kind of work ... In conceptual thinking we fragment the world, and we isolate from the continuum of presentation repeated things, categories of objects, sorts. ... In the visual arts, however, ... we are called upon to concentrate our attention upon individual bits of the world: this canvas, that bit of stone or bronze, some particular sheet of paper scored like this or like that" (Richard Wollheim, "Minimal Art," *Arts Magazine* 39 [January 1965]: 32). The "dismantling of some image," coupled with the sensory specificity traditionally demanded by visual art, would produce the minimalist object. Dismantling reduces qualities; specificity adds qualities (by increasing sensory access to them).

76. See Donald Judd, "Barnett Newman" (written 1964; published 1970), *Complete Writings 1959–1975* (Halifax: Nova Scotia College of Art and Design, 1975), 202.

77. Barnett Newman, statement (23 April 1950), in "Artists' Sessions at Studio 35 (1950)," *Modern Artists in America*, 20.

78. Rosalind E. Krauss, "X Marks the Spot," in Yve-Alain Bois and Rosalind E. Krauss, *Formless: A User's Guide* (New York: Zone Books, 1997), 214. This definition of Minimalism occupies the only site at which Judd appears in *Formless*. Here I have had cause to focus on one of the low points of *Formless*, which nevertheless constitutes a deeply insightful study of major aspects of twentieth-century art.

79. See Richard Shiff, "Judd Through Oldenburg," *Chinati Foundation Newsletter* 9 (October 2004): 33–44.

80. In 1997, John Yau initiated commentary on the entirety of Judd's art by stressing the inappropriateness of applying any metaphorical understanding: "[Judd] had to find a way to make art that could exist on its own terms without the support of metaphor"; Yau, in *Donald Judd's Marfa, Texas,*

produced and directed by Christopher Felver, videodisc (New York: Palm Pictures, 2004 [1997]).

81. Elkins notes that although Krauss's work is well known to academics and art students in universities, journalistic critics and the broader public for art remain largely unaware of it (Elkins, *Master Narratives*, 95–96). Nevertheless, "from the late 1990s perspective, she is, without visible rival, the most influential American critic of her era": David Carrier, *Rosalind Krauss and American Philosophical Art Criticism* (Westport, Conn.: Praeger, 2002), 2.

82. Krauss, *The Optical Unconscious*, 22.

83. Krauss, "Jeu Lugubre," *Formless: A User's Guide*, 113.

84. Georges Bataille, "The Language of Flowers" (1929), *Visions of Excess: Selected Writings, 1927–1939*, ed. and trans. Allan Stoekl (Minneapolis: University of Minnesota Press, 1985), 10, 14.

85. See her own account in Krauss, "We Lost It at the Movies," 578–80.

86. Rosalind E. Krauss, "Corpus Delicti," in Rosalind E. Krauss and Jane Livingston, eds., *L'Amour Fou: Photography and Surrealism* (New York: Abbeville, 1985), 78.

87. Krauss, "Horizontality," *Formless: A User's Guide*, 93–103. As a precedent, Krauss referred to Leo Steinberg's analogous opposition of horizontality to a more traditional sense of pictorial verticality (94). Steinberg's horizontality had a broader compass, however; it was a defining aspect of every kind of work surface on which matter and information could be manipulated, "any content that does not evoke a prior optical event" (Leo Steinberg, "Other Criteria" [1968–72], *Other Criteria: Confrontations with Twentieth-Century Art* [New York: Oxford University Press, 1972], 90).

88. Krauss sometimes represents Greenberg in reverse. She defines his phrase "logical moment" as "that instance of coalescence—which happens in no time at all—of a separate set of facts into a virtual unity" (*Optical Unconscious*, 103). To the contrary, Greenberg speculated that a viewer starts with an aesthetic totality. Subsequent analysis generates a series of aesthetic facts that correspond to "logical moments." Such moments are not the goal, nor do they lead back to the initial aesthetic totality. They are the pitfall of extended looking, antithetical to the "first fresh glance" (which requires relatively little time, not "no time at all)." See Greenberg, "On Looking at Pictures: Review of *Painting and Painters: How to Look at a Picture: From Giotto to Chagall* by Lionello Venturi" (1945), *Collected Essays and Criticism*, 2:34. There have always been those who caution against letting critical analysis stray from the visual object, whether through concepts becoming agents ("modernist visuality wants") or through arguments becoming a contest of concepts (separation versus integration): "Where there is a will there must also be a willer, and this [certain scholars such as Aloïs Riegl] found in those Hegelian collectives, the spirit of the age and the spirit of the race. ... This type of explanation is ... hostile to scholarship because it produces that simulacrum of an explanation which puts an end to further research"; E. H. Gombrich, "Art and Scholarship," *College Art Journal* 17 (Summer 1958): 351–52.

89. There is a curious example in Greenberg's early writing, where he regards repetitious marking as obsessive, leading to an unintended (unconscious) flatness: "Van Gogh became too obsessed by the pattern glimpsed in nature. The frenzied insistence with which he tried to reproduce this pat-

tern in his separate brush strokes and give it the same emphasis over every tiny bit of canvas resulted in pieces of violent decoration the surfaces of which had been ornamented instead of painted into a picture" ("Review of exhibitions of Van Gogh and the Remarque collection" [1943], *Collected Essays and Criticism*, 1:161).

90. Walter Benjamin, "Das Kunstwerk im Zeitalter seiner technischen Reproduzierbarkeit" (1936–39), *Gesammelte Schriften*, eds. Rolf Tiedemann and Hermann Schweppenhauser, 7 vols. (Frankfurt am Main, 1972–1989), 1:500–01.

91. Newman, undated manuscript note, c. 1947, Barnett Newman Foundation, New York.

92. Politically, Newman would expect artists to align with anarchism, which would eliminate national and racial conflict: "It is difficult for the young artist, sensitive to the social problems of our time, to reject ... political calls unless he realizes that ... nationalism in art, whether of the status quo or for the revolution, shows a lack of understanding of what art is about" (Newman, "The Painting of Tamayo and Gottlieb" [1945], *Selected Writings and Interviews*, 72).

93. Newman, undated manuscript (c. 1944; punctuation added, paragraphing suppressed), Barnett Newman Foundation, New York.

94. Newman, "Surrealism and the War" (1945), *Selected Writings and Interviews*, 96.

95. The prewar response to surrealism on the part of Lewis Mumford, who shared with Newman a sympathy for anarchism, was analogous. Mumford's allusion to the Spanish Civil War allowed him to see Goya as the prophet of the surrealism that culminated in Picasso, Dali, and Miró: "Today, Goya's images recur too frequently in the photographic sections of the newspapers to be dismissed as 'unreal,' and it is perhaps no accident that a country that has known brutal irrationality in so many forms should have contributed so many leaders to the surrealist movement today— Picasso, Dali, Miró" (Lewis Mumford, "The Art Galleries: Surrealism and Civilization," *New Yorker*, 19 December 1936, 76).

96. See Newman's response (May 1968) to remarks by William S. Rubin, John Ashbery, and Lucy Lippard, *Selected Writings and Interviews*, 233–37.

97. See the illustrations in books by authors listed in Newman's notes (Barnett Newman Foundation, New York), such as Douglas Houghton Campbell, *The Evolution of the Land Plants [Embryophyta]* (Stanford: Stanford University Press, 1940), and John Walton, *An Introduction to the Study of Fossil Plants* (London: Adam & Charles Black, 1940).

98. With sarcastic understatement, Newman recalled that the surrealists, as Freudians, had been "making claims for themselves as scientists that were a little premature" (interview by Joanna Magloff and Michael Magloff, August 1963, audiotape, Barnett Newman Foundation, New York).

99. Newman, quoted in Thomas B. Hess, *Barnett Newman* (New York: Walker, 1969), 26.

100. Peirce, "Questions Concerning Certain Faculties Claimed for Man," *Writings of Charles S. Peirce*, 2:201.

101. Greenberg, "Introduction to an Exhibition of Barnett Newman," *Collected Essays and Criticism*, 4:54.

102. On the detailed circumstances of creating and titling *Onement I*, see Richard Shiff, "To Create Oneself," in Richard Shiff, Carol C. Mancusi-Ungaro, and Heidi Colsman-Freyberger, *Barnett Newman: A Catalogue Raisonné* (New York: The Barnett Newman Foundation, 2004), 44–67.

103. See Newman, "Interview with David Sylvester," "Interview with Emile de Antonio" (1970), *Selected Writings and Interviews*, 255–56, 306.

104. Newman, "Interview with Emile de Antonio," *Selected Writings and Interviews*, 306 (sentence order reversed).

105. See, for example, Sidney Janis, *Abstract and Surrealist Art in America* (New York: Reynal and Hitchcock, 1944).

106. Newman, "Surrealism and the War," *Selected Writings and Interviews*, 94.

107. When interviewed in 1991, Annalee Newman remembered: "What Barney said about the European painters was that here are these guys living through this terrible war in Europe, and they come over here and their painting doesn't change at all. They painted as if nothing had happened" (in Dodie Kazanjian, "The Decisive Decade," *Vogue*, March 1991, 430).

108. Newman, "Surrealism and the War," *Selected Writings and Interviews*, 95. Greenberg's sense of the cumulative effect of surrealism during the decades of fascism and war—disengaged self-indulgence—was no more sanguine than Newman's. He wrote of the "frivolous, hedonistic pessimism of dada and surrealism (the latter of which was at least optimistic enough to enroll itself behind the revolution)"; Greenberg, "Jean Dubuffet and French Existentialism" (1946), *Collected Essays and Criticism*, 2:92.

109. Newman, "Surrealism and the War," *Selected Writings and Interviews*, 95–96.

110. Newman later regarded Jackson Pollock's "prophetic" status with a similar irony and pessimism: "He has already [in 1967] been thrust into art theory … Pollock 'the picturemaker,' the inventor of 'styles' … Is Pollock the prophet of our [formalist] fate?": Newman, "From 'Jackson Pollock: An Artists' Symposium, Part I'" (1967), *Selected Writings and Interviews*, 191.

111. A set of typescript poems collectively titled "Rhymes for a Bombed Out Nursery" exists at the Barnett Newman Foundation, New York. One of them, "Prayer," is dated September 1945.

112. Clement Greenberg, "Clyfford Still," *Arts* 55 (October 1980): 117.

113. Not entirely atypical: Newman claimed to have had a similar experience during his work on the series of paintings called *The Stations of the Cross*, 1958–66, which revealed their meaning to him in the midst of his effort to paint them; see Newman, "The Fourteen Stations of the Cross, 1958–1966" (1966), *Selected Writings and Interviews*, 189.

114. G. W. F. Hegel, *Phenomenology of Spirit*, trans. A. V. Miller (Oxford: Oxford University Press, 1977 [1807]), 103 (emphasis original).

115. For details of the Newman-Greenberg relationship, see Shiff, "To Create Oneself," *Barnett Newman: A Catalogue Raisonné*, 20–21, 36–38, and passim.

116. Clement Greenberg, in Russell W. Davenport, ed., "A *Life* Round Table on Modern Art," *Life* 25 (11 October 1948): 62.

117. Greenberg, statement in "Clement Greenberg with Peter Fuller," ed. Linda Saunders, *Modern Painters* 4 (Winter 1991): 22. Even Greenberg's initial support may have been less securely grounded in his experience of de Kooning than is usually supposed. Renée Arb, who registered her

enthusiasm for de Kooning's art of the late 1940s shortly in advance of Greenberg (see her "Spotlight on: De Kooning," *Artnews* 47 [April 1948]: 33), recalls that Greenberg was not particularly sensitive to de Kooning's qualities: "Even in 1948, when he wanted to applaud Bill, I don't feel he really liked him" (Renée M. Arb, statement to the author, 17 June 2005).

118. Greenberg, "A *Life* Round Table on Modern Art," 78 (emphasis original). Compare Greenberg's much later statement to Fuller's: "I can't choose what to like and not like. My prejudice is towards realistic [that is, representational] art ... but I'm forced, compelled to like abstract art most in this time" ("Clement Greenberg with Peter Fuller," 20). Apparently, Greenberg did not believe that his preferences were arbitrary (they were "compelled"), but he may have believed that history was arbitrary. See also his statement of 1987: "If I had my way the best painting, the new painting, I think, would be like Fantin-Latour or Vermeer ... If I had my way, yes, that's the way I'd want painting to go"; "A Public Debate with Clement Greenberg" (1987), in Thierry de Duve, *Clement Greenberg Between the Lines* (Paris: Éditions Dis Voir, 1996), 126.

119. De Kooning, statements to George Dickerson (1964), in George Dickerson, "Willem de Kooning," unedited manuscript dated 3 September 1964, Thomas B. Hess papers, Archives of American Art, Smithsonian Institution, Washington, 13, 15–16. These statements were edited out of Dickerson's published article, "The Strange Eye and Art of de Kooning," *Saturday Evening Post*, 21 November 1964, 68–71.

120. De Kooning (1953), quoted in Thomas B. Hess, *Willem de Kooning* (New York: Museum of Modern Art, 1968), 100.

121. Greenberg, "Review of an Exhibition of Willem de Kooning" (1948), *Collected Essays and Criticism*, 2:229. "Bill was very irritated with his facility and he was constantly struggling against it": Elaine de Kooning, "On the Work of Willem de Kooning" (1983–84), *The Spirit of Abstract Expressionism: Selected Writings*, ed. Rose Slivka and Marjorie Luyckx (New York: George Braziller, 1994), 228.

122. Greenberg, "Henri Rousseau and Modern Art" (1946), *Collected Essays and Criticism*, 2:93–95.

123. Greenberg, "A Critical Exchange with Fairfield Porter on '"American-Type" Painting'," *Collected Essays and Criticism*, 3:240.

124. Greenberg, "Review of an Exhibition of Willem de Kooning," *Collected Essays and Criticism*, 2:228–29.

125. Greenberg, "Foreward to an Exhibition of Willem de Kooning" (1953), *Collected Essays and Criticism*, 3:122.

126. Anonymous, "Big City Dames," *Time* 61 (6 April 1953): 80.

127. Greenberg, "'American-Type' Painting" (1955), *Collected Essays and Criticism*, 3:222.

128. See the account of de Kooning's friend Harold Rosenberg, as if to mark the end of the era: Harold Rosenberg, "Masculinity: Real and Put On," *Vogue* 150 (November 1967): 106–07, 159.

129. Thomas B. Hess, "De Kooning Paints a Picture," *Artnews* 52 (March 1953): 66; Elaine de Kooning, statement to George Dickerson (1964), in Dickerson, "Willem de Kooning," 13–14.

130. James Fitzsimmons, "Art," *Arts and Architecture* 70 (May 1953): 8.

131. Grace Hartigan, statement in Cindy Nemser, *Art Talk: Conversations with 12 Women Artists* (New York: Charles Scribner's Sons, 1975), 158–59. Elaine de Kooning said the same: "[The Woman paintings] do have a certain ferocity, but that has to do with paint" (Elaine de Kooning, recorded in the film *De Kooning on de Kooning*, directed by Charlotte Zwerin, produced by Courtney Sale, Direct Cinema, New York, 1981).

132. James Fitzsimmons, "Art," *Arts and Architecture* 71 (February 1954): 4. In an editorial capacity in 1967, Fitzsimmons proposed to commission from Harold Rosenberg a comprehensive account of de Kooning's art, evidence of Fitzsimmons's longstanding interest (letter from Fitzsimmons to Rosenberg, 1 January 1967, "Harold Rosenberg Papers, 1923–1984," Getty Research Institute, Research Library, Special Collections, Los Angeles).

133. James Fitzsimmons, "On the 'peintures sauvages' of Joan Miró," *Miró: "peintures sauvages" 1934 to 1953* (New York: Pierre Matisse Gallery, 1958), n.p.

134. Sidney Geist, "Work in Progress," *Art Digest* 27 (1 April 1953): 15.

135. Fitzsimmons, "Art" (May 1953), 4, 6 (sentence order altered). Marcia Brennan discusses a number of similar statements of the period in her *Modernism's Masculine Subjects: Matisse, the New York School, and Post-Painterly Abstraction* (Cambridge, Mass.: MIT, 2004), 46–75.

136. "There is also a refusal to work with ideas that are too clear. … de Kooning has it in him to attain to a more clarified art": Greenberg, "Review of an Exhibition of Willem de Kooning," *Collected Essays and Criticism*, 2:229–30.

137. Fitzsimmons, "Art" (May 1953), 4, 6.

138. Greenberg, "After Abstract Expressionism" (1962), *Collected Essays and Criticism*, 4:124. This statement originally appeared in *Art International* (6 [25 October 1962], 25), for which Fitzsimmons served as editor. Despite his "I am not a formalist," he and Greenberg were on excellent terms; see Greenberg's memorial statement in Michael Peppiatt, ed., "A Tribute to James Fitzsimmons, Editor and Publisher (1919–1985)," *Art International*, Winter 1988, 42–43.

139. Clement Greenberg, "'American-Type' Painting" (1958; revision of 1955 essay), *Art and Culture* (Boston: Beacon, 1961), 214.

140. De Kooning, quoted in "Willem the Walloper," *Time* 57 (30 April 1951): 63.

141. See, for example, Alfred H. Barr, Jr., *Cubism and Abstract Art* (Cambridge, MA: Harvard University Press, 1986 [1936]), 11; "Introduction," *The New American Painting* (New York: The Museum of Modern Art, 1959), 17. See also, Thomas B. Hess, *Abstract Painting: Background and American Phase* (New York: Viking, 1951), 27.

142. De Kooning's painting and drawing technique involved aspects of mimeticism, even miming, that linked his painter's materiality to bodies in physical action; see Richard Shiff, "The Gravity of Willem de Kooning's Twist," in Enrique Juncosa and Teresa Millet, eds., *Willem de Kooning* (Valencia: Institut Valencià d'Art Modern, 2001), 54–89.

143. "In our everyday life we experience not solid and immediate facts but stereotypes of meaning. … To quite small circles the appeal of modern art—notably painting and sculpture, but also of the crafts—lies in the fact

that in an impersonal, a scheduled, a machined world, they represent the personal and the spontaneous. They are the opposite of the stereotyped and the banalized": Mills, "The Man in the Middle," 70, 75. Schapiro disputed the position of Barr and others on the relatively autonomous nature of abstraction (at least around 1936, the year of *Cubism and Abstract Art*); he argued that the development of art of any kind should be correlated with a history of change in underlying economic and social conditions. To account for artists' attraction to the more rationalistic forms of abstraction during the 1920s, he drew a parallel between abstraction conceived as autonomous and technology "conceived abstractly as an independent force with its own inner conditions"; with the economic crisis of the 1930s, artists shifted to "anti-rationalist ... new romantic styles" (Schapiro, "Nature of Abstract Art," 97–98). Schapiro assumed the position of a critical theorist with an overview, stressing the fact that modern artists of various generations, from the impressionists forward, responded to evident social realities but "did not know the underlying economic and social causes of their own disorder and moral insecurity"; they were generally "ignorant" of "causes" (84, 98). To the contrary, as a sociologist in the field, Mills spoke as if from within the midst of things, emphasizing artists' and designers' conscious intention—a micro-theory rather than a macro-theory. A writer can easily slip from one voice to the other, and many critical accounts consist of both, including Schapiro's own later essay, "The Liberating Quality of Avant-garde Art," which grants to the artists a greater consciousness: "For the [nineteenth-century avant-garde] artists themselves ... each of [their] styles was justified by ideal ends that they served, whether of order, liberty or truth" (Schapiro, "The Liberating Quality of Avant-garde Art," 37). Here, from the same moment, is another statement by a prominent art historian, but in accord with Mills, not Schapiro: "The art historian who sees the styles of the past merely as an expression of the age, the race or the class-situation, will torment the living artist with the empty demand that he should go and do likewise and express the essence and spirit of his time, race, class or, worst of all, of the self. The more we exorcize those spirits which still haunt the history of art, the more we learn to look at the individual and particular work of art as the work of skilled hands and great minds in response to concrete demands"; Gombrich, "Art and Scholarship," 356.

144. Barnett Newman, in Dorothy Gees Seckler, "Frontiers of Space," *Art in America* 50 (Summer 1962): 86. In a letter to Jean Lipman, editor of *Art in America*, 9 July 1962 (Barnett Newman Foundation, New York), Newman confirmed that it was his intent "not to discuss any names" directly.

145. De Kooning, quoted in Anonymous, "Big Splash," *Time* 73 (18 May 1959): 72.

146. De Kooning, audiotaped statement, interview by Michael C. Sonnabend and Kenneth Snelson, summer 1959, typescript, Willem de Kooning Foundation, New York.

147. For more comment along these lines, see Ferrara, "One Giant Leap," 129–130.

148. As recollected by Louis Finkelstein; see Marla Prather, *Willem de Kooning: Paintings* (Washington: National Gallery of Art, 1994), 101.

149. Thomas B. Hess, *Willem de Kooning* (New York: Braziller, 1959), 117.

150. De Kooning, quoted by Bibeb, "Willem de Kooning: Ik vind dat alles een mond moet hebben en ik zet de mond waar ik wil," *Vrij Nederland* (Amsterdam), 5 October 1968, 3 (translation by Mette Gieskes).

151. Willem de Kooning, in Harold Rosenberg, "Interview with Willem de Kooning," *Artnews* 71 (September 1972): 55. This interview–conversation was recorded in 1971, then edited, presumably by Rosenberg, and published in 1972. The sources for de Kooning's sense of Cézanne may be variants of two statements attributed to him by admiring young writers: "The artist doesn't directly perceive [by intellect] all the relationships; he feels them" (Léo Larguier, *Le dimanche avec Paul Cézanne* [Paris: L'Edition, 1925], 137); "Each brushstroke should correspond, here, on my canvas, to a [single] breath of the world, to its spark of illumination, there, on [my model]. We must live in harmonious union—my model, my paints, and me—articulating the very moment that passes" (Joachim Gasquet, *Cézanne* [Paris: Bernheim-Jeune, 1926 (1921)], 195). A related interpretation of Cézanne (discussed below) appeared in Maurice Merleau-Ponty, "Cézanne's Doubt" (1945), *Sense and Non-Sense*, trans. Hubert L. Dreyfus and Patricia Allen Dreyfus (Evanston: Northwestern University Press, 1964), 14–15.

152. Cézanne's words as recalled, not necessarily verbatim, by Gasquet, *Cézanne*, 132.

153. Willem de Kooning, interview by Emile de Antonio, 1970, in *Painters Painting*, film produced and directed by Emile de Antonio, Turin Film Corp., 1972, videotape (Mystic Fire Video, New York, 1989). De Kooning often made his statement about "bright ideas" and had done so, for example, in an interview by David Sylvester, conducted in March 1960 for BBC radio (see David Sylvester, "De Kooning's Women," *Sunday Times Magazine* [London], 8 December 1968, 52).

154. Greenberg, "'American-Type' Painting," *Collected Essays and Criticism*, 3:222.

155. On de Kooning and Picasso, see Rudy Burckhardt, "Long Ago with Willem de Kooning," *Art Journal* 48 (Fall 1989): 222; David Sylvester, "Flesh Was the Reason," in Prather, *Willem de Kooning: Paintings*, 17–19. In the transcript of de Kooning's interview (courtesy Willem de Kooning Foundation, New York), Rosenberg mentions the writings of Cubist theorists Albert Gleizes and Jean Metzinger, a reference omitted from the published version.

156. Willem de Kooning, "What Abstract Art Means to Me," *The Museum of Modern Art Bulletin* 18 (Spring 1951): 7.

157. Greenberg, "How Art Writing Earns Its Bad Name" (1962), *Collected Essays and Criticism*, 4:136.

158. Greenberg, "After Abstract Expressionism," *Collected Essays and Criticism*, 4:124, 128 (order of phrases altered).

159. De Kooning, in Rosenberg, "interview with Willem de Kooning," 55.

160. A youthful work by de Kooning suggests remote formal links to Cézanne, but is exceptional; see Judith Zilczer, *Willem de Kooning from the Hirshhorn Museum Collection* (Washington, DC: Hirshhorn Museum and Sculpture Garden, Smithsonian Institution, 1993), 13, fig. 1.

161. Willem de Kooning, "A Desperate View," in Thomas B. Hess, *Willem de Kooning* (New York: Museum of Modern Art, 1968), 15. De Kooning

presented this lecture at the "Subjects of the Artist" school in New York, 18 February 1949.

162. See Rosenberg's statement in Rosenberg, "Interview with Willem de Kooning," 55. Rosenberg and de Kooning referred the "Don't think, look!" notion to Wittgenstein.

163. De Kooning, quoted in "Willem the Walloper," 63. De Kooning's remark reverberated; it was quoted again by *Time* two years later ("Big City Dames," 80).

164. In a succession of writings on de Kooning, Thomas Hess stressed ambiguity and multiplicity as his interpretive theme, apparently influenced by a similar focus in the literary analysis of the New Critics of the 1930s, '40s, and '50s, such as Cleanth Brooks, William Wimsatt, R. P. Blackmur (cited directly by Hess) and William Empson (author of the famous *Seven Types of Ambiguity*, 1930). Compare Hess, *Abstract Painting: Background and American Phase*, 103–04 ("shapes become ambiguously interpretable ... this continual outpouring of ambiguity"); "De Kooning Paints a Picture," 32 ("the painter makes ambiguity into actuality"). Greenberg also presented ambiguity as a significant factor ("Review of an Exhibition of Willem de Kooning," *Collected Essays and Criticism*, 2:229). In 1993, I interviewed a number of people who had known de Kooning over many years. Several of them (including John McMahon, Joan Ward, and Allan Stone) emphasized his tendency to consider numerous alternatives as he addressed a topic, avoiding conclusiveness and termination; he often shifted or reversed the drift of the conversation. In formal interviews, too, he would argue by association, allowing himself to move from thought to thought without making a definitive judgment. For discussion of these habits of thought, see Richard Shiff, "Water and Lipstick: de Kooning in Transition," in Prather, *Willem de Kooning: Paintings*, 50–55.

165. Merleau-Ponty, "Cézanne's Doubt," *Sense and Non-Sense*, 9. The earlier translation, which is abridged, is by Juliet Bigney, *Partisan Review* 13 (1946): 464–78.

166. Paul Cézanne, letter to Emile Bernard, 21 September 1906, in John Rewald, ed., *Paul Cézanne, correspondance* (Paris: Grasset, 1978), 326–27. Like de Kooning, Cézanne had a great sense of irony. Possibly, his reference to "slow progress" expresses a false modesty. In this instance, however, he would seem sincere, given his rapidly failing health and awareness that many aspects of his cumulative artistic project remained incomplete. In his summary account a year later, Bernard attributed the unsatisfying state of Cézanne's art to the painter's own doubt: "If he had acted without so many doubts over what could be better ... he would have given us magisterial works. ... [He believed] that what he had done up to the present was only the beginning of what he would produce, if he were to live many years more"; Emile Bernard, "Souvenirs sur Paul Cézanne et letters inédites," *Mercure de France* 69 (1 October 1907): 395, 399.

167. See Elaine de Kooning, "De Kooning Memories" (1983), *The Spirit of Abstract Expressionism: Selected Writings*, ed. Marjorie Luyckx and Rose Slivka (New York: Braziller, 1994), 214.

168. See note 150.

169. Compare Hess, "De Kooning Paints a Picture," 31: "He needs such doubt to keep off-balance." See also Ferrara, "One Giant Leap," 129–30.

170. Edmond Jaloux, *Les saisons littéraires*, 2 vols. (Fribourg: Editions de la librairie de l'Université, 1942), 1:75.

171. De Kooning was born in 1904, Merleau-Ponty in 1908. The potential relevance of de Kooning's mimeticism to Merleau-Ponty's sense of corporeality is evident: "My body can assume segments derived from the body of another, just as my substance passes into them; man is mirror for man"; Maurice Merleau-Ponty, "Eye and Mind" (1961), *The Primacy of Perception and Other Essays*, ed. James M. Edie, trans. Carleton Dallery (Evanston: Northwestern University Press, 1964), 168. On the mimetic factor in de Kooning, see Shiff, "The Gravity of Willem de Kooning's Twist."

172. Merleau-Ponty, "Eye and Mind," 185.

173. Merleau-Ponty, "Cézanne's Doubt," 20.

174. Projected into a late twentieth-century context, one thinks of the self-differing and Mallarméan miming in Jacques Derrida, "The Double Session" (1970), *Dissemination*, trans. Barbara Johnson (Chicago: University of Chicago Press, 1981), 173–285.

175. Paul Souriau, *L'esthétique du mouvement* (Paris: Alcan, 1889), 211, n. 1.

176. Greenberg, "A *Life* Round Table on Modern Art," 62.

177. Charles Morice, "Paul Cézanne," *Mercure de France* 65 (15 February 1907): 577, 593 (emphasis original).

178. Greenberg's subsequent account of this phenomenon: "[The formal] problem so absorbed [Cézanne] in the means that he would too often lose sight of the end, his own emotion"(Greenberg, "Review of Exhibitions of Corot, Cézanne, Eilshemius, and Wilfredo Lam" [1942], *Collected Essays and Criticism*, 1:130).

179. Charles Morice, "Le XXIe Salon des Indépendants," *Mercure de France* 54 (15 April 1905): 552.

180. Evidence of a problematic conflation of intellectual and emotional life with the practice of painting came in the form of representations that failed to distinguish one depicted object from another, allowing the pictorial structure of the paint (the texture, the color) to dominate the structure of the objects as it would appear in reality. As an example of this type of observation, common in the nineteenth century, see Thoré-Bürger (Théophile Thoré), "Salon de 1868," *Les Salons*, 3:532: "[Manet's] present vice is a kind of pantheism that values a human head no more than a slipper … that paints everything almost uniformly." For more on the nineteenth-century development of this issue, see Richard Shiff, "Natural, Personal, Pictorial: Corot and the Painter's Mark," in Andreas Burmester, Christoph Heilmann, and Michael F. Zimmermann, eds., *Barbizon: Malerei der Natur—Natur der Malerei* (Munich: Klinkhardt & Biermann, 1999), 120–38; "Something Is Happening," 190–201.

181. Charles Morice, "Le Salon d'Automne," *Mercure de France* 58 (1 December 1905): 381.

182. Judd, in Angeli Janhsen, ed., "Discussion with Donald Judd," *Donald Judd* (St. Gallen: Kunstverein St. Gallen, 1990), 54. De Man investigates self-difference by focusing on a statement from Hegel ("so kann ich nicht sagen was ich nur meine"), which, when analyzed, reduces to "I cannot say what I think," or even "I cannot say I." I, the pronoun, cannot say what I, the person, mean. De Man refers to "the undoing, the erasure of any relationship, logical or otherwise, that could be conceived between what the I

is and what it says it is" (de Man, "Sign and Symbol in Hegel's *Aesthetics*," 768–69). For the passage at issue, see William Wallace, trans., *Hegel's Logic: Being Part One of the "Encyclopaedia of the Philosophical Sciences"* (Oxford: Oxford University Press, 1975), 31. See also Paul de Man, "Reply to Raymond Geuss," *Critical Inquiry* 10 (December 1983): 387–88.

183. Morice, "Paul Cézanne," 593.

184. Wittgenstein, *Zettel*, 71.

185. Greenberg, "Review of an Exhibition of Willem de Kooning," *Collected Essays and Criticism*, 2:229

186. Henri-Edmond Cross, "Le dernier carnet d'Henri-Edmond Cross—II" (1908–09), ed. Félix Fénéon, *Le bulletin de la vie artistique* 3 (1 June 1922): 255.

187. See Richard Shiff, "Apples and Abstraction," in Eliza E. Rathbone and George T. M. Shackelford, eds., *Impressionist Still Life* (Washington: The Phillips Collection, 2001), 42–47.

188. Thomas B. Hess, "U.S. Painting: Some Recent Directions," *Art News Annual* 25 (1956): 98.

189. Wollheim, "Response to James I. Porter," 142 (emphasis added).

190. Greenberg, "The Present Prospects of American Painting and Sculpture" (1947), *Collected Essays and Criticism*, 2:164.

191. Newman, "The Fourteen Stations of the Cross, 1958–1966," *Selected Writings and Interviews*, 189.

192. Judd, "Local History" (1964), *Complete Writings 1959–1975*, 155–56 (order of phrases reversed).

193. See note 83.

194. Cézanne's words as recalled, not necessarily verbatim, by Gasquet, *Cézanne*, 132.

195. Cézanne, quoted in Emile Bernard, "Souvenirs sur Paul Cézanne et lettres inédites," *Mercure de France* 69 (16 October 1907): 614.

196. Georges Lecomte, *Ma traversée* (Paris: Laffont, 1949), 156.

197. On Cézanne's sensitivities, see Richard Shiff, "Sensation, Movement, Cézanne," in Terence Maloon, ed., *Classic Cézanne* (Sydney: Art Gallery of New South Wales, 1998): 13–27.

198. See Cézanne's comments on Gauguin and van Gogh, letter to Emile Bernard, 15 April 1904, in *Paul Cézanne, correspondance*, 300.

199. On "sensation," see Shiff, "Sensation, Movement, Cézanne," 13–14, 26.

200. See Christian Zervos, "Conversation avec Picasso" (1935), in Marie-Laure Bernadac and Androula Michael, eds., *Picasso: Propos sur l'art* (Paris: Gallimard, 1998): 36.

201. Merleau-Ponty, "Cézanne's Doubt," 20, 10–11.

202. Denis, "Quelques notices: A propos de l'exposition de Charles Guérin" (1905), *Théories 1890–1910: Du symbolisme et de Gauguin vers un nouvel ordre classique* (Paris: Rouart et Watelin, 1920), 143.

203. Herbert Read, "Henri Rousseau," *Now* 3 (n.d. [1944]): 32.

204. Greenberg, "Review of the Water-Color, Drawing, and Sculpture Sections of the Whitney Annual" (1946), *Collected Essays and Criticism*, 2:57–58.

205. Read, "Henri Rousseau," 32.

206. Robert Delaunay, letter to Franz Marc, 11 January 1913, "Extraits de H[enri] R[ousseau], Le Douanier" (1913), in *Du cubisme à l'art abstrait*, ed. Pierre Francastel (Paris: S.E.V.P.E.N., 1957), 189, 194.

207. Robert Delaunay, "Mon ami Henri Rousseau," *Les lettres français*, no. 369, 14 August 1952, 9.

208. Arsène Alexandre, "Deux mots historiques," *Comoedia*, no. 551 (3 April 1909): 3.

209. Francis Lepeseur (Emile Bernard), "L'anarchie esthétique: Les Indépendants," *La rénovation esthétique* 1 (June 1905): 92.

210. Maurice Denis, undated personal statement recorded in Charles Chassé, *Dans les coulisses de la gloire: D'Ubu-Roi au Douanier Rousseau* (Paris: Editions de la Nouvelle Revue Critique, 1947), 168.

211. Gauguin's words (1894?), as recalled by Paul Sérusier; see Chassé, 133, n. 1.

212. Henry McBride, in *The Sun* (New York), March or April 1938, paraphrased and quoted in an anonymous review, "Glorifying the 'Masters of Popular Painting'," *Art Digest* 12 (15 May 1938): 6.

213. Gustave Kahn, "Revue de la quinzaine: Exposition Henri Rousseau," *Mercure de France* 164 (1 August 1923): 785–86. On Pissarro's interest in Rousseau, see also John Rewald, *The History of Impressionism* (New York: Museum of Modern Art, 1961), 560. It was extremely common for Cézanne to be invoked as a parallel to Rousseau in one sense or another; see, for example, the opening paragraph of Wilhelm Uhde's monograph (*Henri Rousseau* [Paris: Eugène Figuière, 1911], 5), which suggests analogous mistreatment by journalists.

214. Paul Gauguin, letter to Camille Pissarro, c. 10 July 1884, in Victor Merlhès, ed., *Correspondance de Paul Gauguin, 1873–1888* (Paris: Fondation Singer-Polignac, 1984), 65.

215. Guillaume Apollinaire, "Les Indépendants," *L'Intransigeant* (20 April 1911), reprinted in *Chroniques d'art (1902–1918)*, ed. L.-C. Breunig (Paris: Gallimard, 1960), 162–63.

216. Camille Pissarro, letter to Lucien Pissarro, 9 September 1892, in Janine Bailly-Herzberg, ed., *Correspondance de Camille Pissarro*, 5 vols. (Paris: Presses Universitaires de France [vol. 1], Valhermeil [vols. 2–5], 1980–1991), 3:256 (emphasis original).

217. Gustave Kahn, "Au temps du pointillisme," *Mercure de France* 171 (1 April 1924): 12–13.

218. For an early appreciation of a Rousseau composition, detail by detail, see L[ouis] Roy, "Un isolé: Henri Rousseau," *Mercure de France* 13 (March 1895): 350–51. Chassé divided Rousseau's early enthusiasts into those who marvelled at his utter naiveté and those who marvalled at this knowledgeable understanding of aesthetic principles; see Chassé, 141. Uhde had argued that Rousseau was in full control of whatever style he chose to use; Uhde, *Henri Rousseau*, 54–55.

219. Maximilien Gauthier, "Maîtres populaires de la réalité," in Holger Cahill et al, *Masters of Popular Painting: Modern Primitives of Europe and America* (New York: Museum of Modern Art, 1938), 21. "Popular painting" encompassed art under several designations, including folk art, naïve art, outsider art, and amateur art (Sunday painting). Gauthier later commented: "In proving that a painting may be intensely pleasurable, independently or even in spite of what it represents, Rousseau was paving the way, *without being fully aware of it*, for non-figurative art" (Maximilien Gauthier, "The

Douanier Rousseau," *Henri Rousseau* [New York: Wildenstein, 1963], n.p. [emphasis added]).

220. Max Weber, statement of 11 February 1958, in Carol S. Gruber, ed., *The Reminiscences of Max Weber* (New York: Columbia University, 1958), 227, 242 (emphasis original).

221. Alfred H. Barr, Jr., and Daniel Catton Rich, "Foreword," in Daniel Catton Rich, *Henri Rousseau* (New York: The Museum of Modern Art, 1942), 8. Rich published the foreword to a revised edition of 1946 under his name alone, adding that his view, "so strikingly different from much written on Rousseau, has been strongly contradicted, especially by essayists who admire the 'primitive'" (Daniel Catton Rich, *Henri Rousseau* [New York: Museum of Modern Art, 1946], 8).

222. James Johnson Sweeney, "Two Reviews of the Henri Rousseau Exhibition," *College Art Journal* 1 (May 1942): 110.

223. See Richard Shiff, "Selbst-Interferenz," trans. Kathrin Thiele and Birgit M. Kaiser, in Michael Lüthy and Christophe Menke, eds., *Subjekt und Medium in der Kunst der Moderne* (Zürich: Diaphanes, 2006), 13–21.

224. On Rousseau's academic ambitions and methods, see John House, "Henri Rousseau as an Academic," in Frances Morris and Christopher Green, ed., *Henri Rousseau: Jungles in Paris* (London: Tate Publishing, 2005), 183–89.

225. Ean Lipman, "Masters of Popular Painting,"*Art in America* 26 (July 1938): 141.

226. James W. Lane, "Notes from New York," *Apollo* 28 (August 1938): 90. The artists in question were André Bauchant and René Rimbert.

227. Peirce, "A Definition of Feeling" (c. 1906), *Collected Papers*, 1:153. Compare Paul de Man, *Allegories of Reading* (New Haven: Yale University Press, 1979), 78: "The hour of truth, like the hour of death, never arrives on time, since what we call time is precisely truth's inability to coincide with itself."

228. Henry McBride, "Rousseau le Douanier," *Art and Understanding* 1 (March 1930): 227–28.

229. Read, "Henri Rousseau," 30 (emphasis original).

230. Hence, the appropriateness of Wassily Kandinsky's association of Rousseau with an artistic "realism" that would fit the formula: "Realism = Abstraction; Abstraction = Realism." See Wassily Kandinsky, "On the Question of Form" (from *Der blaue Reiter*, 1912), trans. Peter Vergo, in Kenneth C. Lindsay and Peter Vergo, eds., *Kandinsky: Complete Writings on Art* (New York: Da Capo, 1994), 242–52.

231. Lipman, "Masters of Popular Painting," 141.

232. Rich, "Foreword," *Henri Rousseau* (rev. ed., 1946), 8. Roger Fry, a prominent source for the formal pictorial analysis that Rich himself preferred, may have been among those whom he regarded as offering the "easy explanation": "Here [with Rousseau] is one case where want of skill and knowledge do not completely obscure, though they may mar, expression. And this is true of all perfectly naïve and primitive art"; Roger Fry, "The French Post-Impressionists" (1912), *Vision and Design* (New York: Meridian, 1956 [1920]), 238.

233. Greenberg, "Henri Rousseau and Modern Art," *Collected Essays and Criticism*, 2:93–95. Robert Goldwater had also been struck by the extent of the

acceptance of Rousseau and other "popular" masters: "The replacement of [their] natural public … in the immediate circle of the artist himself … by the public predicated by the Museum's interest, and our interest, in these popular artists, is one of the most curious phenomena of modern taste" (Robert J. Goldwater, "Seeing the Shows: Masters of Popular Painting," *Magazine of Art* 31 [June 1938]: 357 [order of phrasing altered]).

234. Greenberg, "Henri Rousseau and Modern Art," *Collected Essays and Criticism*, 2:93.

235. Greenberg, "Henri Rousseau and Modern Art," *Collected Essays and Criticism*, 2:94. On psychosis and madness in Rousseau, see also Greenberg, "Review of Exhibitions of Corot, Cézanne, Eilshemius, and Wilfredo Lam," "Review of Exhibitions of Van Gogh and the Remarque Collection," 1:130, 161. In the first review (1942), Greenberg associated Louis Eilshemius with Rousseau ("both artists were indeed a little bit mad"). In the second (1943), he linked Van Gogh's "psychopathic state" to Rousseau and Eilshemius. And in 1946, he introduced Eilshemius parenthetically as a possible fourth to join Rousseau, Cézanne, and Van Gogh: "Eilshemius, whose unbalanced mind permitted him a boldness he might have turned to better advantage for modern art had he lived in France and become well acquainted with impressionism" ("Henri Rousseau and Modern Art," 94). Works by Eilshemius show a coarse, amateurish application of paint, fanciful, sometimes risible subjects, but a sophisticated sense of tonal values and compositional organization—in short, the marks of a "primitive" talent. On Eilshemius, see Steven Harvey, *Louis M. Eilshemius* (New York: National Academy of Design, 2001).

236. Arthur Rimbaud, letter to Paul Demeny, 15 May 1871, *Lettres du voyant*, ed. Gérald Schaeffer (Geneva: Droz, 1975), 137.

237. Greenberg, "The Present Prospects of American Painting and Sculpture," *Collected Essays and Criticism*, 2:164–65.

238. Greenberg, "Review of the Water-Color, Drawing, and Sculpture Sections of the Whitney Annual," *Collected Essays and Criticism*, 2:57–58.

239. Greenberg, "Henri Rousseau and Modern Art," *Collected Essays and Criticism*, 2:95.

240. Greenberg, "Review of an Exhibition of School of Paris Painters," *Collected Essays and Criticism*, 2:88.

241. Clarence J. Bulliet, *Apples and Madonnas: Emotional Expression in Modern Art* (Chicago: Pascal Covici, 1927), 12. Bulliet was one of a number of writers who preceded Greenberg in grouping Rousseau with Cézanne and Van Gogh.

242. Greenberg, "Review of an Exhibition of School of Paris Painters" (1946), *Collected Essays and Criticism*, 2:88.

243. Max Weber, "Rousseau as I Knew Him," *Artnews* 41 (15–28 February 1942): 35.

244. Greenberg, "Henri Rousseau and Modern Art," *Collected Essays and Criticism*, 2:95.

245. Greenberg, "Henri Rousseau and Modern Art," *Collected Essays and Criticism*, 2:94.

246. Greenberg, "Religion and the Intellectuals: A Symposium," *Collected Essays and Criticism*, 3:40–41.

247. Judd, in Janhsen, "Discussion with Donald Judd," 54.

248. Peirce, "Illustrations of the Logic of Science: Deduction, Induction, and Hypothesis," *Popular Science Monthly*, 481–82 (emphasis original).
249. Addendum, July 2006: I cited this remarkable text in several publications and numerous lectures, but seemingly without inducing others to follow along. Now, finally, it has appeared elsewhere. Caroline A. Jones uses it as the epigraph for a chapter of her *Eyesight Alone: Clement Greenberg's Modernism and the Bureaucratization of the Senses* (Chicago: University of Chicago Press, 2005), 204. I am likely to have instigated Jones's use, having recommended the Rousseau review to her at a College Art Assocation panel discussion in February 2001. Additionally, the bibliography for *Eyesight Alone* lists an essay of mine in which Greenberg's text appears: Richard Shiff, "Critical Reflections," *Artforum* 34 (October 1995): 124. Jones's comprehensive study includes the other source of citation as well, another possible stimulus: "Clement Greenberg with Peter Fuller," *Modern Painters*. For other recent writing on Greenberg of a comprehensive nature, see de Duve, *Clement Greenberg Between the Lines*.
250. "Clement Greenberg with Peter Fuller," 20.
251. The marked-up publication as well as Greenberg's irritated letter of response (undated) is in "Clement Greenberg Papers, 1928–1995," Getty Research Institute, Research Library, Special Collections, Los Angeles. I thank Michael Schreyach for verifying the content of these documents.
252. See Bernard Berenson, *Aesthetics and History* (Garden City, N.Y.: Doubleday, 1954 [1948]), 69–71.
253. Krauss, "The Crisis of the Easel Picture," *Jackson Pollock: New Approaches*, 160, 169. Many of Greenberg's statements belie such an assessment of his position. Here he describes the very physical materiality of postwar New York painting: "There is no insulating finish, nor is pictorial space created 'pictorially,' by deep, veiled color, but rather by blunt corporeal contrasts and less specifiable optical illusion. … Every fresh and productive impulse in painting since Manet, and perhaps before, has repudiated received notions of finish and unity, and manhandled into art what until then seemed too intractable, too raw and accidental"; Greenberg, "Symposium: Is the French Avant-Garde Overrated?" (1953), *Collected Essays and Criticism*, 3:156. Of course, the phrase "manhandled into art" can be read with the stress on "art" rather than "manhandled," but the context renders this interpretation quite willful, that is, manhandled.
254. "Clement Greenberg with Peter Fuller," 20.
255. William James, *The Principles of Psychology* (Cambridge, Mass.: Harvard University Press, 1983 [1890]), 435 (emphasis eliminated).
256. I Have discussed this constellation of issues—dreams, realities, identities, sensations, feelings—in relation to specific works of abstract art in Richard Shiff, "Love Her as Herself," in Kevin Mullins, ed., *David Reed: Leave Yourself Behind: Paintings and Special Projects 1967–2005* (Wichita: Ulrich Museum of Art, 2005), 24–65.
257. Greenberg, "A *Life* Round Table on Modern Art," 62.
258. Vincent Gille, "Illusion of Sources—Sources of Illusion: Rousseau Through the Images of His Time," in *Henri Rousseau: Jungles in Paris*, 63. Gille's characterization captures the charm and fascination that Rousseau holds today, but also alludes to the social concerns of the painter's era and to an early anecdote reported in Uhde, *Henri Rousseau*, 43.

259. Greenberg, "The Necessity of the Old Masters" (1948), *Collected Essays and Criticism*, 2:250–51.

260. Greenberg, "Religion and the Intellectuals: A Symposium," *Collected Essays and Criticism*, 3:40–41.

261. Greenberg, "Henri Rousseau and Modern Art," *Collected Essays and Criticism*, 2:95.

262. De Man, "Sign and Symbol in Hegel's *Aesthetics*," 768. The reading is of Hegel's *Enzyklopädie der philosophischen Wissenschaften*, vol. I, para. 20. For more details, see above, note 180. Terry Eagleton cautions against de Man's radical doubt as itself an unhealthy absolutism, motivated by a desire to purge himself of his early writings of fascist orientation; see Terry Eagleton, *The Ideology of the Aesthetic* (Oxford: Basil Blackwell, 1990), 9–10, 311.

263. Greenberg, "Cézanne and the Unity of Modern Art" (1951), *Collected Essays and Criticism*, 3:88; Clement Greenberg, "Convention and Innovation" (1976), *Homemade Esthetics: Observations on Art and Taste* (New York: Oxford University Press, 1999), 54.

264. "You intuit quality. But you can't analyze it": Greenberg, "The Bennington College Seminars" (1971), *Homemade Esthetics*, 99.

265. Donald Judd, "Questions to Stella and Judd," interview by Bruce Glaser (February 1964; emended by Judd and Glaser, December 1965), ed. Lucy Lippard, *Artnews* 65 (September 1966): 61.

266. Gene Currivan, "Nazi Death Factory Shocks Germans on a Forced Tour," *New York Times*, 18 April 1945, 1.

267. On beginnings (like Newman's), Irwin states a position that might be shared by pragmatists, phenomenologists, and existentialists, as well as modernists and postmodernists: "We do not begin at the beginning, or in an empirical no-where. Instead we always begin somewhere in the middle of everything"; Robert Irwin, "Notes Toward a Model," *Robert Irwin* (New York: Whitney Museum of American Art, 1977), 24 (emphasis eliminated).

268. Newman, quoted by Cohen, introduction to "Barnett Newman Talks to David Sylvester" (see note 58). Newman made this statement to Harold Cohen in May 1964, when brothers Harold and Bernard Cohen were restretching *Uriel* in the London flat of Alan Power, who had purchased it. Within this context, his use of *stretch* may have constituted a pun. Power remembers that Newman extended his enunciation of the word *far* while gesturing with his hand from left to right, as if to indicate the materiality of the "stretch"—art as physical risk as much as emotional and intellectual risk (Alan Power, statement to the author, 27 August 2006).

269. Newman, statement in "A Conversation: Barnett Newman and Thomas B. Hess" (1966), *Selected Writings and Interviews*, 274. On judgment and the lack of guidance, compare Bridget Riley: "My main activity in the studio is the exercise of judgment—pure judgment. ... Like pure color, such judgment is distinguished by having no referential role outside the work itself [no standard to guide it]. It seems that many people feel that there is something 'there' in good Abstract painting that can neither be assessed objectively nor dismissed as mere mystification"; "Bridget Riley in Conversation with Jenny Harper, April 2004," in Beat Wismer, ed.,

Bridget Riley: Bilder und Zeichnungen 1959–2005 (Aarau: Aargauer Kunsthaus, 2005), 222.

Seminar

1. *Stanford Encyclopedia of Philosophy*, internet version, accessed May 5, 2004.
2. Shiff, "Flexible Time," *Art Bulletin* 76 (December 1994): 583-87.
3. Elkins, *What Happened to Art Criticism?* (Chicago IL: Prickly Paradigm Press distributed by University of Chicago Press, 2003).
4. Heinrich von Kleist, "Über die allmähliche Verfertigung der Gedanken beim Reden," in Siegfried Streller, ed., *Heinrich von Kleist: Werke und Briefe*, 4 vols. (Berlin: Aufbau-Verlag, 1978), 3: 453-59.
5. Elkins, *Why Art Cannot be Taught: A Handbook for Art Students* (Urbana-Champaign IL: University of Illinois Press, 2001).
6. Shiff, "Realism of Low Resolution: Digitisation and Modern Painting," in Terry Smith, ed., *Impossible Presence: Surface and Screen in the Photogenic Era* (Chicago: University of Chicago Press, 2001), 124-56.
7. Elkins, "What Does Peirce's Sign System Have to Say to Art History?" *Culture, Theory, and Critique* 44 no. 1 (2003): 5-22.
8. "When I think as a 'critic,' I doubt that any of the three perspectives can be found in a pure state": Shiff, "Flexible Time," 587.
9. Shiff, "Criticism at Odds with Its Art: Prophecy, Projection, Doubt, Paranoia," *Common Knowledge* 9 (Fall 2003): 461.

PUBLICATIONS BY RICHARD SHIFF

Books

Cézanne and the End of Impressionism: A Study of the Theory, Technique, and Critical Evaluation of Modern Art (Chicago: University of Chicago Press, 1984); French edition: *Cézanne et la fin de l'impressionnisme: théorie, technique et evaluation critique de l'art moderne*, trans. Jean-François Allain (Paris: Flammarion, 1995); Spanish edition: *Cézanne y el fin del impresionismo: Estudio de la teoría, la técnica y la valoración crítica del arte moderno*, trans. Daniel Aguirre Oteiza and Roser Vilagrasa (Madrid: A. Machado, 2002).

Paul Cézanne (New York: Rizzoli, 1994).

Barnett Newman: A Catalogue Raisonné [co-authored with Carol C. Mancusi-Ungaro and Heidi Colsman-Freyberger] (New York: The Barnett Newman Foundation, 2004).

Reprinted Excerpts

"Defining 'Impressionism' and the 'Impression'," in Francis Frascina and Jonathan Harris, eds., *Art in Modern Culture: An Anthology of Critical Texts* (London: Phaidon, 1992), 181–88.

"The Poussin Legend" [in Japanese], trans. Takanobu Tobishima and Shin'ichiro Matsuoka, *Eureka* 28 (September 1996): 136–47.

Edited Book

Critical Terms for Art History [co-edited with Robert S. Nelson] (Chicago: University of Chicago Press, 1996). Second edition: (Chicago: University of Chicago Press, 2003); includes my essays "Originality" (103–15; 2nd ed.,

145–59) and "Afterword: Figuration" (323–28; 2nd ed., 479–85); Japanese edition: Tokyo: Brücke, 2002; Slovakian edition: Bratislava: Soros Center for Contemporary Art, 2004. Korean edition: Seoul: Artbooks, 2006; Serbian edition: in preparation (SVETOVI).

Journal Articles, Essays, Book Chapters, Book Introductions

"Seeing Cézanne," *Critical Inquiry* 4 (Summer 1978): 769–808.

"Art and Life: A Metaphoric Relationship," *Critical Inquiry* 5 (Autumn 1978): 107–22.

Reprinted in: Sheldon Sacks, ed., *On Metaphor* (Chicago: University of Chicago Press, 1979), 105–20; Sally Everett, ed., *Art Theory and Criticism* (Jefferson, N.C.: McFarland, 1991), 154–69.

"The End of Impressionism: A Study in Theories of Artistic Expression," *Art Quarterly*, NS, 1 (Autumn 1978): 338–78.

"The Art of Excellence and the Art of the Unattainable," *Georgia Review* 32 (Winter 1978): 829–41.

"History and Innovation" [co-authored with Carl Pletsch], *Critical Inquiry* 7 (Spring 1981): 634–38.

"Miscreation," *Studies in Visual Communication* 7 (Spring 1981): 57–71.

"The Technique of Originality: 'Innocence' and Artifice in the Painting of Corot, Monet, and Cézanne," *Studies in Visual Communication* 8 (Autumn 1982): 2–32.

"Mastercopy," *Iris* (Paris) 1, no. 2 (1983): 113–27.

"Representation, Copying, and the Technique of Originality," *New Literary History* 15 (Winter 1984): 333–63.

"The Original, the Imitation, the Copy, and the Spontaneous Classic: Theory and Painting in Nineteenth-Century France," *Yale French Studies*, no. 66 (1984): 27–54.

"Making a Find: An Argument for Creativity, Not Originality," *Structuralist Review* 2, no. 3 (Spring 1984): 59–80.

"Remembering Impressions," *Critical Inquiry* 12 (Winter 1986): 439–48.

"The End of Impressionism" (revised version), in Charles Moffett, ed., *The New Painting: Impressionism 1874–1886* (San Francisco: The Fine Arts Museums of San Francisco, 1986), 60–89.

"Handling Shocks," *New Observations*, no. 47 (1987): 14–19.

"Performing an Appearance: On the Surface of Abstract Expressionism," in Michael Auping, ed., *Abstract Expressionism: The Critical Developments* (New York: Harry N. Abrams, for the Albright-Knox Art Gallery, 1987), 94–123.

"Anamorphosis: Jasper Johns," in James Cuno, ed., *Foirades / Fizzles: Echo and Allusion in the Art of Jasper Johns* (Los Angeles: Wight Art Gallery, 1987), 147–66.

"On Criticism Handling History," *History of the Human Sciences* 2, no. 1 (1989): 63–87.

Preliminary version: "On Criticism Handling History," *Art Criticism* 3, no. 1 (Autumn 1986): 60–77.

"Painting, Writing, Handwriting: Roger Fry and Paul Cézanne," introduction to Roger Fry, *Cézanne: A Study of His Development* (Chicago: University of Chicago Press, 1989), x–xxviii.

"Phototropism (Figuring the Proper)," *Studies in the History of Art* 20 (1989): 161–179.

Abridged version: "Phototropism (Figuring the Proper)," *Photographic INsight* 1, nos. 2–3 (Winter–Spring 1988): 19–34.

"Picasso's Touch: Collage, *Papier collé, Ace of Clubs*," *Yale University Art Gallery Bulletin*, 1990, 38–47.

["To Create Oneself: Barnett Newman's Writings"], introduction to John P. O'Neill, ed., *Barnett Newman: Selected Writings and Interviews* (New York: Alfred A. Knopf, 1990), xiii–xxviii; German edition: *Barnett Newman: Schriften und Interviews 1925–1970*, trans. Tarcisius Schelbert (Bern and Berlin: Gachnang & Springer, 1996), 11-29; French edition: in preparation (Paris: Macula).

"Constructing Physicality," *Art Journal* 50 (Spring 1991): 42–47.

["Gasquet's Portrait of Cézanne"], introduction to *Joachim Gasquet's Cézanne: A Memoir with Conversations*, trans. Christopher Pemberton (London: Thames and Hudson, 1991), 15–24.

"Cézanne's Physicality: The Politics of Touch," in Salim Kemal and Ivan Gaskell, eds., *The Language of Art History* (Cambridge: Cambridge University Press, 1991), 129–80; French translation of this essay: Flammarion, 1995; Spanish translation of this essay: Machado, 2002; Japanese translation of this essay: *Art Trace*, 2007.

"The Necessity of Jimmie Durham's Jokes," *Art Journal* 51 (Fall 1992): 74–80.

"'Il faut que les yeux soient émus': impressionnisme et symbolisme vers 1891," *Revue de l'art*, no. 96 (1992): 24–30; This essay republished by Flammarion, 1995; Spanish translation of this essay: Machado, 2002.

"Handling Shocks: On the Representation of Experience in Walter Benjamin's Analogies" (expanded version), *Oxford Art Journal* 15, no. 2 (1992): 88–103.

"The Work of Painting: Camille Pissarro and Symbolism," *Apollo* 136 (November 1992): 307–10.

"Cézanne and Poussin: How the Modern Claims the Classic," in Richard Kendall, ed., *Cézanne & Poussin: A Symposium* (Sheffield: Sheffield Academic Press, 1993), 51–68.

"Water and Lipstick: de Kooning in Transition," in Marla Prather, ed., *Willem de Kooning: Paintings* [exh. cat., National Gallery of Art, Washington] (New Haven: Yale University Press, 1994), 32–73.

Reprinted excerpt: Ellen G. Landau, ed., *Reading Abstract Expressionism: Context and Critique* (New Haven: Yale University Press, 2005), 594–615.

"Original Copy," *Common Knowledge* 3 (Spring 1994): 88–107.

"Flexible Time," *Art Bulletin* 76 (December 1994): 583–87.

"Imitation of Matisse," in Caroline Turner and Roger Benjamin, eds., *Matisse* [exh. cat.] (Brisbane: Queensland Art Gallery, 1995), 41–51.

["Judgment of History"], Critical Reflections series, *Artforum* 34 (October 1995): 82–83, 124–25.

"Ascribing to Manet, Declaring the Author," introduction to Bradford R. Collins, ed., *Twelve Views of Manet's 'Bar'* (Princeton: Princeton University Press, 1996), 1–24.

"On Passing Through Skin: Technology of Art and Sensation," *Public* 13 (1996): 14–31; Excerpt republished as "Switches," *Public* 20 (2000): 78–81.

"Light's Articulation: *Solomon's Temple*," introduction to James Alinder, ed., *Solomon's Temple: The European Building-Crafts Legacy, Photographs by Laura Volkerding* (Tucson: Center for Creative Photography, 1996), 9–19.

"Strates," in Suzanne Pagé, ed., *Georg Baselitz* [exh. cat., Musée d'Art moderne de la Ville de Paris] (Paris: Paris Musées, 1996), 39–47.

"Realism of Low Resolution," *Apollo* 144 (November 1996): 3–8.

"Willem de Kooning: Painting's Potential," in *Willem de Kooning: Paintings 1983–84* [exh. cat.] (New York: Matthew Marks Gallery, 1997), 7–17.

"La touche de Cézanne: entre vision impressionniste et vision symboliste," in Françoise Cachin, Henri Loyrette, and Stéphan Guégan, eds., *Cézanne aujourd'hui*, (Paris: Réunion des Musées Nationaux, 1997), 117–24.

"Breath of Modernism (Metonymic Drift)," in Terry Smith, ed., *In Visible Touch: Modernism and Masculinity* (Chicago: University of Chicago Press, 1997), 184–213.

"To Move the Eyes: Impressionism, Symbolism, and Well-being, c. 1891," in Richard Hobbs, ed., *Impressions of French Modernity: Art and Literature in France 1850–1900* (Manchester: Manchester University Press, 1998), 190–210.

"Cézanne's Blur, Approximating Cézanne," in Richard Thomson, ed., *Framing France: Essays on the Representation of Landscape in France, 1870–1914* (Manchester: Manchester University Press, 1998), 59–80.

"From Primitivist Phylogeny to Formalist Ontogeny: Roger Fry and Children's Drawings," in Jonathan Fineberg, ed., *Discovering Child Art: Essays on Childhood, Primitivism, and Modernism* (Princeton: Princeton University Press, 1998), 157–200; Japanese translation (by Mariko Kaname): *Art/Criticism* (Tokyo) 3 (Spring 2007).

"Corot and the Painter's Mark: Natural, Personal, Pictorial," *Apollo* 147 (May 1998): 3–8.

"Originality in the Visual Arts," "Photography/Catechresis," in Michael Kelly, ed., *Encyclopedia of Aesthetics*, 4 vols. (New York: Oxford University Press, 1998), 3:408–13, 502–06.

"Closeness," in Naomi Salaman and Ronnie Simpson, eds., *Postcards on Photography* [exh. cat.] (Cambridge: Cambridge Darkroom, 1998): 11–36.

"Sensation, Movement, Cézanne," in Terence Maloon, ed., *Classic Cézanne* [exh. cat.] (Sydney: Art Gallery of New South Wales, 1998), 13–27.

"Homeopathic Criticism," *Common Knowledge* 7 (Winter 1998): 4–13.

"L'expérience digitale: Une problématique de la peinture moderne," trans. Jean–François Allain, *Les Cahiers du Musée national d'art moderne* 66 (Winter 1998): 50–77; Italian translation: "L'esperienza digitale: Una problematica della pittura moderna," *Ipso facto* 8 (September–December 2000): 68–101.

"Natural, Personal, Pictorial: Corot and the Painter's Mark" [expanded version], in Andreas Burmester, Christoph Heilmann, and Michael F. Zimmermann, eds., *Barbizon: Malerei der Natur — Natur der Malerei* (Munich: Klinkhardt & Biermann, 1999), 120–38.

"Mark, Motif, Materiality: The Cézanne Effect in the Twentieth Century," in Felix Baumann, Evelyn Benesch, Walter Feilchenfeldt, and Klaus Albrecht Schröder, eds., *Cézanne: Vollendet — Unvollendet* (Ostfildern–Ruit: Hatje Cantz, 2000), 99–123; Reprinted in: Mary Tompkins Lewis, ed., *Critical Readings in Impressionism and Post–Impressionism* (Berkeley: University of California Press, 2007), 286–321.

"Chuck Close: Mark, Image, Medium, Interference," in *Chuck Close*, exh. cat. (New York: PaceWildenstein, 2000), 4–15; Reprinted excerpt: Mildred Glimcher, ed., *Adventures in Art: 40 Years at Pace* (Milan: Leonardo International, 2001), 615–17.

"Autonomy, Actuality, Mangold," in Richard Shiff, Robert Storr, Arthur Danto, Nancy Princenthal, and Sylvia Plimack Mangold, *Robert Mangold* (London: Phaidon, 2000), 7–57, 282–88.

"Donald Judd: Fast Thinking," in *Donald Judd: Late Work*, exh. cat. (New York: PaceWildenstein, 2000), 4–23.

"Behind and Underneath," in Kosme de Barañano and Maita Cañamas, eds., *Georg Baselitz: Escultura frente a pintura*, exh. cat. (València: Instituto Valenciano de Arte Moderno, 2001), 36–51.

"Introduction," in Michael Doran, ed., *Conversations with Cézanne* (Berkeley: University of California Press, 2001), xix–xxxiv, 215–22.

"Realism of Low Resolution: Digitisation and Modern Painting," in Terry Smith, ed., *Impossible Presence: Surface and Screen in the Photogenic Era* (Chicago: University of Chicago Press, 2001), 124–56.

"The Gravity of Willem de Kooning's Twist," in Enrique Juncosa and Teresa Millet, eds., *Willem de Kooning*, exh. cat. (Valencia: Institut Valencià d'Art Modern, 2001), 54–89.

"Apples and Abstraction," in Eliza E. Rathbone and George T. M. Shackelford, eds., *Impressionist Still Life*, exh. cat. (Washington: The Phillips Collection, 2001), 42–47, 227–28.

"De Kooning Controlling De Kooning," in Cornelia H. Butler and Paul Schimmel, eds., *Willem de Kooning: Tracing the Figure*, exh. cat. (Los Angeles: Museum of Contemporary Art, 2002), 152–67.

"'With Closed Eyes': De Kooning's Twist," *Master Drawings* 40/1 (2002): 73–88.

"Whiteout: The Not-Influence Newman Effect," in Ann Temkin, ed., *Barnett Newman*, exh. cat. (Philadelphia: Philadelphia Museum of Art, 2002), 77–111.

"Georg Baselitz Grounded," in Jay Clarke, ed., "Negotiating History: German Art and the Past," special issue of *The Art Institute of Chicago Museum Studies* 28/1 (2002): 52–65, 109–10.

"Expression: Natural, Personal, Pictorial," in Paul Smith and Carolyn Wilde, eds., *A Companion to Art Theory* (Oxford: Blackwell, 2002), 159–72.

"Puppet and Test Pattern: Mechanicity and Materiality in Modern Pictorial Representation," in Bruce Clarke and Linda Dalrymple Henderson, eds., *From Energy to Information: Representation in Science and Technology, Art, and Literature* (Stanford: Stanford University Press, 2002), 327–50, 420–26.

"A Space of One to One," in *Donald Judd: 50 x 100 x 50, 100 x 100 x 50*, exh. cat. (New York: PaceWildenstein, 2002), 5–23.

"The Young Painter," in Terence Maloon, ed., *Picasso: The Last Decades*, exh. cat. (Sydney: Art Gallery of New South Wales, 2002), 25–41.

"'La pittura per se stressa'. Cézanne e la natura morta" ["'Painting for Itself': Cézanne and Still Life"], trans. Viviana Tonon, in Marco Goldin, ed., *L'impressionismo e l'età di Van Gogh*, exh. cat. (Conegliano: Linea d'ombra, 2002), 253–56.

"Derangement of Clouds," *Van Gogh Museum Journal* (2002): 60–62.

"Mark, Sign, and Gesture in the Impressionist Context" [in Japanese], *Bijutsu Forum 21* 7 (Winter 2002): 47–54.

"Digital Experience in Modern Art," *Jinbun: Memoirs of the Faculty of Engineering and Design, Kyoto Institute of Technology* 51 (2002): 85–94.

"A Compelling Uniqueness," in Dean Sobel, ed., *Robert Mangold: Paintings, 1990–2002*, exh. cat. (Aspen: Aspen Art Museum, 2003), 16–29.

"Photographic Soul," in David Green, ed., *Where Is the Photograph?* (Brighton: Photoforum and Photoworks, 2003), 95–111.

Spanish edition: "El alma fotográfica," David Green, ed., Joana Furió, trans., *Qué ha sido de la fotografía?* (Barcelona: Gustavo Gili, 2007), 102–23.

"Bridget Riley: The Edge of Animation," in Paul Moorhouse, ed., *Bridget Riley*, exh. cat. (London: Tate Gallery, 2003), 80–91.

"Inventer les moyens," in Jean-Claude Lebensztejn and Patrick Javault, eds., *Les Hyperréalismes USA 1965–75*, exh. cat. (Strasbourg: Les Musées de Strasbourg, 2003), 60–77.

"Gego's Materialism," in Mari Carmen Ramirez, ed., *Questioning the Line: Gego in Context* (Houston: The Museum of Fine Arts, 2003), 117–49.

"Digitized Analogies," in Hans Ulrich Gumbrecht and Michael Marrinan, eds., *Mapping Benjamin: The Work of Art in the Digital Age* (Stanford: Stanford University Press, 2003), 63–70.

"Criticism at Odds with Its Art: Prophecy, Projection, Doubt, Paranoia," *Common Knowledge* 9/3 (Fall 2003): 434–62.

"Through a Slow Medium," in Terrie Sultan, ed., *Chuck Close Prints: Process and Collaboration* (Princeton: Princeton University Press, 2003), 18–43.

"Monet and the Mark," in Rodolphe Rapetti, MaryAnne Stevens, Michael Zimmermann, and Marco Goldin, eds., *Monet: Atti del convegno* (Conegliano: Linea d'ombra, 2003), 164–69.

"Preference without a Cause," in Joan Rothfuss, ed., *Past Things and Present: Jasper Johns Since 1983*, exh. cat. (Minneapolis: Walker Art Center, 2003), 12–27.

"Unfinished and Abstracted: Paul Cézanne, Twentieth-Century Painter in Spite of Himself" ("Inacabado y Abstraído: Paul Cézanne, pintor del siglo veinte a pesar de sí mismo"), trans. Juan Luis Delmont, *Cuaderno 7* (Caracas: Fundación Cisneros, 2003), 5–43.

"Classic and Modern Mastercopies," in Javier Arnaldo, ed., *Clasicismo y modernidad* (Madrid: Fundación Colección Thyssen-Bornemisza, 2003), 29–55.

"Tychic Motitif: Baselitz in History" ("Tychisches Motitiv: Baselitz in der Geschichte"), in *Georg Baselitz: Recent Paintings*, exh. cat. (New York/Cologne: Michael Werner, 2003), n.p.

Reprinted in: Susanne Kleine, ed., *Georg Baselitz: Bilder, die den Kopf verdrehen*, exh. cat. (Bonn: Kunst-und Ausstellungshalle der Bundesrepublik Deutschland, 2004), 164–85.

"Donald Judd, Safe From Birds," in Nicholas Serota, ed., *Donald Judd*, exh. cat. (London: Tate Publishing, 2004): 28–61.

"Abstraction not Abstraction," in *De Kooning: A Centennial Exhibition*, exh. cat. (New York: Gagosian Gallery, 2004), 7–16.

"Manual Imagination," in Adam D. Weinberg, ed., *Terry Winters: Paintings, Drawings, Prints 1994–2004* (New Haven: Yale University Press, 2004): 18–33.

"Eine Amerikanisierung deutscher Kunst," trans. Jürgen Blasius, in Cornelia Homburg, ed., *German Art: Deutsche Kunst aus amerikanischer Sicht*, exh. cat., (Cologne: DuMont, 2004), 21–35.

"Rasters in Paradise," in *Bridget Riley: Recent Paintings*, exh. cat. (New York: PaceWildenstein, 2004), 5–19.

German trans.: "Raster im Paradies," trans. Suzanne Schmidt, in Beat Wismer, ed., *Bridget Riley, Bilder und Zeichnungen 1959–2005*, exh. cat. (Aarau: Aargauer Kunsthaus, 2005), 26–41.

"The Primitive of Everyone Else's Way," in Guillermo Solana, ed., *Gauguin and the Origins of Symbolism* (Madrid: Fundación Colección Thyssen–Bornemisza, 2004), 64–79.

"Judd Through Oldenburg," *Chinati Foundation Newsletter* 9 (October 2004): 33–44. Reprinted in: *Tate Papers*, no. 2 (Autumn 2004).

"Index and Counterfeit," in Shinichiro Osaki, ed., *Traces: Body and Idea in Contemporary Art* exh. cat. (Kyoto: National Museum of Modern Art, 2004), 337–43 [Japanese trans., 39–47].

"Evolution," in *Terry Winters: Paintings and Drawings 1981–1986*, exh. cat. (New York: Matthew Marks Gallery, 2004), 4–14.

"Love Her as Herself," in Kevin Mullins, ed., *David Reed: Leave Yourself Behind: Paintings and Special Projects 1967–2005*, exh. cat. (Wichita: Ulrich Museum of Art, 2005), 24–65.

French trans.: "Aime–là pour elle–même: Sur David Reed," trans. Catherine Vasseur *Les Cahiers du Musée national d'art moderne* 97 (Autumn 2006): 41–63.

"La marionnette et la mire," trans. Jean–François Cornu, in Sylvie Ramond, ed. *Impressionnisme et naissance du cinématographe* (Lyon: Fage, 2005), 201–41.

"Newman's Time," in Melissa Ho, ed., *Reconsidering Barnett Newman* (Philadelphia: Philadelphia Museum of Art, 2005), 161–79.

"It Shows," in Madeleine Grynsztejn, ed., *The Art of Richard Tuttle*, exh. cat. (San Francisco San Francisco Museum of Modern Art, 2005), 253–76.

"Il caparbio impressionismo di Gauguin. Futuro, passato, presente" ["Gauguin's Willful Impressionism: Future, Past, Present"], in Marco Goldin, ed., *Gauguin/VanGogh L'avventura del colore nuovo* (Conegliano: Linea d'ombra, 2005), 76–99.

"Something Is Happening," *Art History* 28 (November 2005): 752–82; Reprint: in Deborah Cherry, ed., *About Stephen Bann* (London: Blackwell, 2006), 180–210.

"The Restless Worker," in Terence Maloon, ed., *Camille Pissarro*, exh. cat. (Sydney: Art Gallery of New South Wales, 2005), 32–45.

"*Cézanne's Composition*: Its Criticism, Its Art," foreword to Erle Loran, *Cézanne's Composition* (Berkeley: University of California Press, 2006), xi–xx.

"Das Physische des Abbildens," trans. Torben Lohmüller, in Gertrud Koch and Christiane Voss, eds., *Zwischen Ding und Zeichen: Zur ästhetischen Erfahrung in der Kunst* (Paderborn: Wilhelm Fink Verlag, 2006), 118–34.

"Space Is Made," in *Donald Judd: Single Stacks 1964–1969*, exh. cat. (New York: Van de Weghe Fine Art, 2006), 8–13.

"Techo/Sublime: The Physicality of Picturing," in Lisa Tamaris Becker, ed., *Techno/Sublime An Exhibition and Symposium* (Boulder: CU Art Museum, 2006), 30–41.

"Willem de Kooning: Same Change," in Karen Painter and Thomas Crow, eds., *Late Thoughts: Reflections on Artists and Composers at Work* (Los Angeles: Getty Research Institute 2006), 36–53.

"Selbst–Interferenz," trans. Kathrin Thiele and Birgit M. Kaiser, in Michael Lüthy and Christophe Menke, eds., *Subjekt und Medium in der Kunst der Moderne* (Zürich: Diaphanes, 2006), 13–35.

"Die Zwei Seiten eines jeden Augenblicks" ["Two Sides to Every Instant"], in Carla Schulz–Hoffmann, ed., *Baselitz Remix*, exh. cat. (Munich: Pinakothek der Moderne, 2006) 31–48.

"Cézanne in the Wild," *Burlington Magazine* 148 (September 2006): 605–11.

"Looping," trans. Thomas Raab, in Ingried Brugger and Florian Steininger, eds. *Markus Lüpertz*, exh. cat. (Vienna: Kunstforum, 2006), 15–31.

"Force of Myself Looking," in Gary Garrels, ed., *Plane Image: A Brice Marden Retrospective*, exh. cat. (New York: Museum of Modern Art, 2006), 28–75.

"Curves Evolve," in *Robert Mangold: Column Structure Paintings*, exh. cat. (New York: PaceWildenstein, 2007), 4–19.

"Risible Cézanne," in Eik Kahng, ed., *The Repeating Image: Multiples in French Art from David to Matisse* (Baltimore: Walters Art Museum, 2007), 127–71.

"Johns Metanoid, Metanoid Johns," in James Rondeau, ed., *Jasper Johns: Gray*, exh. cat. (Chicago: Art Institute of Chicago, 2007), 20–41.

"Pissarro: Dirty Painter," in Karen Levitov, ed., *Camille Pissarro*, exh. cat. (New York: The Jewish Museum, 2007), 15–29, 82–83.

"Seurat Distracted," in Jodi Hauptman, ed., *Seurat Drawings*, exh. cat. (New York: Museum of Modern Art, 2007), 17–29.

"Tangible Datum," in Paloma Alarcó, ed., *Estudios de Historia del Arte en honor de Tomàs Llorens* (Madrid: Machado, 2007), 509–27.

"Gauguin: Abstraction and Dream," in Guillermo Solana, ed., *Gauguin y los orígenes del Simbolismo* (Madrid: Fundación Colección Thyssen–Bornemisza, 2007).

"To Risk Not Naming," in John C. Welchman, ed., *The Aesthetics of Risk* (Los Angeles Southern California Consortium of Art Schools, 2007).

"Bridget Riley in Particular," in Lynne Cooke, ed., *Robert Lehmann Lectures on Contemporary Art 4* (New York: Dia Art Foundation, 2008).

"Sensation in the Wild: On Not Naming Newman, Judd, Riley, and Serra," in Francis Halsall ed., *(Re)Discovering Aesthetics* (New York: Columbia University Press, 2008).

"Barnett Newman: Drawing a Space for Self–Awareness," in Angela Lammert, ed., *Raum Räume der Zeichnung* (Berlin: Akademie der Künste, 2008).

"Grave Seurat," in Paul Smith, ed., *Seeing through Science: Recent Perspectives on Seurat* (University Park: Pennsylvania State University Press, 2008).

Review–Essays

"Father of the Twentieth Century" (William Rubin, ed., *Cézanne, The Late Work*), *Times Literary Supplement*, 25 August 1978, 954.

"Review Article" (five books on Pissarro), *Art Bulletin* 66 (December 1984): 681–90.

"Art History and the Nineteenth Century: Realism and Resistance" (field review), *Art Bulletin* 70 (March 1988): 25–48.

Review (John House, *Monet: Nature into Art*), *Art Bulletin* 73 (March 1991): 149–56 [printer's correction, June 1991, 344].

"Break Dancing" (Yve–Alain Bois, *Painting as Model*), *Arts Magazine* 65 (April 1991): 25–26, 29, 31, 35.

"Dense Cézanne" ("Cézanne," Tate Gallery), *Apollo* 143 (June 1996): 51–54.

Review (John Rewald, *The Paintings of Paul Cézanne: A Catalogue Raisonné*), *Art Bulletin* 80 (June 1998): 384–89.

Criticism

"Insistent Matter: The Art of Irwin Kremen," in *The Art of Irwin Kremen*, exh. cat. (Durham Duke University Museum of Art, 1990), 1–6; Reprinted in: Sarah Schroth, ed., *Irwin Kremen: Beyond Black Mountain, 1966 to 2006*, exh. cat. (Durham: Nasher Museum of Art, 2007), 63–83.

"Crafting Concentration: Three Artists at Davidson," in *Herb Jackson, Cort Savage, Russ Warren*, exh. cat., Van Every Gallery, Davidson College, 1993, 5–17.

"Drawing Thick: Serra's Black," in *Richard Serra: Weight and Measure Drawings*, exh. cat. (New York: The Drawing Center, 1994), 17–28.

Review ("Franz Kline: Black & White, 1950–1961"), *Artforum* 33 (December 1994): 78–79 105.

"Vija Celmins's Play of Imitation," *Parkett* 44 (1995): 48–49.

Review (Best & Worst, 1995), *Artforum* 34 (December 1995): 65, 67.

"The Subject in Question" ("Howard Hodgkin: Paintings 1975–1995"), *Artforum* 34 (January 1996): 62–67, 99.

"Jasper Johns, *Alley Oop*, 1958," *Artforum* 34 (March 1996): 88–89.

Review ("Negotiating Rapture: The Power of Art to Transform Lives"), *Artforum* 35 (October 1996): 112–13.

Review ("Lucian Freud: New Work"), *Artforum* 35 (January 1997): 76–77.

"A Family of Relations," in *Georg Baselitz: Recent Paintings*, exh. cat. (New York PaceWildenstein, 1997), 5–17.

"Infractions at Hand" ["Gesetzesverstösse"], in *Georg Baselitz: Fracture Paintings*, exh. cat., (New York/Cologne: Michael Werner, 1997), n.p. [3–21].

Review ("L'empreinte"), *Artforum* 35 (Summer 1997): 132–33.

"Allover You: The Art of Chuck Close," *Artforum* 36 (April 1998): 92–99, 135, 138.

"New York and Columbus: Willem de Kooning," *Burlington Magazine* 141 (May 1999): 315–17.

Review ("Brice Marden: Work of the 1990s"), *Artforum* 37 (May 1999): 173.

"Fort Lauderdale: Willem de Kooning," *Burlington Magazine* 142 (June 2000): 398–99.

Review ("1900: Art at the Crossroads"), *Artforum* 39 (October 2000): 138–39.

"Raster + Vector = Animation Squared," *Parkett* 60 (2000): 44–49.

Review ("Gego 1955–1990"), *Artforum* 40 (October 2001): 152.

Review ("Agnes Martin: The Nineties and Beyond"), *Artforum* 40 (April 2002): 131.

"Line, Loop, Loop, Line," *Markus Lüpertz: Rückenakte*, exh. cat. (New York: Michael Werner, 2005), n.p.[5–15].

Dutch (Flemish) translation: *MDD* (Deurle: Museum Dhondt–Dhaenens, 2005), n.p.

"To Purge Negativity: A Skill Beyond Skill," *Markus Lüpertz: Maleri/Painting*, exh. cat. (Copenhagen: Galleri Bo Bjerggaard, 2005), n.p.

Review ("Frank Stella 1958"), *Artforum* 44 (Summer 2006): 343.

"Thinking by Hand," *Herb Jackson: "Veronica's Veil"*, exh. cat. (Charlotte: McCall Center Center for Visual Art, 2007).

Book Reviews

"Radicalizing Impressionism" (T. J. Clark, *The Painting of Modern Life*), *New York Times Book Review*, 3 March 1985, 16.

"The Myth Behind the Man" (Bernard Zurcher, *Vincent Van Gogh*), *New York Times Book Review*, 9 February 1986, 16.

"The Art of Painting" (Richard Wollheim, *Painting as an Art*), *Partisan Review* 57 (1990) 326–29.

"The Misogyny of American Modernists," (Ronald Paulson, *Figure and Abstraction in Contemporary Painting*), *Times Literary Supplement*, 24 May 1991, 17.

Review (Donald Preziosi, *Rethinking Art History*), *Journal of Modern History* 63 (June 1991): 364–66.

"Cézanne" (Sidney Geist, *Interpreting Cézanne*; Mary Tompkins Lewis, *Cézanne's Early Imagery*), *Art Journal* 50 (Summer 1991): 82–83.

"Subversive Stickers" (Christine Poggi, *In Defiance of Painting*), *Times Literary Supplement*, 2 April 1993, 8.

"Go Figure" (Fred Orton, *Figuring Jasper Johns*), *Artforum Bookforum*, Summer 1995, 1, 26 33.

Review (Jeremy Gilbert–Rolfe, *Beyond Piety*), *Artforum Bookforum*, Summer 1996, 4, 7.

"Hermetic Zeal" (Michael Fried, *Manet's Modernism*), *Bookforum*, Winter 1996, 20–21, 32, 34.

"Modest Proposals" (David Sylvester, *About Modern Art*), *Bookforum*, Winter 1997, 5, 51.

Review (Jonathan Crary, *Suspensions of Perception*), *Journal of the History of the Behavioral Sciences* 37 (Spring 2001): 209–10.

"Flying Colors" (Leo Steinberg, *Leonardo's Incessant Last Supper*), *Artforum* 39 (May 2001): 23–24.

Notes, Catalogue Entries, Letters, Discussions, Interviews, Pedagogy

"Comments on Theoretical Perspectives" [concerning artificial intelligence], *Leonardo* 19 (1986): 269.

"Photographic Realism," *Social Science: An Interdisciplinary Digest of Research* 71 (Fall 1986): 103–09.

"Representational Reciprocity," in *Inheriting the Theory: New Voices and Multiple Perspectives on DBAE* (seminar proceedings) (Los Angeles: The Getty Center for Education in the Arts,1990), 5–7 (summary); complete essay on diskette.

Reply to Sidney Geist, *Art Journal* 51 (Spring 1992): 125.

"On Modernism: An Interview with Richard Shiff" (conducted by Jill Beaulieu and Mary Roberts), *Art Monthly Australia* 81 (July 1995): 7–9.

"Cézanne au miroir de ses critiques," *Le Monde* (Paris), 29 September 1995, 30.

"Paul Cézanne, *Portrait of a Woman*," "Willem de Kooning, *Police Gazette*," in Libby Lumpkin, ed., *The Bellagio Gallery of Fine Art: Impressionist and Modern Masters* (Las Vegas: The Bellagio Gallery of Fine Art, 1998), 58–63, 174–81. Revised ed., 1999, 88–93, 206–13.

"Chuck Close: la réalité dévisagée," *Beaux-arts*, no. 183 (August 1999): 36–41.

"About Recent Painting: A Critical Exchange Among Thierry de Duve, Lane Relyea & Richard Shiff," ed. Lane Relyea, in Annette DiMeo Carlozzi, *Negotiating Small Truths*, exh. cat. Jack S. Blanton Museum of Art, Austin, 1999, 129–37.

"Paul Cézanne, Las grandes bañistas," *El Cultural* (Madrid), 9 January 2000, 38–39.

Introductory remarks and commentary for panel discussion, *Art in the Landscape* (Marfa: The Chinati Foundation, 2000), 115–31.

Statement on Leo Steinberg, *Encounters with Rauschenberg*, *Artforum* 39 (December 2000): 35.

"Paul Cézanne, 'Still Life: Flask, Glass, and Jug,'" in Matthew Drutt, ed., *Thannhauser: The Thannhauser Collection of the Guggenheim Museum* (New York: Guggenheim Museum 2001), 88–90.

"Digital Experience in Modern Art," in Takanori Nagai, ed., *Report on Research: Cézannisme in Japan* (Kyoto: Kyoto Institute of Technology, 2002), 87–94.

"To Change," in *De Kooning: Paintings 1967–1984*, exh. cat. (San Francisco: John Berggruen Gallery, 2002), 7–11.

"Entretiens: Chuck Close et Richard Shiff," in Jean–Claude Lebensztejn and Patrick Javault, eds., *Les Hyperréalismes USA 1965–75*, exh. cat. (Strasbourg: Les Musées de Strasbourg, 2003), 164–85.

"Drawing Modern: Works from the Agnes Gund Collection," *Artforum* 42 (September 2003) 75.

"Talk" [contributions to group discussion], in Katy Siegel and Paul Mattick, *Money* (New York: Thames and Hudson, 2004), 181–93.

"Georg Baselitz," in Klaus Gallwitz, Isabel Greschat, and Judith Irrgang, eds., Stefan Barmann trans., *Sammlung Frieder Burda* (Ostfildern–Ruit: Hatje Cantz, 2004), 136–41.

"Flicker in the Work: Jasper Johns in conversation with Richard Shiff," *Master Drawings* 44 (Autumn 2006): 275–98.

"'Problem creation is more important than problem solving': Chuck Close in conversation with Richard Shiff," in Klaus Kertess, ed., *Chuck Close Paintings: 1968–2006* (Madrid Museo Nacional Centro de Arte Reina Sofia, 2007), 49–61.

"De Kooning and *Woman, 1949*," in *Willem de Kooning: Women*, exh. cat. (New York: Craig F. Starr, 2007), n.p.

"Willem de Kooning: *Untitled I, 1981*," in *Willem de Kooning Untitled I*, exh. cat. (New York Christie's, 2007), 7–9.

"*Attic, 1949*," "*Untitled*, c. 1946," "*Untitled*, c. 1948," "*Two Women, 1953*," in Lisa Mintz Messinger and Gary Tinterow, eds., *Abstract Expressionism and Other Modern Works: The Muriel Kallis Steinberg Newman Collection in The Metropolitan Museum of Art* (New York Metropolitan Museum of Art, 2007).

INDEX